GW01606444

Published by KunstAM GmbH
Edited by Adam Fuss

Designed by Collettiva Design
Maurizio Poletto, Vienna, www.collettiva.com
Printed by Venturini DMC, Maniago, Italy
on Munken Pemium White 90g, Hanno Art
Matt 130g, Fedrigoni Woodstock Grigio 110g.

ISBN 10: 3-200-00749-4
ISBN 13: 978-3-200-00749-9
Printed in Italy, September 2006

Skate's Art Investment Handbook
by Sergey Skaterschikov

Skate's Art Investment Handbook

by Sergey Skaterschikov

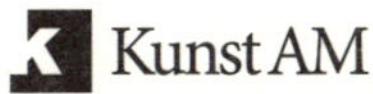

Kunst AM

"it is not possible to measure with any particular accuracy the entire international art market"

Sotheby's Holding Inc disclosure to SEC, Page 4, form 10K for the period ending Dec 31, 2005 filed on March 16, 2006

Contents

Preface to the US Edition

Much has been written about the international art market, and many indices have been created that track the history, provenance and sales of art assets.

Professionals with impressive backgrounds in the art world have written most of those articles and books. Well-informed analysts whose income comes in part from the art world they report on prepare most of the indices.

My interest comes from a different point of view. In the early 1990's, while a student at Moscow State University (MGU), I created the first index to Russia's stock markets. Using the first five letters of my last name, I formed a business, Skate Press, to market that data, which turned out to be quite a success.

On my thirty-second birthday, seven years after selling that first financial data service and four months after receiving my MBA from Duke University's Fuqua School of Business, the news on Picasso's Garçon À La Pipe sale for over USD 100 million at a public auction captured my attention. The sale fascinated me, and I sought to understand how such a price could be possible, and why that particular artist's creativity could be valued so highly.

In my initial research, I noticed that the art assets segment of the alternative investment market was barely analyzed in comparison to other alternative investments. Furthermore, there was practically no professional research coverage that met the standards of mainstream financial markets. The illiquid and non-transparent nature of the global art trade reminded me of the Russian stock market in the 1990s.

Curious about what a new approach to analyzing the highest end of the art market might reveal, I began collecting and analyzing data from the top art sales of recent decades. I closely studied two notable aspects: art's stratospheric transaction costs, far higher than any other financial market, and the high degree of irrational behavior patterns that drive art sales, including the weight placed on provenance (past ownership).

Skate's Art Asset Pricing Model (AAPM) is the result, and Skate's Art Investment Handbook is the explanation of how I arrived at my art valuation algorithm. It also includes Skate's Masterpieces Peer Group, which allows for sampling of comparable transactions involving the world's most valuable art. This Handbook reviews in greater detail how tangible art valuation drivers (artist name, year of creation, size, genre, etc.) determine the price of an artwork and provide the basis for measuring the influence of intangible valuation drivers like provenance and irrational premium. The research for this Handbook provides convincing evidence to support our claim that a so-called irrational premium (i.e. emotional price attached by a specific buyer to a particular artwork) is by far the most important driver for market prices of the most valuable masterpieces. The ability to maximize this premium gives a key competitive advantage to the most successful art market intermediaries.

I wrote Skate's Art Investment Handbook for investors interested in works in the USD 3-25 million price range, most of whom are collectors and institutional investors. My purely rational approach differs from those found in other indices and analyses currently applied to the high-end segment of the art market and for this reason merits serious consideration.

The first edition of the Handbook was published in Russian by Alpina Business Books, a leading publisher of business literature in Russia. Financially supported by Deutsche Bank, the Russian edition was designed to help Russia's new class of high net worth individuals make informed decisions about their art purchases. The book turned out to be an instant success.

This second, U.S. edition is being published independently by a new company I have established in New York to market and sell unbiased art investment research and audit services that focuses on internal controls in art asset management, as well as on governance of art institutions. This new company carries the name of my first business, Skate Press, to highlight my personal commitment to the cause of bringing more transparency to the world of art investment and finance, as well as to continue what is now a fourteen-year tradition of entrepreneurship and shareholder value creation achieved by my time.

For more information about Skate Press, updates to this Handbook and further research publications, please visit our website at www.skatepress.com.

Introduction

The art market is one of the oldest investment markets in the world. Wealthy individuals and various special purpose vehicles, including royal and imperial museums, began purchasing paintings, sculptures and tapestries long before railway stocks became known to the investing public and well ahead of the textbook tulip bubble. In his highly entertaining book *Le métier de peintre au Grand Siècle*, Antoine Schnapper, Professor Emeritus of art history in Sorbonne[1], provided a detailed overview of the art market's infrastructure in France roughly 400 years ago. His work included data on the markets for art and real estate, as well as descriptions of buy-side income levels, capital allocations for art assets and distribution of margins made on artworks among artists, dealers, curators and actual art investors and collectors.

While the infrastructure of all major investment markets, including real estate, evolved into forms that would have been unrecognizable four centuries ago, the art market turned out to be magically immune to social changes, new technologies or any other drivers that fueled the evolution of other types of investment markets. Centuries ago, the investment process for buying art, real estate or underwriting the cost of geographical expedition was largely the same, relying on expert opinions, connections and subjective judgments on the part of investors about exit opportunities, holding horizons and expected rates of return. In today's contemporary investment markets, however, only the art market is largely free from the scientific, rational and disciplined approach to institutional investing that is standard for how equity, debt,

1. Antoine Schnapper, *Le métier de peintre au Grand Siècle*, (Éditions Gallimard, 2004)

commodities, foreign exchange, real estate and derivatives markets work these days.

On the one hand, the "archaic" nature of the art market's infrastructure and investment patterns is well justified. In 2005, the total trading volume on the global art market measured by the transaction volumes at the world's two largest art auction houses ("exchanges") equaled USD 5.8 billion.[2] In comparison, this figure roughly equals the average daily turnover in the market for shares of just two NASDAQ listed companies – Google and Microsoft. The rating of the world's 1000 most valuable works of art, created and maintained by Skate Press on the basis of data for public auctions since 1985, leads to an estimate of the public investable art market capitalization standing at USD 9.2 billion as of July 1, 2006 (a detailed description of the calculation methodology for art market capitalization is provided in section 2.1). Again, by way of comparison, the initial public offering of PartyGaming PLC on the London Stock Exchange on June 30, 2005 valued this company alone at GBP 4.64 billion (USD 8.17 billion). The entire public market of investment quality art is valued at barely more than a single online poker company.

An even more interesting comparison can be found in the market capitalizations of eBay Inc and Sotheby's Holding Inc. At the time this book went to press, the New York Stock Exchange listed Sotheby's Holding Inc, which controls over 50% of the trading volumes at public art auctions, at approximately USD 1.95 billion, or approximately 20% of the entire investable art market's capitalization. On the very same day, the market capitalization of eBay, the world's largest online auction company, stood in excess of USD 35.29 billion. Art and antiques is one of eBay's auction categories, but in the firm's entire history, no single painting or other work of art has been sold on eBay that could have made it into Skate's rating of world's 1000 most valuable works of art. This fact clearly shows that the market for art masterpieces is a very small world for a limited number of participants in terms of trading volumes and combined value.

While the public fraction of the global art market remains small, the entire value of art assets amassed by society and held largely by government sponsored collections is enormous. Skate Press estimates that the free float of the market for investment quality art is no more than 2%, with the combined value of this market[3] in excess of USD 250 billion.

2. Calculated based on 2004 annual reports of Christies International PLC and Sotheby's Holding Inc

3. For the purpose of this edition "investment quality art" is defined as paintings and sculptures whose market price is equal to or exceeds the threshold price of the 1000th most valuable painting based on the rating of world's most valuable artworks prepared by Skate Press on the basis of public auction data. As of July 1, 2006, this price equaled USD 3,969,500 in nominal terms.

The lion's share of this wealth resides in the ownership or management of state-sponsored museums and galleries around the world. The dominant role of government ownership in the area of collecting, storage and management of investment quality art is arguably the most fundamental reason for the immunity of the art investment market to innovation and infrastructure evolution that has been observed elsewhere in investment markets over the last several centuries.

Governments' control over significant portions of the supply and demand sides of the market for investment quality art has helped to nourish and preserve the closed-circuit "clan" nature of art markets worldwide. Developing in the shadow of state ownership and protectionism, fueled with "national cultural heritage" rhetoric, the art investment market finds itself handicapped in comparison to other investment markets, including alternative investment categories to which the art market traditionally belongs. Trading in investment quality art is conducted with far higher transaction costs (10-15% commissions and other transaction costs for art trades versus less than 2% for securities trades) and in an archaic information environment where price information about most art dealings is not equally available to all market participants. Basic things like public registers of artworks produced by the world's most renowned artists also do not exist. Art deals involving the most significant players, most importantly state-sponsored museums and galleries, are not audited and are not assessed in a rational manner, despite the fact that art asset management by state institutions is done at the public's expense and for public benefit.

The objective of this book (heavily based on research and data produced by Skate Press) is to describe the rational approach to investing in the world's most valuable works of art. In addition to a thorough description of the global art market's most important institutions and how the art market compares to other alternative investment markets, this book includes a rating of the world's 1000 most valuable works of art, published here for the first time, as well as a detailed introduction to Skate's Art Asset Pricing Model (AAPM).[4]

4. Skate's Art Asset Pricing Model (AAPM) is the intellectual property and protected trademark of Skate Press

Chapter 1
Infrastructure of the Market for Investment Quality Art

The art investment market generates approximately USD 3.9 billion in annual revenues for its participants – auction houses, art dealers, information vendors and financial service providers.[1] Comparing this figure to the roughly USD 9.3 billion combined market value of the world's 1000 most valuable artworks and to the nearly USD 5.8 billion in annual turnover at the world's major auction houses, one can see that the market's infrastructure comes at an enormous cost to art investment market participants. The overall level of transaction costs and the accompanying limited transparency are perhaps the most important reasons for the art market's consistent failure to develop into a true alternative investment market accepted by institutional investors around the world.

Any investment market is a complex system with a simple function, namely, to balance the interests of buyers and sellers. The elements of this complex system are traditionally described as combining a legal, tax and trading infrastructure, clearing and settlement systems and an information environment. Further adding to the complexity, an investment market fuses state regulation – the setting of general norms, a tax regime and a required level of information disclosure – with self-regulation, which determines how trade is organized and how information exchange works. And, of course, private entrepreneurship of various forms drives the evolution of investment markets around the world.

1. In this book, all figures concerning the art market's various indicators refer to the market for fine art unless otherwise stated.

Both in theory and in reality, the more efficiently constructed the market, the fewer expenditures its participants incur in transaction costs and the lower the gain for intermediaries, resulting in a greater advantage for investors and issuers. An efficient investment market allows its participants to focus on predicting the dynamics of an investment's value (and, correspondingly, on evaluating investment yields) while developing new approaches to eliminating or minimizing risks associated with the investment process. The advent and rapid adaptation of information technologies to the securities trade during the 1990s has radically reduced traditional costs for investing in and dealing with securities and significantly increased the number of market participants. And although the process of redistributing the economic benefits that flow from securities market transactions was painful to many participants who saw their business model go from the most profitable "granting access" to a very competitive "offering advice and a variety of services," in the end, perhaps ironically, these efficiency laden forces ultimately produced a stronger, more vibrant and indeed larger market. Sellers (companies), buyers (investors) and even intermediaries have all done well as a result of a consolidated market for intermediary services and the radical growth of the securities market in general. In the ten to fifteen years during which the securities market experienced its deep restructuring in terms of trading and information infrastructure, only weak intermediaries, irresponsible investors and less efficient issuers found themselves on the losing end. What remained was a market with a new level of efficiency in corporate governance and investing, as well as a new standard for professional services.

Introducing innovations, such as automated securities trading and more transparent accounting or increased depth and timeliness of information disclosure by issuers, would have been impossible, however, without two driving forces in the investment market – an increasing need in the capital markets from the sell side (issuing companies) wishing to attract large volumes of capital under optimal conditions and greater sensitivity of the buy side (investors) to how investment risks are disclosed and managed.

It is worth beginning our discussion of the infrastructure supporting the market for investment quality art precisely with an insight into the motives of buyers and sellers in this market. The main reasons for buying and selling works of art, as well as the investment strategies on which the decisions are based, are primarily discussed in Chapter 5 of this book. Here it is worth mentioning only that the policies of state-owned or affiliated museums are aimed at cornering the market and acquiring masterpieces. Against this background, the state, generally the natural regulator of investment markets and the main participant in the process of developing their infrastructure, unfortunately has no interest in forming a transparent art market in so far as it not only has no intention of selling artworks belonging to its institutions, but also because of its interest in buying these works at the lowest possible price.

Whereas the absence of state support for developing the art market's infrastructure is unusual in the general evolution of investment markets, the formidable opposition to this evolution on the part of market intermediaries is a traditional and more ingrained problem. The absence of public information sources on registers of artworks, the low quality of pricing information, the additional expenses related to masterpieces' authentication and the secrecy of buyers and sellers are all factors that foster uncertainty, irrationality and emotion in the art market, creating an advantage for professional intermediaries. Due to these conditions, an exaggerated level of importance has long existed in favor of the intermediaries in the art investment process, justifying their enormous fees in comparison to the commissions and transaction costs found in other investment markets.

In this context, it is not surprising that very few parties are seeking to develop the art market's infrastructure and improve its efficiency. Perhaps only buyers of art (and even only those who do not have problems with the origin of their capital or who are not afraid of information being published about their art investments), as well as contemporary artists concerned with increasing the investment attractiveness of their works can honestly support major revisions to the infrastructure comprising the market for investment quality art.

Given the imbalance between supporters and opponents of the art market's evolution, it is obvious that significant changes in its infrastructure can hardly happen unless buyers of world masterpieces demand a more efficient venue or a shift occurs in the investment interests in new segments of the art market. In Chapter 6, we will discuss in greater detail the likelihood that such change in the balance of interests among the art market's participants will occur.

1.1. Business models in the art market

As with any investment market, there are two general types of participants that can be found in the art market. The most prevalent participants are private, state and professional investors who make use of every possible type of investment and collection strategy. These strategies are described in greater deal in Chapter 5. The second group of participants is the service providers, namely, the companies or private individuals who in some way provide art investment-related services and, in so doing, represent the art market's infrastructure. The primary business models present in the art market are shown in Exhibit 1.1 and are discussed in greater detail throughout this chapter.

Exhibit 1.1 Main business models in the art market

Segment	*Annual revenues (USD bln)*	*Company*
Auction trade	1.3*	Sotheby's, Christie's, eBay, Dorotheum, Bukowskis, etc.
Financial services	0.5**	AIG, Allianz, UBS, Deutsche Bank, AXA and others
Information	0.08***	Sotheby's, Christie's, Artprice, Artnet, Skate Press
Art dealers (including private galleries and museums)	Approximately 2*	Tens of thousands of companies – highly fragmented market

* Auction and over-the-counter (including galleries and art shows) trade measured by commissions charged based on results of statistical sampling
** Includes art loans, insurance, art banking and so forth
*** For a detailed discussion on how this value has been calculated, please see section 1.4
Source: www.skatepress.com

In its filings with the U.S. Securities and Exchange Commission, Sotheby's Holdings Inc, the world's largest public company specializing in the art market, acknowledges that "it is not possible to measure with any particular accuracy the entire international art market" due to the lack of disclosure and regulatory reporting requirements for art market participants.[2] Exhibit 1.1, which is based on continuous research and data acquisition, confirms our view that most of the revenues and volumes in art trading occurs outside auction houses – in dealer rooms and private galleries. Sotheby's also expresses this view in the same disclosure document quoted above: "although dealers and smaller auction houses generally do not report sales figures publicly, the Company believes that dealers account for the majority of the volume of transactions in the international art market."[3]

The number of publicly traded companies in the art industry that specialize in servicing the art market is quite small, a phenomenon that will be discussed further in Chapter 5. Information about the revenues and expenditures of players in the art market is closed for the most part, making comparisons difficult. Many public companies that service the art market – from auction-based firms like eBay to those that provide financial services like Deutsche Bank, UBS, AXA and Allianz – do not separate economic indicators related to activity in the art market when disclosing their general financial information. The principal reason is that this type of activity is quite small when compared to the overall size of these companies' revenues.

A variety of statistics from companies that service the art market is cited in this chapter. These statistics provide a general idea as to the market's size and its economic trends. While neither detailed nor exhaustive, this analysis does allow the possibility of creating a systemic representation of how value is allocated in different parts of the "food chain" that comprises the world's art market (see Exhibit 1.1)

1.2. The infrastructure of trade

In general, the global art market does not revolve around a single center. The overwhelming majority of transactions involving works of art are conducted directly between their owners or through the mediation of professional dealers and galleries. A significant part of the art trade is nevertheless localized at large art exhibitions that

2. Form 10K for the period ending December 31, 2005, filed on March 16, 2006, pg. 4

3. Ibid, pg. 2.

occur year-round in different cities around the world. The giant art shows like Art Basel (Switzerland) and Maastricht Art (the Netherlands) each draw thousands of professional intermediaries and tens of thousands of investors and collectors. Unlike regional financial markets, however, these art markets last a maximum of one to three weeks. There is neither a single clearing and settlement infrastructure at these markets nor a well-formed system of organized entry for artworks and market participants. In other words, these exhibitions do not fulfill the function of organized and permanent markets that eliminate or reduce contractor risks and assure liquidity and a continuous market price for the art assets that are traded on them.

While exhibitions today are a recognized and successful form of commercial activity in the art market, this model is not examined separately in this chapter, as large international art shows, organized on the basis of a private-state partnership, frequently have a "noncommercial" format. Reliable information about the economics of these art shows is also frequently lacking. In so far as large art shows actually serve as a substitute for organized markets, however, well-developed exhibitions that receive support from municipal budgets can still be an attractive form of commercial activity.

Large auction houses attempt to perform the duties of organized markets. Unlike exhibitions, auction houses have one or more permanent locations, conduct trading year-round and are able to operate globally. They are also able to perform the functions of a clearing and settlement center, eliminating the counterparty risk, and, in the case of the largest auctions, the risk of counterfeit artworks. Worldwide, there are approximately 30 recognized and relatively long-functioning auction houses. With the exception of one sale, only six of these houses have handled works that have fallen into Skate's Top 1000 most valuable artworks (see Chapter 2, Exhibit 2.2 for more details).

Exhibit 1.2 - Total aggregate auction sales: 1989–2005

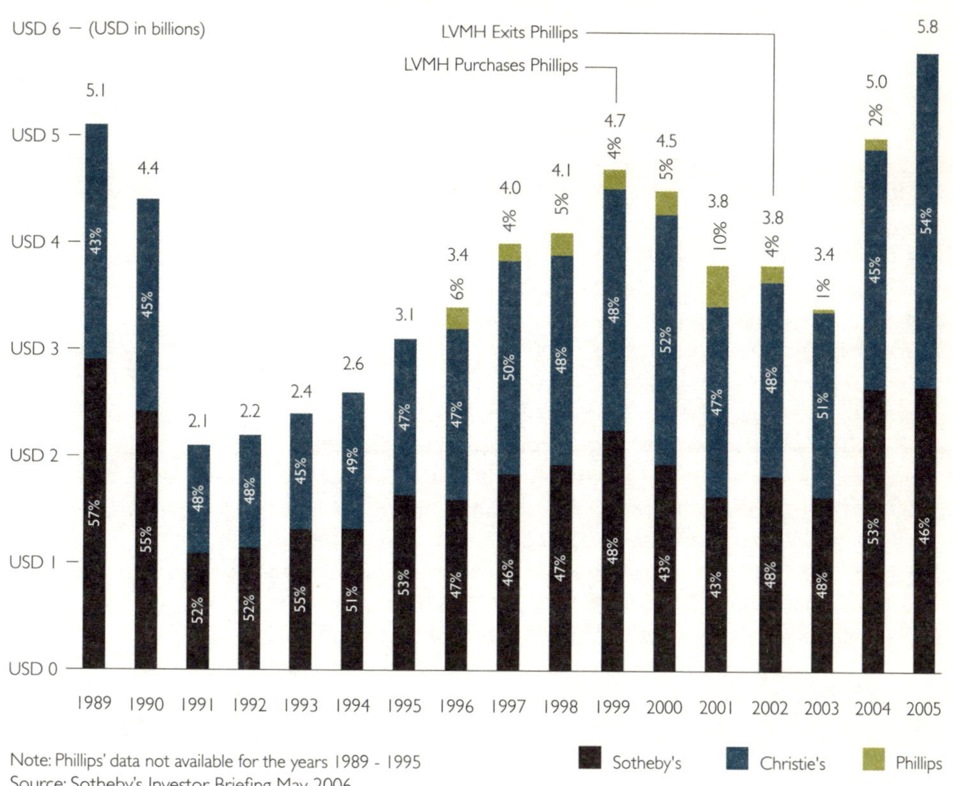

Note: Phillips' data not available for the years 1989 - 1995
Source: Sotheby's Investor Briefing May 2006

Exhibit 1.2 shows how the auction houses' market shares have evolved over the last sixteen years. Clearly, the world's art auctions are currently enjoying their best times ever. The volume of art trading activity has risen dramatically in the last two years, reaching an all-time record high of USD 5.8 billion in 2005. This volume increase occurred against the backdrop of the auction market's consolidation, resulting in a textbook oligopoly following the Phillips' exit in 2002. Only two international auction houses that trade in masterpieces – Sotheby's and Christie's – remained, and for the 20 months ending September 1, 2006, 99.5% of art sales that made their way into Skate's Top 1000 most valuable artworks were sold at one of these two auction houses.[4]

4. See detailed description of Skate's Top 1000, also called the Skate's Masterpieces Peer Group, in Chapter 2. The actual list of world's most valuable artworks is published in Schedule A.

Sotheby's and Christie's both date back to the eighteenth century. Sotheby's first auction, conducted by its founder, Samuel Baker, took place in London on March 11, 1744. Its name came from the founder's nephew, John Sotheby, who became one of the company's two heirs after Baker's death in 1778. The Sotheby family continued to manage the auction house for eighty years after Samuel Baker's death. In the beginning, the company specialized in trading rare books, and only in 1917 did paintings and sculptures begin to dominate its auctions. Around this time Sotheby's moved to London's fashionable New Bond Street.[5] In 1977, the company went public, with demand at its initial public offering in New York exceeding the offer by 26 times, a level of demand similar to the recent debut of Google on the NASDAQ market.[6]

Twenty-two years after Sotheby's first auction, James Christie organized Christie's first auction on December 5, 1766 in a building on Pall Mall Street, a ten-minute walk from his future main competitor. Christie's main objects were not paintings either, but rather much more commonplace items like irons and bed linens. Until the end of the twentieth century, Christie's was also a public company, but in 1998, French billionaire Francois Pinault purchased its controlling stake for slightly more than USD 1 billion.[7] The new owner wittingly returned the company to private ownership, halting public share trading (and, at the same time, public disclosure of information on its activities).

Interestingly, clients from Russia have played historically important roles in both companies. Christie's became the largest auction company in the world after Robert Walpole's sizable collections were auctioned in the eighteenth and nineteenth centuries. Catherine the Great was the main buyer at these auctions, placing her acquisitions primarily in St. Petersburg's Hermitage museum. In 2004, Russian businessman Viktor Vekselberg greatly aided in the financial recovery of Sotheby's, taking the Faberge egg collection off the auction and concluding a private transaction on its purchase with the Forbes family through Sotheby's. This deal allowed Sotheby's to significantly correct its financial position, which had been weakened by payments made in the European and American lawsuits described below.

5. To this date, the main Sotheby's auctions continue to take place in this building.

6. Sotheby's is included in Skate's art stock index. Some information about its current financial indicators is presented in Chapter 4.

7. According to Forbes magazine, Francois Pinault's net worth is estimated at USD 6.3 billion. Pinault-Printemps, Yves Saint Laurent, Gucci and Samsonite are among the other companies he controls.

Income from commissions charged to both buyers and sellers of art lies at the heart of the business model governing auction houses. According to Sotheby's financial statements, the average level of commissions paid in 2005 was 18.7%, up from 16.4% in 2004.[8] According to all indications (e.g. published premiums on the part of buyers), Christie's charges comparable commissions. For both auction houses, commissions generate an overwhelming part of their revenues (over 80%). Art investors are generally able to receive significant discounts when making transactions at either auction house. Whereas the published level of commissions for buyers is around 12%, and on average it has been slightly over 10% in recent years, statistical analysis of commission payments actually paid by buyers of the 1000 most valuable works of art shows that the average size of the buyer's premium has equaled 9.7% (Exhibit 1.3).

8. Sotheby's shares are listed on the New York Stock Exchange, which requires the company to disclose information on its activities through a centralized system of information disclosure in the United States (EDGAR). EDGAR is the source of further information about Sotheby's, unless stated otherwise in the text.

Exhibit 1.3 – Growth of the buyer's premium rate paid to auction houses on sales of the most valuable paintings

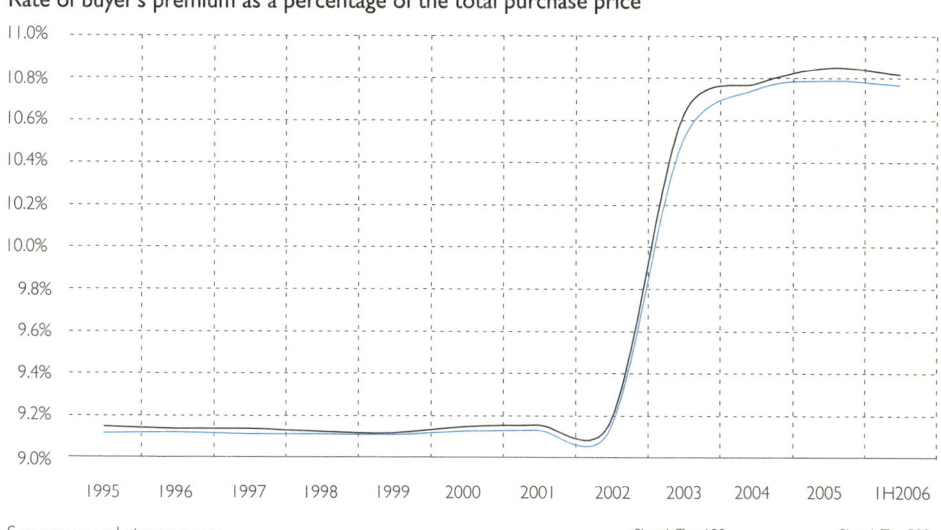

Source: www.skatepress.com

These commissions translate into gigantic revenues for the auction houses. From sales of the world's 1000 most valuable works of art alone, the auction houses earned USD 903,242,215. In other words, investors paid an average commission of USD 903,242 for each artwork included in Skate's Masterpieces Peer Group (detailed in Chapter 2). Sotheby's is the world's leader in terms of collecting commissions on sales of world masterpieces, taking 52.2% of the total commissions paid on the top 1000 artworks. Christie's holds an unchallenged second place with 44.8%.

The commission levels in the art market are unprecedented in comparison to other investment markets where commissions rarely exceed 5% and, in the past several years on the highly competitive debt and equity capital markets have fallen to 1% and lower. It is no surprise, therefore, that the oligopolistic character of the global auction houses and their large commissions constantly come into the view of state regulatory agencies in various countries.

Thunder crashed on the quiet world of the auction oligopoly in 2000 when a scandal arose over a price fixing agreement between the two supposedly competing auction houses. The goal of this agreement was to maintain the high level of commission revenues. In a collective lawsuit filed by Sotheby's and Christie's clients, the auction houses were accused of maintaining high commissions in a coordinated pricing policy throughout the better part of the 1990s, and following a court inquiry, Sotheby's and Christie's were forced to admit to the charges and each pay their clients USD 512 million. Both companies underwent a change in management, and as a result of further court proceedings, the owner of the controlling stake in Sotheby's at the time, seventy-six-year old Alfred Taubman, was imprisoned.[9] It took a few more years, however, before the complex capital structure of Sotheby's could be reformed. Only after the signing of the so-called "Transaction Agreement" on September 7, 2005 was the dual class super-voting share structure of Sotheby's Holdings Inc eliminated, resulting in the introduction of a corporate governance structure in line with market standards. Prior to the Transaction Agreement, Alfred Taubman and his family were able to exercise more than 62% effective control over Sotheby's essentially through the use of discriminating voting power against other shareholders.

The speed with which both companies recovered from this knockout punch speaks of the economic power of their business model, especially considering that they were not only on the edge of bankruptcy, but also that they had completely lost their clients' trust (see

9. The most intriguing details of this scandal are described in Christopher Mason's *The Art of the Steal: Inside the Sotheby's-Christie's Auction House Scandal*, G.P. Putnam's Sons (New York, 2004).

Exhibit 1.4). In 2005, both companies finished the year with record financial results over the previous five years, and in 2006, they have every chance of recovering the international credit agencies' investment grade ratings that they had lost in 2000. The auction house oligopoly has been restored, and the market positions of Sotheby's and Christie's are especially solid today. Whether this dominant position can be maintained in the future is discussed in Chapter 6.

Exhibit 1.4 – Sotheby's market capitalization over the last ten years

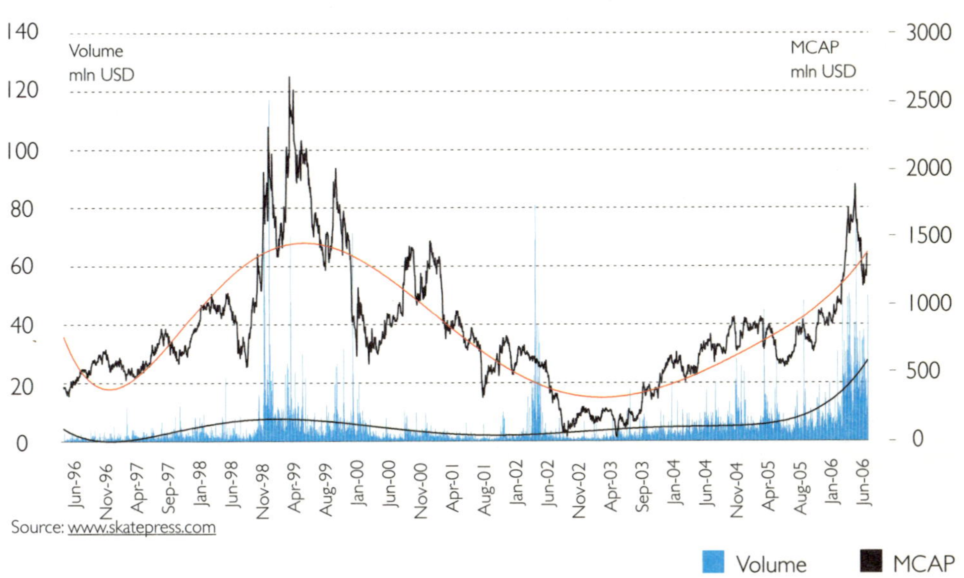

Source: www.skatepress.com

1.3. The business of financial services

Information on the revenues and yields of transactions involving financial services in the art market is incomplete. Estimating the size of this market is extremely difficult, as there is not a single public company in the world whose main business is financing or insuring transactions in the art market.

Research by Skate Press nevertheless shows that insurance is the dominant type of business in the market for financial services. Ninety-five percent of all revenues derived from providing financial services in the art market comes from insurance, including insurance against risks related to storage and transport (see Exhibit 1.1, which shows the total amount of financial service revenues). The main risks associated with investing in artworks, however, namely those involving authenticity and expropriation, are not insurable.

Perhaps unexpected, financing transactions with artworks or using them as collateral is not significant in terms of volume. In 2005, for example, Sotheby's revenue from clients' loans made on the security of artworks, including interest bearing revenue, totaled USD 8.3 million, and the total size of its credit portfolio equaled USD 102.6 million. Over the last fifteen years, Sotheby's has made on average USD 125 million in loans to its clients, for the most part in the form of short-term loans on the eve of auctions. On balance, the low liquidity of artworks and their high price volatility limits financing in the form of short-term loans. The collateral value of artworks in loan transactions never exceeds 50% of the price paid by an owner for a work of art and, in fact, is often considerably lower.

Whereas insuring artworks is carried out by a comparably greater number of companies capable of sorting out the requirements for lowering risks associated with storage and transport, financing with artworks as collateral is a specific business. Credit committees at most of the world's largest banks are in no position to evaluate and manage risks in the art sector. From the point of view of commercial lending on the security of art assets, these risks include:

- Risk of incorrect evaluation of an art asset's base value (market value from which a loan rate is determined by calculating the collateral value at a discount rate that is equal to 50% or more of the market price).

- Risk of macroeconomic changes that might have a negative effect on the purchasing ability of art investors and collectors.

- Risk of forgery or of damage to the art asset.

- Risk of "portability" of the collateral – collateral in the form of an artwork is considerably easier to steal than, for example, collateral in the form of shares in a publicly traded company.

• Risk of previous obligations and encumbrances. The absence of a transparent information infrastructure, especially concerning the history of ownership and transactions with artworks, in many cases does not allow for documented confirmation of an art asset being free of previously acquired obligations and encumbrances.

• Risk of claims regarding the legality of an artwork's export or resale.

1.4. The business of information

The quality, size and level of globalization of information companies servicing an investment market are the signs of that market's maturity. The aggregate annual sales volume of professional financial information offered by global giants such as Bloomberg, Reuters and Thomson Financial Services is no less than USD 10 billion and provides direct evidence of the maturity of the global markets for capital, currency and commodities serviced by these companies.

The landscape of the art market's information infrastructure is a miniature copy of the global investment markets and is clear evidence of the art market's small and narrow focus, which, with the exception of the market for the world's masterpieces, exists as a collection of local art markets. The combined annual revenues of companies specializing in selling information to art market investors in various countries is around USD 75 million. This figure excludes artists' albums and the production of general art interest media such as thematic journals. According to Skate Press research, about one third of this market is attributed to the Art Loss Register (ALR), an art market industry association whose founding members include the International Foundation for Art Research and various national art associations, major auction houses such as Christie's, Sotheby's and Bonhams, as well as venture capital and financial services groups such as 3i, AXA and Aon. ALR is an online database of lost and stolen art, which charges USD 75 per search, thus providing a vetting mechanism for art market professionals to check on good title risk before entering a related transaction.

ALR serves as sort of a centralized register, but it does not address the risk of authenticity, however. There are about 300,000 searches conducted on ALR annually.[10]

Approximately 47% percent of the art investment information market is divided among four companies – the information subdivisions of Sotheby's and Christie's,[11] which each control approximately 15% of the market, and information vendors Artnet and Artprice, which have 10% and 7% market share, respectively. Both Artnet and Artprice are publicly traded companies that support gigantic databases with information on auctions and over-the-counter transactions around the world. Interestingly, according to our research on business model of auction houses, revenue from information services has far exceeded that from financial services in recent years.

In addition to the small aggregate sales volumes of the companies (which is an unfortunate measure of this sector), the information sector of the art market remains blatantly defective in terms of what information it can supply to market participants. It is impossible to obtain the following from companies servicing the art market's information segment:

- Access to databases of owners of significant artworks of a single author or period. Instead, investors can only obtain information on works in large collections of the more famous museums, as well as information about the seller and the general history of an individual work or series of works, which is not always reliable. On capital markets, access to information about those who own publicly-traded securities is a standard product.

- Comprehensive information about registers of all well known works of a single artist. Instead, investors are offered catalogues that generally contain incomplete information about the price of transactions involving works of a particular artist in the past. These catalogues often contradict publications of competing expert groups, especially with regard to dating of works, the history of their background and even their authenticity. Needless to say, in traditional investment markets, information about issuance conditions and the number of securities outstanding for each issue is easy to find in public sources and is available free of charge.

10. All data related to Art Loss Register is taken from the ALR's website and other public disclosure materials.

11. Auction catalogues and internet databases are the main form of information products offered by these companies. In 2005, Sotheby's revenues from information products stood at USD 9.7 million, Artnet's revenue from information sales (classified as online gallery network and price database revenue line in company's financials) equaled USD 7.0 million in the same year, and Artprice earned EUR 3.5 million or approximately USD 4.2 million in revenue from art information sales in 2005. Source – annual reports of the companies.

• Detailed descriptions of attributes of famous masterpieces. The process of authentication and attribution of artworks is the know-how of individual experts and is nontransparent for market participants, creating significant risk of abuse and error in authentication and valuation by experts. On capital markets, one can find central information disclosure databases, sponsored either by the state or by market participants themselves. These databases contain information about all publicly-traded securities and their issuers, including information describing issuers and their contact information. In the art market, confirmation of an art asset's authenticity is not a standard information service, but a comparably expensive procedure that does not always provide an unambiguous or reliable result (see section 1.6 for a more detailed description of authentication services).

The experience of other investment markets shows that the number of participants increases only when there is a developed information infrastructure, equal access among investors to pricing information, and transparency in the market with respect to both the product and the buyers. Until now, the closed nature of transactions involving artworks has imposed a major obstacle to significant investment in art assets. It also does not allow for artists and their heirs to receive proper payment for their intellectual property in the same way that musicians and actors are compensated.

Some authorities and market regulators, however, are trying to change this situation. In February 2006, a new law in the United Kingdom introduced a royalty concept of sorts for living artists. This concept, also known as droit de suite or DDS, provides for royalty payments to living artists each time their original artworks are bought or sold by an art market professional.[12] A royalty-like charge that the auction house imposes on the buyer, DDS is typically calculated on the hammer price (excluding buyer's premium and VAT). The qualifying threshold from which DDS applies in the UK is EUR 1,000 (or about USD 1,200). The DDS rate is calculated as a percentage of the hammer price (using a sliding scale from 4% to 0.25%) subject to maximum royalty payable of EUR 12,500 (approximately USD 15,000) per transaction with any one work of art for any one sale. This maximum royalty applies to works sold for EUR 2 million (approximately USD 2.4 million) and above.

12. The droit de suite was established in France in the 1920s to assist the widows of artists killed in World War I. It supplemented a special tax on the overall turnover of art dealers that has been used for a special arts social welfare fund. Droit de suite provisions were subsequently incorporated into the copyright legislation of most countries in what is now the European Union and reflected in the Berne Convention for the Protection of Literary & Artistic Works. The EU Resale Royalty Directive harmonizes legislation in the various EU states, including the UK. The droit is a peculiarity that has not found much favor in Australia, the United States (although a form of the droit is in place in California), Canada, New Zealand or Asia (see http://www.caslon.com.au/droitprofile.htm).

This new DDS provision and the regulatory thinking behind it are interesting for three reasons:

1) DDS applies only to living artists who make the higher priced segment of the contemporary art market less cost efficient compared to other market segments;

2) In percentage terms and in its ability to affect investment returns, DDS becomes less relevant for higher priced works of art. In fact, if any of the living artists present in Skate's Top 1000 artworks are sold or bought in London, the DDS cost will be at 0.25%, and for artworks over USD 6 million, it will actually go below 0.25%, as the amount of DDS royalty is capped to USD 15,000;

3) Due to the lack of unitary regulatory standards for art investment markets around the world, the UK legislative initiative is unlikely to have any significant effect on the amount of royalties paid on auction sales to living artists. Applicable only in the UK, it creates an incentive for auction houses to sell contemporary art in other jurisdictions that do not impose DDS. Affluent buyers clearly can with equal ease purchase an artwork of their choice in London, New York and Zurich, thus rendering country-sponsored art market regulation initiatives rather impotent endeavors.

1.5. The business of the art dealer

Art dealers who buy artworks as professional intermediaries intending to quickly resell them embody the market for art assets outside the organized auction house market, large art exhibitions and direct sales between artists and collectors.

The art dealers' form of business, remaining relatively unchanged over a number of centuries, has survived largely due to the presence of a strong competitive advantage in comparison to other means by which investors can effect the purchase and sale of art assets.

Exhibit 1.5 – Competitive advantage of art dealers in comparison to other means of effecting transactions with artworks

Type of market access	*Competitive advantages of art dealers*
Auction	**1.** No commission is taken from the buyer **2.** No payment for insurance during the auction or for publication of works in a catalogue **3.** Immediate conclusion of transaction (no need to wait for the auction to begin) **4.** Confidentiality of transaction, including the price
Exhibit/art show	**1.** No need to make decisions during the short period of time the exhibit is occurring **2.** Enough time to study the work prior to its purchase **3.** No expenditures on transport and insurance that are sold or purchased at the exhibit
Access to artist's studio	**1.** The opportunity to compare the works of many artists simultaneously **2.** The possibility of not only purchasing, but also selling a work of art **3.** A dealer's reputation is on the line, meaning that dealers screen artworks before showing them to clients, selecting only those that they believe meet certain quality criteria

Source: www.skatepress.com

Worldwide, tens of thousands of art dealers and hundreds of dealer companies with a serious reputation in the international market exist. Curiously, however, the market for dealer services is de facto non-corporate in nature and remains fragmented between single owner shops or small partnerships that are built around the names and reputation of certain individuals, with "personal touch" always being the key element of art investment transactions. While several large contemporary investment banks and famous art dealers began their operations at approximately the same time centuries ago, the investment banks underwent an evolution analogous to that of the capital markets in the last several centuries, transforming into professionally organized international companies that respond to the demands of the investment markets. At the same time, art dealerships have retained their closed, often family-oriented status. Skate Press has identified only two publicly-traded companies whose primary business is that of dealing in art. These two companies – Britain's Partridge Fine Arts PLC and Luxembourg's Artemis Fine Arts S.A. – were always below the sight of professional market analysts due to their low market capitalization. While Partridge Fine Arts ceased to exist as an independent public company in 2006 and Artemis Fine Arts has suffered financial ruin to the extent that its shares have practically ceased trading, both companies are nevertheless of interest to us in the context of being models of the dealer business.

Partridge Fine Arts, established in London at the turn of the nineteenth and twentieth centuries, owns galleries in a mansion located in one of London's more prestigious neighborhoods, just across the street from Sotheby's. At the time of this book's publication, Partridge Fine Arts was in a difficult financial position. Having barely broken even in 2003, the company experienced significant losses in 2004 of GBP 1.6 million against a total sales volume of GBP 7.6 million, which itself was a 25% reduction over 2003 sales. In the first half of 2005, the company's operational losses decreased by GBP 588,000 during a sales increase of one-third in comparison to the same period in 2004. The company, however, was forced to recognize an impairment of the value of the artworks stored in its warehouses and record an additional GBP 10 million in losses as a result of this impairment.[13] In other words, the company's auditors required it to reflect the real value of the artworks purchased from clients rather than sold to them. As a result of this impairment, the value of its inventory (artworks in its galleries and warehouses) fell by nearly 40% to GBP 16 million. Unsurprisingly, trade in the company's shares practically ceased in 2005, with Partridge shares effectively becoming as illiquid and worthless as most of the artworks in the Partridge inventory.

The financial health of Partridge Fine Arts is interesting for a number of reasons. First, Partridge serves as an example of the art market's volatility and the unpredictability of turnovers. In one year, the company's sales fell by 25% and in the next half year increased by 33%. Second, it demonstrates the risks inherent in the dealer business. In purchasing works of art from a client, dealers risk not being able to resell them quickly and, in the event of an unsuccessful acquisition, the risk of freezing a significant portion of working capital and experiencing significant losses. One of Partridge's obvious mistakes was

13. All financial data for Partridge Fine Arts PLC are taken from the company's financial statements for 2004 and the first half of 2005.

its lack of financial discipline. By the end of 2004, the company had accumulated an artwork inventory valued at 3.5 times its total annual revenues – a classic example of the risk of "excessive inventory" and one that is also present in the business of books and game publishers when they fail to balance circulation with demand and end up stocking the warehouse with finished goods. In the absence of proper risk management, freezing large financial resources in the form of working capital leaves an art dealer unprotected from negative changes in the business environment, allowing the dealer's financial position to rapidly worsen as a result.

Approximately 150 years ago, Cézanne's sole dealer "papa Tango" went bankrupt. As a result of this bankruptcy, Cézanne's first personal exhibit took place. The financial position of Partridge Fine Arts underwent the same type of development. In its interim report from July 29, 2005, John Partridge, the company's chairman of the board, explained the company's significantly worsening financial situation by stating: "We have continued to experience the most difficult and unpredictable trading conditions. Although there has been some welcome strengthening of the US dollar exchange rate in recent weeks and trading has improved, there has not yet been a marked change in many of our American clients' reluctance to make commitments to purchase at current rates of exchange." The real reason for the company's difficult financial condition could have been tied to the irresponsible management of currency risks, a task that any professionally organized business must perform.

The annual report of Partridge Fine Arts also contains some interesting data with respect to the business model of the art dealer. The company's annual revenues were not enough to purchase even six paintings from Skate's Top 1000. In other words, not a single significant work of art listed in Skate's Top 1000 was handled by a transaction involving Partridge Fine Arts. An analysis of its artwork sales by geographic segment shows that although the volume of art asset sales to American buyers fell significantly (nearly twofold from GBP 5.9 million to GBP 2.8 million) in 2004, at the same time sales to European countries other than the United Kingdom sharply increased (by 70% from GBP 1 million to GBP 1.7 million). The timely globalization of the trade in artworks could have allowed a dealer like Partridge Fine Arts to more easily survive the cyclical fall in demand for art assets in the United States by switching its focus to other regions.

As a perfect end to this case study of poor risk management in the art dealer business, Partridge Fine Arts was acquired in 2006 by Amor Holdings Ltd. (an arts and antiques investment company), which has the financial backing of Christie's. Amor acquired a 51% stake for USD 6.9 million or USD 0.60 per share. When the acquisition agreement was announced, the market price of Partridge shares was approximately USD 0.95 per share. Partridge's listing on the LSE was canceled, and according to the Partial Offer, the company should be re-registered as a private limited company. In return for Christie's financing of the acquisition, Partridge's art inventories were sold through Christie's in May 2006 for USD 14,855,600.

Interestingly enough, in the art investment business, large auction houses, enjoying their comfortable position as large corporations with solid access to capital and a strong grip on their core market, seem to provide an exit of last resort for shareholders of large art galleries and dealers. The Partridge transaction is not the first case when an investment company backed by an auction house has taken over and liquidated a failed art dealer. In May 1990, Sotheby's entered a similar transaction, purchasing Pierre Matisse Gallery Corporation for USD 153 million and entering into a 50/50 partnership agreement with Acquavella Contemporary Art Inc. (another art investment group) to manage the entire process of disposing the Matisse Gallery's inventory, a process that continues to this day (this agreement is scheduled to expire only on March 31, 2007).[14] In cases such as these, the auction house targets not only interest income, but more importantly income from auction sales of a failed dealer's inventory.

Unfortunately, financial information on Amor Holdings Ltd and Acquavella Contemporary Art has not been publicly disclosed. We have reason to believe, however, that art dealers who enjoy the partnership and financial backing of the world's largest auction houses live in a much more secure and predictable world and are far more immune to the significant operational and financial risks to which independent small art dealers are exposed.

14. All values are quoted as per Sotheby's 10K filings with the U.S. SEC / EDGAR.

In many ways, the history of Partridge has been repeated with Artemis. Unlike Partridge Fine Arts, however, Artemis Fine Arts is one of several art dealers with a diverse and tangibly functioning network. Since its purchase of Germany's C.G. Boerner in the 1990s, a company with a 175-year history, Artemis Fine Arts has conducted business in four major world cities – New York, London, Paris and Düsseldorf. Its international network, however, did not suffice to protect it from the same risk management problems involving liquidity and excessive inventory that Partridge encountered. The volume in storage (artworks in galleries and warehouses) exceeded the annual revenues of Artemis Fine Arts by nearly threefold, leaving the company particularly vulnerable to changes in the market environment.

The management of Artemis Fine Arts was also able to craft an elegant explanation for the company's financial problems. In presenting to shareholders the company's decreased revenues by 19% in 2003 over the previous year, the management attributed the decline to changing tastes in art among the public. Like Partridge, excessive inventory was the reason for the company's significantly worsened financial indicators (in this case, in 2003). On the sixth page of the company's annual report, the management affirms that "where previously a strong German economy had provided a good market…today paintings by Rembrandt, Van Goyen and Salomon van Ruysdael amongst others, for which top prices were paid in prior years, remain unsold." While there may be an element of truth in this statement, when taking into account the structure of sales of Artemis Fine Arts (approximately 50% of turnover was related to sales of artworks to large international museums like the Metropolitan, The Getty, The Art Institute of Chicago, The Museum of Fine Arts in Boston, the Smithsonian in Washington and the National Gallery in London),[15] it is obvious that the company could have been more responsible in managing its purchases, forecasting the interests of purchasing museums and not allowing the inventory levels to exceed critical ratios.

As a result, at the time of this book's publication, Artemis Fine Arts was also in the process of changing hands. On May 17, 2006 it was announced that El Rocio Investments Ltd. and AXA Versicherung AG had signed an agreement for the sale of a controlling stake in Artemis Fine Arts by AXA Versicherung to El Rocio Investments. The agreement covers the sale and purchase of 872,789 shares (55.49% of all

15. Information on the company's sales structure was taken from an interview with Artemis Fine Arts S.A.'s chairman of the board of directors, Walter Lanssens, at http://www.twst.com/notes/articles/lss009.html

shares outstanding), for a price of USD 11.75 per share. The agreed price represents a premium of 9.23% on the preceding month's average share price and a premium of 11.06% on the closing price of May 16, 2006.

Apparently the financial problems that the above art dealers experienced illustrate the price that many art dealers pay for not introducing modern corporate governance and risk management practices into their operations. In itself, the art dealer business model is undoubtedly sound. An analysis of the financial reports produced by Artemis Fine Arts and Partridge Fine Arts shows that gross margins in the art dealer business vary on the order of 18-25% and, in this way, match the profits enjoyed by the large international auction houses. In Chapter 6, we will discuss some of the more exciting opportunities in the art dealership market.

1.6. Professional services

While the art dealer business is fragmented and lacks large international dealers resembling the investment banks on the world's capital markets, the business of professional services (authentication, restoration, valuation, etc.) has remained at the level of artisan labor. Practically all large dealers and auction houses have corresponding specialists on their staffs or enjoy an alliance with experts who offer these professional services. The institution of experts as the main evaluators and authenticators of artworks is discussed in greater deal in the following chapters.

Chapter 2
Measuring the Market for Investment Quality Art

Applying objective and professional financial metrics to the world of art investment yields eye-opening results. Of the world's top 1000 most valuable artworks, only 93 have been sold more than once in the last 21 years. Effective annualized investment returns on the world's most significant masterpieces (measured by repeat sales) stand at a disappointing -1.63%, with no single artwork purchased for more than USD 10.9 million generating a positive investment return over the last two decades.

In this chapter, we will examine the limitations of the existing benchmarks in the market for investment quality art and then focus on the following two proprietary tools that Skate Press successfully developed to measure market performance:

1) Skate's Masterpieces Peer Group (Skate's Top 1000), a database of the world's 1000 most valuable works of art, which is continuously updated using information on market transactions whose details have been made public; and

2) Skate's Index of Repeat Sales, which tracks true effective returns on investments in the world's most significant artworks on the basis of repeat sales (i.e., when important artworks change hands at public auctions more than once in the past 25 years, allowing for more than one data point to be fixed and annualized effective investment returns calculated on that basis).

2.1. Existing art indices

As with every other investment market, responsible art investors need access to trustworthy and objective information, as well as professional research. *What are the current prices for the world's most significant works of art? What are the true effective historical returns? What are the projected price trends? How do the forward-looking dynamics that influence demand drivers look?* These are among the typical questions art investors should ask. Understanding the nature of supply and how it changes is equally critical. When investing in art, one should be aware of how many artworks a particular master has created, how many of these works are in free float and what proportion is closely held by national museums and trusts.

While asking all of these standard financial questions is relatively simple, finding answers relevant to the world of art investment is a far more complex task. As we discussed in the first chapter, ascertaining the price of the world's most significant art is a discrete process confined to an oligopoly of major auction houses, a series of major international art shows and a very quiet over-the-counter dealer market. All market participants do not have equal access to information, and no regulation prescribes how auction houses and market intermediaries must operate or how artworks as investment products are treated. With few exceptions, there are no publicly accessible centralized registers of significant artists' works. There is also a great degree of subjectivity involved in confirming the authenticity of art. Finally, major art investors are not subject to the same disclosure and accountability requirements that govern institutional investors in other markets. These limitations make it extremely difficult to track ownership data and the effective returns that art investors achieve.

Fascination with the world of art investment, fueled by the mystique surrounding it and the eye-catching price records set by masterpieces at public auctions, has encouraged many different parties, from scholars to entrepreneurs, to suggest various tools to measure and monitor art market performance. The art investment indices of Mei-Moses, Artnet, Artprice and others, all widely covered in the press and specialized literature, attempt to describe and benchmark price performance in the art market. We have elected not to describe these indices in this book for two principal reasons – (1) plentiful information readily exists about these indices, making it likely that our readers are already familiar with them, and (2) as explained further below, we believe these price indices have little practical use.

From a professional investment standpoint, any index designed to measure the performance of one segment of an investment market is only useful from a practical point of view when the index can be purchased. In other words, an index portfolio can be established to track the market without trying to beat it (over-perform the index). If an index is not investable, meaning that an index portfolio cannot be created by allocating funds into the index constituents according to prices and weights used in the index calculation process, then the practical value of the index is nil. It remains no more than an indicative market measurement tool that may not necessarily reflect the true "average" performance of the investment market the index claims to benchmark.

All existing price indices fall into the same trap. In tracking overall price levels on the art market and indexing the art markets' performance, these indices effectively view all artworks as a standard investment product differentiated by no more than two or three factors, such as artist name, genre or period. We believe this approach is fundamentally wrong, and in the next chapter we will discuss why it is impossible to look at art as a standard investment product in the same way that we look at stocks, bonds or mortgage-backed securities. Given the way art valuation works, one must examine each masterpiece individually. While averaging price performance for all of Picasso's works or all nudes painted in France during the nineteenth century can yield fairly interesting interesting (and often intellectually intriguing) results that describe price levels in related art market segments, these results have very little to do with effective rates of investment returns. Very few artworks are sold repeatedly, and an increase in overall price levels does not necessarily mean one can buy and sell a work of art at returns comparable with changes in the price indices developed by companies like Artprice or Artnet. Unlike stocks or bonds, where each individual security is identical as long as it belongs to a single class of shares or bonds (and unique identification codes such as ISIN and CUSIP in capital markets are assigned to each class, not to each individual security), artworks are unique, making it useless to treat all works by Picasso or Matisse as the same "investment asset" class. Each work will have fundamentally different valuation drivers and subsequently different prices within each single "class" (artist, period, and genre).

None of the art market indices available today meets the criteria of an investable index, and hence these indices not only possess little practical use from an investment point of view, but also produce rather misleading benchmarks. The issue at hand is one of liquidity. While art prices may rise in general, the increases are largely the result of new works being bought by new investors at higher prices. At the same time, the dynamics of repeat sales, which are very few in number, suggest that the annualized effective rates of return achieved on investments in significant masterpieces are far more modest and do not correlate at all with overall changes in art prices. We will provide evidence to support this statement further in this chapter.

Finally, today's art indices ignore a very specific feature of the market for investment quality art, namely, the enormous transaction and ownership costs that are simply not an issue for investments made in more efficient traditional capital markets. To adequately understand potential returns on art assets when compared to stocks or bonds, an investor must also compare commissions paid to auction houses, insurance, physical security and so forth with expenses such as broker commissions, settlement fees and depositary charges that are incurred when investing in mainstream assets.

2.2. Skate's Top 1000 — the masterpieces peer group and the proxy for the investment quality art market

In the world of finance, three principal approaches are used to value an asset – liquidation value (the price paid by the market for an asset offered in a "fire sale"), discounted free cash flow (DCF) value (value based on the sum of all future cash flows generated by an asset, discounted to reflect the time value of money and the fundamental risks surrounding an asset), and analogue valuation (based on prices paid for comparable assets under similar circumstances).

Analogue based valuation (also known as valuation based on multiples of a peer group of companies) is widely considered one of the most practical ways of quickly determining the valuation range for an asset without conducting significant research and modeling. All that is required is the ability to correctly identify a list of comparable companies (a peer group) and assemble high-level data on their values from public sources. The pertinent data could include price to earnings, price to sales and other financial ratios (referred to a multiples-based analysis or valuation) on a range of publicly traded companies comprising a peer group. Solving for proportion and benchmarking the asset in question against a peer group of companies then allows one to make a "napkin test" of a valuation range based on a simple high-level comparison to a peer group of companies. As simple as it seems, the analogue valuation approach is almost universally used in the financial world alongside fundamental DCF valuation models. It is also an approach of choice for buy-side professionals who often initially screen planned investments with multiples-based analysis to avoid building time-consuming financial models for every investment opportunity they see.

In this book we describe our approach to the multiples-based valuation of the world's most significant art. Skate Press has developed the pioneering Skate's Masterpieces Peer Group, which is a formalized process of benchmarking the world's most significant art against Skate's proprietary database of the world's 1000 most valuable artworks (based on price records for public transactions). Essentially a rating of the world's 1000 most valuable artworks (published in Schedule A of this edition as of September 1, 2006 and updated at www.skatepress.com), Skate's Masterpieces Peer Group serves as the nucleus of the database describing the world's most valuable art assets alongside a series of parameters detailed further in this chapter. Every significant work of art that appears on the market (at a major art auction or trade show, in a large gallery or over-the-counter) can be mapped against Skate's Masterpieces Peer Group (if it does not belong to it already), allowing one to quickly assemble not only the valuation range but also certain valuable data on liquidity and historical effective investment returns on similar artworks. Skate Press actively makes use of analogue valuations based on Skate's Masterpieces Peer Group when working with large private banks and their customers. Standing alone, the rating of the world's 1000 most expensive artworks paints an interesting and intriguing picture of the world of art finance.

Exhibit 2.1 – Key indicators of the market for the world's most valuable artworks

Indicator	*Value*
Market capitalization in nominal prices (1)	USD 9,332,754,827
Market capitalization in real prices (2)	USD 10,700,220,287
Number of "investment quality artists" (artists in the Top 1000)	171
Artist with the greatest "capitalization"	Pablo Picasso (USD 1.6 bln)
Artist with the largest number of works listed in the Top 1000	Pablo Picasso (123)
Artist with the largest average price	Georges Seurat (USD 35.2 mln)
Nominal threshold price for Top 1000 entrance	USD 3,986,820
Real price threshold price for Top 1000 entrance	USD 4,562,399
Average annual turnover (3)	USD 733 mln
Average annual top 100 index growth (4)	5.05%
Average annual top 300 index growth (5)	5.50%
Average annual top 500 index growth (6)	5.84%

(1) Auction prices converted to USD and including buyer's premium with no time value adjustment made
(2) Auction prices converted to USD and excluding buyer's premium, indexed to reflect the time value of money as per the real terms prices calculations methodology described in section 2.4.1
(3) Averaged on the basis of a period of 21 years, from 1985 to 2005 and reflecting trading volumes with works of art included in Skate's Top 1000
(4) 100 most valuable works in nominal prices in USD, including buyers' premiums, from January 1, 1995 to December 31, 2005
(5) 300 most valuable works in nominal prices in USD, including buyers' premiums, from January 1, 1995 to December 31, 2005
(6) 500 most valuable works in nominal prices in USD, including buyers' premiums, from January 1, 1995 to December 31, 2005
Source: www.skatepress.com

The USD 9.3 billion market for the world's 1000 most significant masterpieces is based on publicly recorded prices for art sales, with 96.7% of all entries in terms of combined value (and 96.9% in terms of number of artworks) compiled from the world's two largest art auction houses – Sotheby's and Christie's. As such, Skate's Masterpieces Peer Group largely reflects the price trends, valuations and liquidity patterns existent within and set on the global auction markets.

Exhibit 2.2 – Allocation of works from Skate's Top 1000 by auction house

Auction house	*Number of works*	*Total value, USD*
Sotheby's	503	4,846,862,586
Christie's	466	4,177,908,563
Phillips, de Pury & Luxembourg / Phillips	21	190,432,000
Binoche & Godeau	2	61,895,900
Ader, Tajan / Ader, Picard, Tajan	3	24,974,030
Piasa	3	20,388,111
Others	2	10,293,647

Source: www.skatepress.com

A key but critical difference distinguishes Skate's Masterpieces Peer Group dataset and the massive databases that information vendors like Artprice and Artnet operate. Significant third party academic research supports every entry in Skate's dataset, and the provenance multiple (the discount rate reflecting risks of authenticity and export restrictions described in great detail in Chapter 4) of each work in Skate's dataset is close or equal to 1. In other words, Skate's Masterpieces Peer Group is a quality comparables group that can be used for analogue-based valuations without worry over forgeries. It also allows one to factor in transaction costs when calculating effective investment returns – a good starting point to objectively benchmark the performance of art assets as an investment class.

2.3. Repeat sales

Skate's Masterpieces Peer Group also permits us to measure effective investment returns on the world's most significant art. An index of repeat sales designed by Skate Press tracks transactions for all of the artworks included in Skate's Masterpieces Peer Group that have subsequently been returned to the market, potentially several times. As of September 1, 2006, there were only 93 repeat sales[1] in Skate's Masterpieces Peer Group (based on data covering the period since January 1, 1985). In other words, only 9.3% of the

1. Taking into account only repeat sales of artworks that were already listed in Skate's Top 1000

world's most valuable artworks were sold more than once on the public market during the last 21 years.

Given that repeat sales create at least two price data points on a timeline, information on them allows us to extract valuable information on actual (effective) rates of return achieved by art investors on the basis of completed transactions. Skate Press uses the Annualized Effective Rate of Return (ERR) as the metric of actual investment returns on art investments. The ERR reflects actual returns achieved from investment in art assets - net commissions paid to auction houses - before net VAT adjustments, personal taxes and ownership costs, with all values calculated in nominal rates and not adjusted to inflation.

Amazingly, it turns out that the weighted average ERR based on the 93 repeat sales in Skate's Masterpieces Peer Group lies in negative territory, equal to -1.63%. With the exception of works by the Old Masters and postmodernists, negative returns are observed across every period. Even those in positive territory yield less than 8% on an annualized basis.

Exhibit 2.3 – Weighted average ERR for the world's most significant art by period

Period	*Year of creation*	*Number of repeat sales**	*Average purchase price (USD)*	*Weighted average annualized ERR, %*	*Weighted average holding period (years)*
From Renaissance to Classicism	1487 - 1866	1	9,077,500	7.7%	3.0
Rise and golden age of Impressionism	1867 - 1887	20	8,522,780	(2.0%)	9.1
Neo-impressionism, Venetian Renaissance, Nabism, Fauvism, Modernism	1888 - 1903	16	6,677,267	(2.9%)	6.9
Cubism, expressionism, suprematism, Dadaism	1904 - 1921	24	7,717,709	(0.6%)	9.3
Surrealism and abstract art	1922 - 1946	7	8,112,800	(2.1%)	7.0
Action painting and pop-art	1947 - 1970	17	4,453,364	(2.1%)	7.6
Postmodernism	1971 - 2002	3	7,071,736	3.0%	6.8
Other repeat sales	n/a	5	6,664,464	(4.6%)	5.9
Total		**93**	**7,082,029**	**(1.6%)**	**8.1**

* Taking into account only repeat sales of artworks that were already listed in Skate's Top 1000
Source: www.skatepress.com

Analyzing repeat sales also supports certain important beliefs widely accepted in the art investment market, including that (1) investments made beyond a certain price level are largely driven by irrational motives, meaning that an investor purchasing an individual work of art at a price over a certain threshold[2] should not expect a positive return if he attempts to return the artwork back to the market; and (2) an art investment requires relatively long holding periods, with optimal exit after one or more cycles from the date of the investment.

2. As of September 1, 2006, there have been no repeat sales recorded in Skate's Masterpieces Peer Group for artworks sold for more than USD 26.4 million.

Exhibit 2.4 – Skate's Masterpieces Peer Group: effective returns based on repeat sales

Distribution of annualized ERR connected to the initial purchase

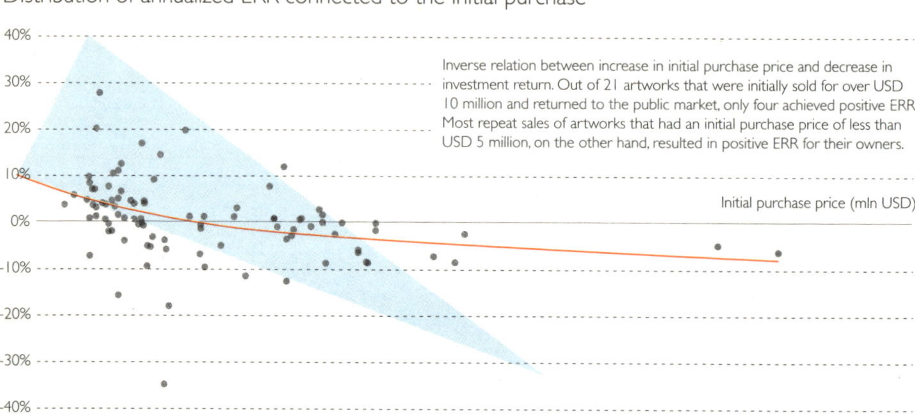

Source: www.skatepress.com

Exhibit 2.4 provides convincing statistical evidence that paying more than USD 10.9 million for a work of art leaves virtually no chance of achieving a positive ERR on such an investment. Transactions over USD 10 million are largely made to remove a work of art from the market. Decisions on these types of purchases are largely driven by motives so unique to a buyer that finding another buyer with the same motives and prepared to pay an even higher price is statistically improbable.

As shown in Exhibit 2.4, if historical repeat sales of significant art provide any guide, a realistic target annualized rate of return should be below 20% for works of art priced at a few million dollars (but below the ceiling of USD 10.9 million, above which no positive returns have been recorded thus far), making art investments (without yet factoring in ownership costs!) in general far less attractive than venture capital or private equity deals.

As clearly demonstrated in Exhibit 2.5, the longer the holding period, the greater the probability of realizing a positive return on an art investment. While this return will not necessarily become consider-

Exhibit 2.5 – Skate's Masterpieces Peer Group: effective returns and holding period

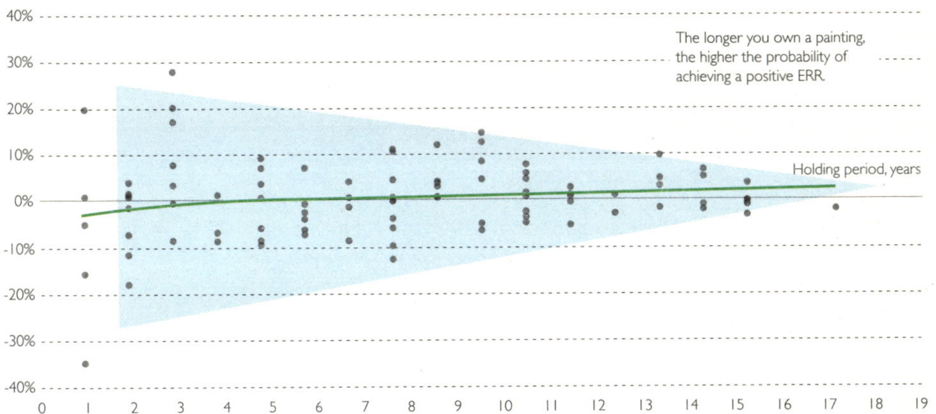

Source: www.skatepress.com

ably more attractive over the years, the repeat sale is at least more likely to generate a positive effective return. Once ownership costs are added to the calculation, however, it becomes rather obvious that longer holding periods aimed at achieving positive returns are offset by a buildup in such costs (e.g. insurance, storage, security fees) over the years. Increased yields over longer investment horizons are unlikely to help recoup the ownership costs incurred over the same period. For these reasons, a rational investment strategy might actually favor short-term art investment tactics that play on current price trends and demand patterns. Most art dealers actually work this way when committing capital to art assets, rarely having more than an 18-month investment horizon for their purchases, with commissions secured from sellers and guaranteed minimums promised to them.

In later chapters, we will use repeat sales statistics extensively to benchmark the performance of certain segments in the art market. The entire listing of repeat sales recorded for Skate's Masterpieces Peer Group as of September 1, 2006 is published in Schedule C and is updated online at www.skatepress.com.

2.4. Data and calculations

Elsewhere in this book, we will only use two primary art market measurement tools – Skate's Masterpieces Peer Group (Skate's Top 1000) and Skate's Index of Repeat Sales – to illustrate the rules and principles of art investing. In this section, however, we provide inquisitive readers with a detailed overview of how Skate Press gathers and processes the data underlying these measurement tools.

2.4.1. Price data

Skate Press updates its database as soon as it discovers reliable and objective information on a work of art valuable enough to be included in Skate's Top 1000. The Top 1000 listing includes information on the artist and the work's period of creation, literature describing the work, an image, the year of creation, size, technique and provenance. It also includes price, date and the currency of sales, as well as information on commissions paid and any available information on the buyer. Price data is always verified at the place where a public transaction with an artwork originally occurred. When archiving information on a given work, Skate Press uses the masterpiece's original name, avoiding translation into a single language.[3] This principle of data archiving gives Skate Press analysts a uniform means of processing information on pricing and calculating a number of derived indices on all works appearing in the company's database.

After initially entering data, Skate Press specialists begin processing the pricing information, which proceeds as follows:

1. An artwork's value is divided into net price for the seller, net price for the buyer, and general price (including commissions paid by both buyers and sellers). As we saw in the first chapter, the actual size of the transaction costs considerably exceeds the so-called "buyer's premium" in so far as the oligopolistic nature of the market allows the auction houses to levy substantial commissions on both buyers and sellers.

2. With the help of an automated algorithmic search of conformities, a new artwork in the database is tested for its uniqueness. Skate Press conducts this test because repeat sales of the same works often occur on the market, but under different names (i.e.

3. In the literature one can find different translations of the names of artworks, a fact resulting from the lack of recognized translation standards for many works.

different languages) and with different years attributed to their creation. Copies of the same work are also occasionally found on the market. In the event that doubts arise as to the authenticity of a work sold, Skate Press specialists perform additional research, turning to art authenticators and critics to confirm a work's uniqueness.

3. Prices are converted into USD (the standard currency used by Skate Press) based on the official exchange rates on the date a work is purchased. General prices (buyer's prices, including premiums) can readily be compared with historical data. On this basis, the Skate's Top 1000 is actually built and updated in nominal prices.

4. To convert the index of the 1000 most valuable works into real prices (i.e., prices that take into account inflation[4]), the prices of all works in the Skate Press database – excluding buyers' premiums – are multiplied by an index of the U.S. dollar's purchasing power. The Bureau of Labor Statistics at the U.S. Department of Labor[5] serves as the source of information for calculation, with the Consumer Price Index – All Urban Customers (CPI-U) being used as the deflator for calculating real prices of artworks.

Archiving and processing pricing information for artworks in this way allows us to create a number of high-quality statistics for comparing individual artworks sold on the open (auction) market. These statistics can be then be used to form a number of key and second-level indicators for the market of investment quality art. We will examine these indicators in greater detail in the section below.

2.4.2. Derivative price indices: key market indicators

The goal in creating key indicators of the market for investment quality art is the maximum objective representation of current price trend dynamics and the "depth" (liquidity) of the public market for the most valuable artworks. These key indicators also allow one to evaluate the market's composition (structure of market capitalization according to industry by analogy with the stock market), as well as the allocation of value, trading volumes and growth rates in the outward value of artworks.

4. If a work is sold for USD 10 million in 1989 and another for USD 10 million in 1997, then the former is obviously more valuable to the extent that the U.S. dollar's purchasing power decreased over those eight years. Purchasing power is one means of measuring the temporary value of money at any given time.

5. See http://www.bls.gov/cpi/home.htm

Skate Press has developed the following list of the main key indicators in the market for investment quality art. All indicators are reflected in both nominal and real prices, allowing those using the statistics to choose a preferred indicator.

a. Capitalization of the market for investment quality art, calculated as the aggregate value of all artworks included in Skate's Top 1000.

b. Average value of the top 1000 artworks, calculated as the average of Skate's Top 1000.

c. Threshold price, corresponding to the 1000th work in Skate's Top 1000.

d. Index of market breadth – number of artists in the rating.

e. Index of market depth – turnover in the past twelve months as a percentage of market capitalization. Turnover is calculated as the aggregate value of all new works included in Skate's Top 1000 over the past twelve months and is intended to be a measure of liquidity in the art market.

f. Index of repeat sales – this index reflects the turnover of the most significant works on the open market and is calculated as the number of repeat sales of works in Skate's Top 1000 over a ten-year period as a percentage of 1000.

g. Average annual yield, calculated as the change in market capitalization over a respective period and expressed in annual percentages.

Exhibit 2.6 – General indicators in the global market for investment quality art

Indicator[6]	*September 1, 2005*	*September 1, 2006*	*Change over previous year (%)*
Market capitalization (USD)	8,618,941,667	9,332,754,827	8.28
Average value of a work (USD)	8,618,942	9,332,755	8.28
Threshold price	3,632,500	3,986,820	9.75
Index of market breadth	177	171	-3.39
Index of market depth	10.6%	10.0%	-58 bps
Index of repeat sales	7.8%	9.3%	150 bps

Source: www.skatepress.com

2.4.3. Derivative price indices: market segmentation (second-level indicators)

To analyze the market for investment quality art, Skate Press segments the list of the 1000 most valuable artworks into the categories described further in this section. On their basis, the art market's second-level indicators are calculated. Several examples of using second-level indicators are presented in the tables below, which include an analysis of Skate's Top 1000 as of September 1, 2006.

a. Market capitalization of individual artists, calculated as the aggregate value of all works by an individual artist that have entered the Top 1000 (prices are calculated and updated simultaneously in both nominal and real prices). These statistics are presented as a rating of top 50 most valuable artists in Schedule B.

b. "Productivity index" of historical periods, calculated as the aggregate market value of works from Skate's Top 1000 that were created in a particular period (see Exhibit 2.7).

c. "Subject popularity index," calculated as the aggregate market value of works from Skate's Top 1000 that depict a particular standard subject (see Exhibit 2.8).

6. All indicators are calculated in nominal terms as described in section 2.4.1.

d. "Size popularity index," calculated as the aggregate market value of works from Skate's Top 1000 that were created according to a standard size.

e. Historical statistics of general capitalization dynamics, average and threshold prices by century, as well as actual yields of portfolios composed of works from Skate's Top 1000 (see Exhibit 2.9 for some statistics on selected Top 1000 subsegments).

f. Historical dynamics of first and second-level indicators from the entire period of research (since 1985).

g. Index of individual markets' capitalization, calculated as the aggregate market value of works from Skate's Top 1000 that were sold at individual auctions or in individual cities.

Exhibit 2.7 – Skate's Top 1000 by period of creation

Period	*Year of creation*	*Number of works*	*Length of period in years (inclusive)*
From Renaissance to Classicism	1487–1866*	60	380
Rise and golden age of Impressionism	1867–1887	120	21
Neo-impressionism, Venetian Renaissance, Nabism, Fauvism, Modernism	1888–1903	157	16
Cubism, Expressionism, Suprematism, Dadaism	1904–1921	235	18
Surrealism and abstract art	1922–1946	130	25
Action painting (9) and pop art	1947–1970	170	24
Postmodernism	1971–2002	43	32

* There are also three works prior to the year of 1487 (primarily Leonardo de Vinci)
Source: www.skatepress.com

Exhibit 2.8 – Skate's Top 1000 by subject (genre)

Subject	*Number of works*	*Subject*	*Number of works*
Landscape	239	Other portrait	40
Female portrait	146	Self-portrait	16
Abstraction	148	Female with a child portrait	12
Nude	86	Religious subject	19
Male portrait	56	Installation	1
Still life	56	*Others*	129
Sculpture	52		

Source: www.skatepress.com

Exhibit 2.9 – Historical data for the Top 100, Top 300, Top 500 and Top 1000 groups

	2001	*2002*	*2003*	*2004*	*2005*
Top 100					
Capitalization, mln USD	2,424	2,522	2,594	2,778	2,839
*Top 100 MCAP index**	*139*	*145*	*149*	*159*	*163*
Annual growth, mln USD	48	98	72	184	61
Top 100 annual growth index	*2%*	*4%*	*3%*	*7%*	*2%*
Annual turnover, mln USD	151	205	185	345	201
*Top 100 annual turnover index**	*93*	*126*	*114*	*213*	*124*
Annual turnover, % of MCAP	*6%*	*8%*	*7%*	*13%*	*7%*
Threshold price, USD	12,980,000	13,752,500	14,306,000	14,850,500	16,256,000
*Top 100 threshold price index**	*146*	*155*	*161*	*167*	*183*
Top 300					
Capitalization, mln USD	4,242	4,420	4,575	4,866	5,045
Top 300 MCAP index	*143*	*149*	*154*	*164*	*170*
Annual growth, mln USD	142	177	156	291	178
Top 300 annual growth index	*3%*	*4%*	*4%*	*6%*	*4%*
Annual turnover, mln USD	375	311	344	540	433
Top 300 annual turnover index	*140*	*116*	*128*	*201*	*161*
Annual turnover, % of MCAP	*9%*	*7%*	*8%*	*12%*	*9%*
Threshold price, USD	6,820,000	7,098,083	7,272,325	7,891,454	8,362,500
Top 300 threshold price index	*155*	*161*	*165*	*179*	*190*

	2001	*2002*	*2003*	*2004*	*2005*
Top 500					
Capitalization, mln USD	5,370	5,595	5,812	6,187	6,457
Top 500 MCAP index	*146*	*153*	*158*	*169*	*176*
Annual growth, mln USD	215	225	217	376	270
Top 500 annual growth index	*4%*	*4%*	*4%*	*6%*	*4%*
Annual turnover, mln USD	488	393	434	698	597
Top 500 annual turnover index	*149*	*120*	*133*	*214*	*183*
Annual turnover, % of MCAP	*9%*	*7%*	*8%*	*12%*	*10%*
Threshold price, USD	4,840,000	4,959,500	5,280,000	5,509,500	6,010,427
Top 500 threshold price index	*166*	*171*	*182*	*189*	*207*
Top 1000					
Capitalization, mln USD	7,197	7,525	7,840	8,367	8,814
Top 1000 MCAP index	*100*	*105*	*109*	*116*	*122*
Annual growth, mln USD	-	328	316	527	447
Top 1000 annual growth index		*5%*	*4%*	*7%*	*5%*
Annual turnover, mln USD	674	605	553	936	896
Top 1000 annual turnover index	*92*	*83*	*76*	*128*	*122*
Annual turnover, % of MCAP	0%	8%	7%	12%	11%
Threshold price, USD	2,862,500	3,080,921	3,228,767	3,515,660	3,746,000
Top 1000 threshold price index	*100*	*108*	*113*	*123*	*131*

* Threshold price, annual turnover and market cap indices are indexed from a base of 100 points on January 1, 1995 except for Top 1000, which has a base of 100 points on January 1, 2001.
Source: www.skatepress.com

Chapter 3
Art Valuation Drivers

With all of its imperfections, especially its poor liquidity (only 1-2% of repeat sales per annum in Skate's Top 1000 when measured by number of artworks) and its low level of transparency (at least half of the dealings in the world's most significant art are often barely traceable and leave no public records), investors can hardly rely on the infrastructure of the art investment market when trying to discern the appropriate price of an asset. The price discovery process is tortuous, which is unfortunate given that the ability to understand art valuation drivers and develop one's own set of arguments defending a valuation range is the key competence of people and organizations making transactions on the art market. What is left is a small number of art experts playing the central role in determining prices. In cases of non-forced transactions (when there is no urgency to sell and no need to enter financial pledge agreements), expert opinions about art valuation set the basis for negotiations. Auction houses function to drive valuations even higher whenever more than one bidder seeks a given work of art.

This book attempts to demystify the work of art experts and condense their collective knowledge and experience into a pragmatic procedure for use in art valuation. In this chapter, we will examine all of the key valuation drivers applicable to the art asset class, and in Chapter 4, we will introduce the practical art valuation tools developed by Skate Press.

3.1. The role of experts in art valuation

Expert knowledge remains at the core of the art valuation process. The lack of a transparent information infrastructure allows experts to play a vital role as sources of knowledge about an artwork's provenance and authenticity. Expert knowledge is often supported by both the name and personal reputation of an individual, which in turn stems from his or her academic credentials, family roots (it is customary for famous artists' heirs to serve as authenticity experts, for example) and track record to date.

Reliance on expert opinion in art asset valuation leaves the art market on shaky ground, as human error becomes a major risk factor in a way that is not the case with traditional investment markets where such risks do not affect the process of determining the authenticity of investment products or objectivity of information. Expert errors have been known to be both unintentional and intentional, with cases of the latter often being driven by conflicts of interest. Given that very little regulation exists in the art market, professional ethics can be notorious, meaning that due to personal financial considerations experts are prone to take sides with either buyers or sellers in the valuation process. Moreover, multiple examples exist of competing experts performing valuations and authenticity checks for certain individual artists. Because significant transactions with art, including museum purchases, are often made on the over-the-counter market, the lack of transparent pricing coupled with an art expert's ability to compromise professional integrity in the cozy nature of the art world (often based on personal rather than professional relationships), it can be very easy and tempting for museum curators, art dealers and experts to enter into agreements that inflate art valuations at the expense of museum (or public trust) funds, splitting the proceeds for personal use.

Albeit late and incomplete, the recent arrival of useful information technologies has made some inroads into the still fairly strong market position of expert opinion with respect to art valuation. At least three elements of the information infrastructure partially described in Chapter 1 make it easier to value art on the basis of objective and verifiable data rather than subjective expert opinion:

1) Art Loss Register – Described in section 1.4, the Art Loss Register allows a work of art to be checked against a database of lost and stolen art, including art placed under 1933-1945 cultural spoliation claims.[1]

2) Object ID – An international standard for describing cultural objects and essentially the equivalent of an individual security code (CUSIP/ISIN) that exists for traditional investable assets, Object ID was developed through the collaboration of the museum community, police and customs agencies, the art trade, the insurance industry and appraisers of art and antiques. Currently being implemented by the Council for the Prevention of Art Theft (CoPAT), the Object ID project was initiated by the J. Paul Getty Trust in 1993, with the standard being launched in 1997. Object ID is being promoted by major law enforcement agencies, including the FBI, Scotland Yard and Interpol.

3) Price databases – Price record databases, developed and operated by companies like Artprice and Artnet, have helped spread knowledge about prior sales of artworks, making it possible for many investors and intermediaries to conduct their own research into historical price data and comparable sales, thus reducing dependency on art experts.

Art valuation remains more an art than a science, however. An individual's experience in practical art valuation will remain at the heart of successful art investment. As we will see later in this chapter, the mechanical use of art valuation drivers should allow for a disciplined approach to an art investment decision, although there will still be considerable room for judgment calls about final transaction prices.

3.2. Practical approaches to art valuation

As in the world of traditional investments, the use of valuation methods is driven by the economic interests of the person performing the valuation, a person who can represent either a buyer or seller or be positioned independently.

In this context, the valuation methods used extensively throughout this book are based on an independent valuation approach. Before

1. Such claims are defined as objects confiscated by Nazi looting agencies, the Soviet "trophy brigades" or through individual acts of looting by Allied troops.

we dive into these methods, however, it might make sense to give a brief overview of the alternative approaches to valuation and the reasons for their usage.

1) Valuation at cost – This method is perhaps one of the most widely used "back-of-the-envelope" approaches to art valuation. Tracking sales of significant art since 1985, Skate Press has observed that in at least one-third of cases sellers of important artworks name their value-at-cost as a so called "reserve price"[2] to art auctions. This figure rarely reflects ownership costs, however, and it is often simply a purchase price that includes a buyer's premium for artworks purchased at an auction. The valuation at cost approach is one vivid demonstration of the mindset behind art investment decisions. Many art buyers, while hoping for positive returns, do not consider or treat their art purchases as investments and find it perfectly acceptable to sell at cost, in reality admitting negative returns on their investments (when all transaction and ownership costs are taken into account).

• From a pragmatic point of view, this method helps quantify an essential art valuation driver known as the "joy of art ownership." An art investor who agrees to sell a masterpiece "at cost" in essence accepts the joy experienced from owning an artwork as being equal to what he or she would normally expect to earn on a similar size investment of comparably high risk over an equivalent holding period.

2) Accounting value of art investments – there is no standard under IFRS (International Financial Reporting Standards) or US GAAP (United States Generally Accepted Accounting Principles) specifically regulating the accounting for art assets by business enterprises.

Under IFRS, if a company's business is to trade with art assets then these assets will likely meet the definition of inventories under IAS 2 "Inventories" and should be accounted for at the lower of cost or net realizable value, in accordance with IAS 2. If the art assets are held as long-term investments then they do not seem to fall into the scope of any existing IFRS standard. Nevertheless, applying the guidance of IAS 16 allows either the cost model or

2. The reserve price is the lowest acceptable price for a seller to agree to sell a work of art, always pre-agreed between a seller and an auction house before the start of an auction.

the revaluation model. Under the cost model the assets would be carried at cost less any depreciation. Art assets having unlimited useful life would not be depreciated. Under the revaluation model the assets are regularly revalued to their fair value, and any revaluation gain is charged to a revaluation reserve in equity. In case of any impairment indications, the entity needs to assess the recoverable value of the asset in accordance with IAS 36 "Impairment of assets" and write it down to its recoverable amount, if it is lower than the carrying amount.

US GAAP (Statements Financial Accounting Standard ## 93, 116 and certain other pronouncements) provides specific guidance on accounting for art investments by nonprofit organizations, including the works of art in Skate's Top 1000. Generally, nonprofit organizations are required to initially record such assets at acquisition cost if they were purchased and at estimated fair value if they were contributed or donated. FAS 93 says that art works should not be depreciated on the books as long as "their 'economic' benefit or service potential is used up so slowly that their estimated useful lives are extraordinarily long." According to the same FAS 93, a work of art should be deemed to have such characteristics "only if verifiable evidence exists demonstrating that (a) the asset individually has cultural, aesthetic, or historical value that is worth preserving perpetually and (b) the holder has the technological and financial ability to protect and preserve essentially undiminished the service potential of the asset and is doing that." Recorded work of art assets will be subject to impairment testing.

• A good way to interpret the accounting view of art investments is that a masterpiece's depreciation is matched by its ownership costs, or that a major work of art does not depreciate in accounting value as long as it is being insured, stored and protected properly. Accounting rules applied for long-term art investments simply ignore the volatility of global art prices and are more consistent with the "valuation at cost" approach adopted by many art buyers and sellers.

3) Liquidation value – There are quite a few standard situations when the liquidation value approach is used to assess the value of art assets. Among these include acceptance of artworks as

collateral for term loans, cleaning up art dealers' inventories or need-to-sell circumstances that occasionally hit the owners of significant works of art. While no consistent data is available on liquidation / collateral value being used on the market for the world's masterpieces, based on information gathered through continuous research by Skate Press, the liquidation value is rarely above 30% of the market value (often determined by the recent auction sale adjusted to expert opinions on current value) and is often as low as 10% of the last auction price. These figures suggest huge liquidity risks associated with art investments.

• Because demand often has to be groomed in order to command a good price and because a buyer has to feel privileged at having the chance to purchase a work of art, fire sales are the worst selling tactic on the art market. Traditional banks also rarely accept art as collateral for a loan due to the specialist knowledge required to understand and value an art asset, as well as the ownership costs and hassle involved in accepting art as collateral. Those banks that do accept art as collateral often demand fairly substantial hedge over price fluctuations and grant loans with principal amounts equal to a mere fraction of an art asset's market price.

3.3. Art valuation drivers in non-forced market transactions

In Chapter 4, we will discuss in greater detail Skate's art asset valuation approach based on a proprietary analogue-based valuation method. This section covers in detail individual art valuation drivers. Each artwork included in Skate's Top 1000 Masterpieces Peer Group is described according to these drivers, making it possible to compare works of art across a set of descriptive factors (valuation drivers).

Analysis of the world's most significant artworks and the valuations they command suggests that an artwork's value is driven by two sets of factors. One group is made up of simple unequivocal numbers and facts, such as the artist's name, subject matter, size, year of creation and artist's age at the time of creation. Another group is made of two far less tangible drivers – provenance and transaction context.

Skate's approach to art valuation simply involves taking one step at a time and meticulously analyzing first the tangible valuation drivers, after which a judgment can be made on the intangible qualitative valuation drivers.

Maintaining Skate's Top 1000 Masterpieces Peer Group generates sufficient comparable data to properly identify and map the fact-based valuation drivers for significant artworks. These five factors, detailed in section 3.4, are:

1) Artist name
2) Size of the work
3) Subject (genre)
4) Historical period
5) Artist maturity

The critical intangible valuation drivers – provenance and transaction context (also described as irrational premium) – are covered in section 3.5.

3.4. Tangible art valuation drivers

3.4.1 Artist name

Nobody disputes the fact that prices for artworks made by the same artist can differ significantly. Mapping the distribution of a single artist's works by price levels is nevertheless quite revealing. Exhibit 3.1 shows the distribution for works included in Skate's Top 1000. Here we took the six highest valued artists by market capitalization and looked at the distribution of their works in the Top 1000 by value ranges. These data are benchmarked against Top 1000 averages. The results of this exercise clearly support the rule that the valuation of a single artist's work will be widely dispersed.

The key idea to take away from this chart is not only that none of the 10 price categories we used can absorb more than 25% of an artist's masterpieces included in the Top 1000, but also that the prices for the works of each artist from the sampling spanned nearly the entire valuation spectrum.

Exhibit 3.1 – Distribution of single artist masterpieces market values

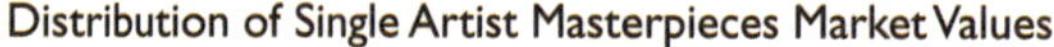

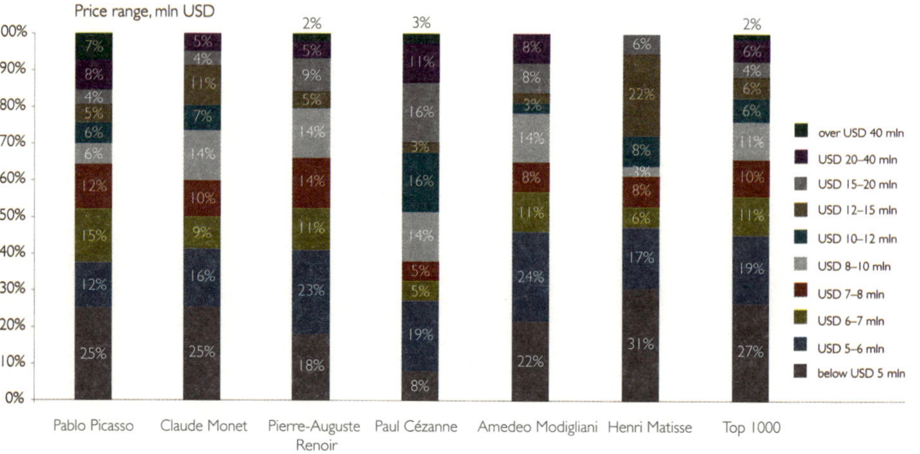

Source: www.skatepress.com

While a full technical analysis comparable to those widely used in financial markets is hardly applicable to art prices due to the inadequate depth and the non-comparable quality of data from a statistical point of view, certain observations are simply too obvious to ignore.

First, USD 6 million seems to be the price level that captures a significant share of the valuation spectrum even for the world's most valuable artists. Forty-eight percent of works by Matisse included in Skate's Top 1000 are valued at USD 6 million or less.

Second, distribution patterns also vary widely, but Cézanne stands out as being the only master that has nearly half (49%) of his works in the Top 1000 priced over USD 10 million. Picasso, who is the undisputed champion in terms of combined market capitalization, has only 30% of his works from the Top 1000 priced in the same range. The benchmark for the Top 1000 as a whole is just 24%, meaning that only about 240 artworks are priced over USD 10 million.

As Exhibit 3.1 demonstrates, simply taking an artist's name is definitely not a compelling option for establishing a valuation range for his or her works. There are several more subtle ways, however, to consider an artist's name as a valuation driver. While these variants will not yield an accurate valuation for every artist's work, they do offer some food for thought on how an artist's name can drive an artwork's price. Three of these ways are reviewed further in this section, and the fourth one – looking at valuation of artworks by living artists as a separate group – is covered in Chapter 6.

Analyzing the breadth of an artist's market is the first way to look at an artist's name as a valuation driver. As shown in Exhibit 3.2, artists can be classified into five market size (free float) categories. Clearly having 20 or more artworks in the Top 1000 provides enough reference points to justify valuation levels for significant artists. In Wall Street terminology, there are nine "blue chip" artists with a broad market (a large free float) of their artworks priced over the Top 1000 threshold.

Exhibit 3.2 - Market free float of artists

Category	*Number of works*	*Number of Artists*	*Names*
"Blue Chips"	≥ 20	9	Monet, Picasso, van Gogh, Matisse, Cézanne, Renoir, Modigliani, Degas, Warhol
"Second Tier"	8–19	18	Léger, Miró, Bacon, Rothko, Johns, Kooning, Mondrian
"Third Tier"	4–7	25	Klimt, Brancusi, Rembrandt, Twombly, Pollock, Rubens, Moore
"Rare appearances"	2–3	49	Turner, Bellows, Smith, Leonardo da Vinci, Kline, Soutine, Munnings
"Guests"	1	70	Titian, Sarto, Waterhouse, Heem, Tissot, Malevich, Wood

Source: www.skatepress.com

The second approach, widely adopted by some of our rival art market information suppliers, involves looking at average prices for an individual artist's works. Unlike our competition, however, we would only look at average prices for Skate's Top 1000 artworks and only include in the ranking the artists with four or more masterpieces in this top sampling. This approach singles out names like Rubens, Klimt[3] and Beckman as leading the pack of top valued artists, which would not be obvious if one were to look only at the market capitalization of an artist (combined value of all artworks included in the Top 1000).

Finally, a third way to address the artist's name factor is to consider the angle of nationality. Exhibit 3.4 ranks artists' nationalities, reflecting the combined value and averages for artworks created by artists of the same nationality and included in Skate's Top 1000. Again, this approach highlights the strength of Rubens and the Flemish masters in terms of artist name as an art valuation driver, a conclusion that is counterintuitive to what statistics on artist market caps or individual price records suggest.

3. Calculations for Klimt exclude the sensational sale of Golden Adele (the image on the cover of this edition) for USD 135 million reported in June 2006. This sale was conducted outside of the auction market, and the price was never officially announced. The sale is covered in greater detail in Chapter 4.

Exhibit 3.3 – Artists' average prices

Rank	*Artist name*	*Free float category*	*Average price, USD*	*Number of works*
1	Sir Peter Paul Rubens	"Third tier"	17,369,122	6
2	Edouard Manet	"Second tier"	16,861,148	8
3	Vincent van Gogh	"Blue Chips"	16,843,548	35
4	Gustav Klimt	"Third tier"	13,486,791	7
5	Paul Cézanne	"Blue Chips"	13,055,941	37
6	Pablo Picasso	"Blue Chips"	12,819,732	123
7	Max Beckmann	"Third tier"	12,343,468	4
8	Constantin Brancusi	"Third tier"	12,300,500	7
9	Canaletto	"Second tier"	11,701,768	11
10	Rembrandt Harmensz van Rijn	"Third tier"	11,625,491	7

Source: www.skatepress.com

The artist average in Exhibit 3.4 reflects the average market capitalization of an artist of a particular nationality, with Picasso driving Spanish dominance. The work average column essentially means that a work by an Austrian artist would on average be twice as expensive as one by an Irish master. French and Italian artworks, by contrast, generally command similar valuations.

Exhibit 3.4 – Art averages by nationality

Rank	*Nationality*	*Artists in Top 1000*	*Total Value*	*Total works*	*Work average*	*Artist average*
1	Spanish	12	1,803,967,583	158	11,417,516	150,330,632
2	Irish	1	118,015,994	18	6,556,444	118,015,994
3	French	35	3,361,711,028	371	9,061,216	96,048,887
4	Austrian	2	186,709,773	15	12,447,318	93,354,887
5	Rumanian	1	86,103,500	7	12,300,500	86,103,500
6	Dutch	17	913,363,544	75	12,178,181	53,727,267
7	Russian / French	2	99,809,917	13	7,677,686	49,904,959
8	Swiss	3	116,167,515	16	7,260,470	38,722,505
9	Flemish	3	113,641,804	8	14,205,226	37,880,601
10	Italian	19	718,894,453	79	9,099,930	37,836,550

Source: www.skatepress.com

Taken by themselves, these statistics have little practical use for art valuation purposes. An artist's name is clearly an important contributing factor, but it cannot be used as the only valuation driver to define an artwork's valuation range with any acceptable degree of accuracy.

3.4.2 Size of the work

Could adding the factor of size to the artist's name factor make valuation more accurate? The intuitive answer is "no." Major artists' works are not sold on a per square meter basis, a finding which, along with others discussed further in this section, supports this intuitive "no."

Exhibit 3.5 depicts the relation between artwork sizes and their values, with very little correlation between average artwork values and their sizes. The only exception is the "grand oeuvres," or works larger than four square meters in size. The discounting of G-size paintings versus smaller size peers highlights the importance of ownership costs in the art investment world. Unlike conventional investment assets, art assets absorb significant maintenance costs, and for larger size paintings the costs of storage and restoration can be particularly large. The discriminating average for G-size paintings also reflects their lack of "portable asset" utility, a valuation consideration that is a rudimentary leftover from previous eras when it was important for wealthy owners that some of their significant assets could be evacuated easily and on short notice.

Exhibit 3.5 – Average values of Skate's Top 1000 artworks grouped by size

Size group	*Square meter*	*Square inch*	*Number of works*	*Total value, USD*	*Average value, USD*
A	0 - 0.25	0 - 387.5	92	770,683,563	8,376,995
B	0.25 - 0.50	387.5 - 775	264	2,240,732,043	8,487,621
C	0.50 - 0.75	775 - 1162.5	196	1,846,077,954	9,418,765
D	0.75 – 1	1160.5 – 1550	94	1,093,045,189	11,628,140
E	1 – 2	1550 – 3100	168	1,703,268,889	10,138,505
F	2 – 4	3100 – 6200	100	1,019,321,212	10,193,212
G	> 4	> 6200	30	203,910,390	6,797,013
sculptures, mobiles, installations			56	455,715,587	8,137,778

Source: www.skatepress.com

In applying per square meter averages for individual artists' paintings and looking at the consistency of those ratios within size groups, it becomes clear that there is very little correlation between size and actual value. As we see in Exhibit 3.6, the value dots are spread widely, suggesting that if only an artist's name and artwork size is known, a work of art cannot be valued with any meaningful degree of accuracy.

Exhibit 3.6 – A blurred picture: per square meter valuation of masterpieces offers no clues to art valuation[4]

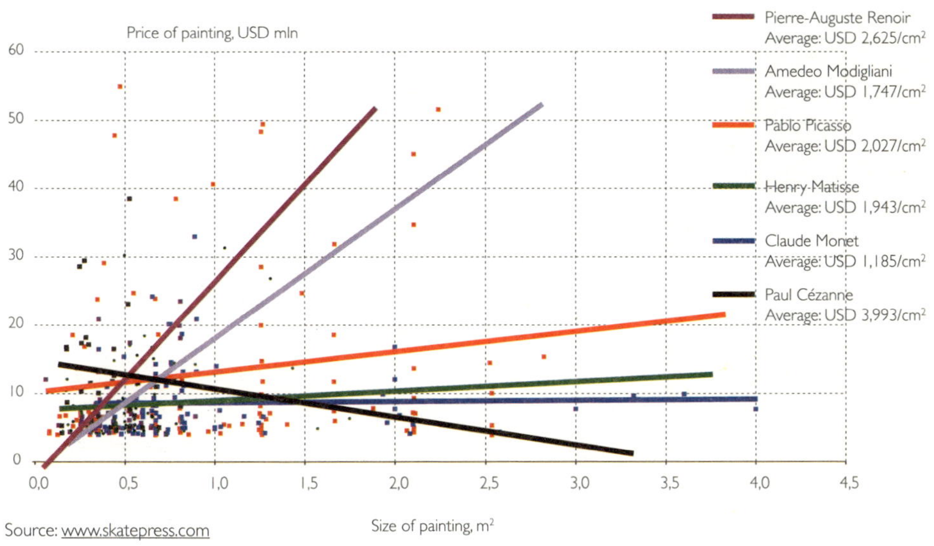

Source: www.skatepress.com

4. In Exhibit 3.6 value dots of different colors map the market price of various artists' works from Skate's Top 1000, with each artist being represented by a unique color. The X-axis reflects size in square meters, and the Y-axis the recorded market price in USD. The charts are drawn for the six most valuable artists based on their market capitalization in Skate's Top 1000.

There is at least one fairly consistent relation between size and valuation, however. Exhibit 3.7 demonstrates that per square meter valuation of important artworks drops significantly and consistently as the painting grows in size. This tendency essentially means that art buyers and sellers never benchmark artworks around any per square metrics and instead use other valuation drivers to determine the differences in price. While it may be interesting that per square meter valuation of works by Renoir, Picasso and Modigliani spike at certain sizes, we would not advise trying to devise any kind of price rules related to size.

Clearly, size is not a reliable valuation driver. While size does provide a useful descriptive factor that allows works of art to be standardized for valuation purposes, the size factor alone is not an important valuation driver.

Exhibit 3.7 – No consistency in per square values for the world's most expensive art

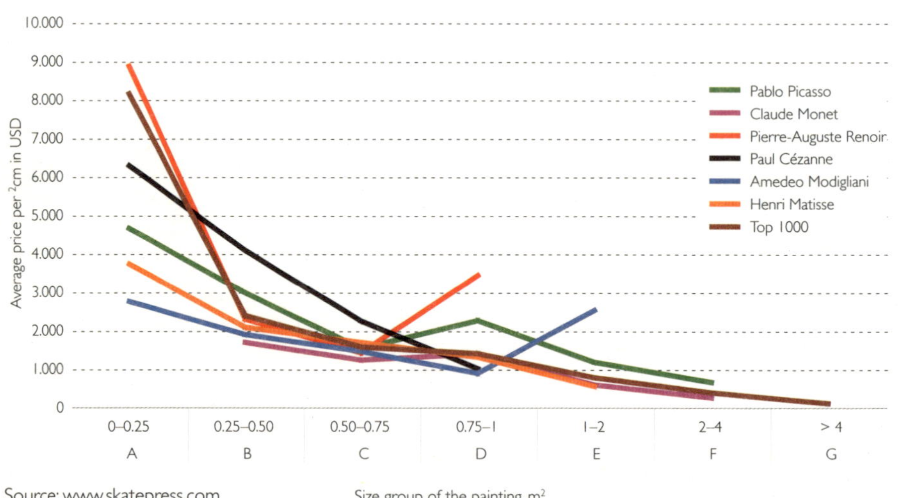

Source: www.skatepress.com Size group of the painting, m²

3.4.3 Subject (genre)

If an artist's name and the size of his or her works are not enough, then perhaps adding a third factor – the subject of an artwork – will help narrow the valuation range and establish a certain degree of accuracy and system in the valuation process? Again, the answer is a clear "no." Across the various artist-size-subject combinations, there is a consistent lack of correlation, suggesting that knowing the artist's name, the size of the work and its genre brings one no closer to any accurate estimate of an artwork's value on the basis of only these three factors.

Exhibit 3.8, which analyzes four artist-size-subject combinations for the "blue chip" artists and their artworks in the Top 1000, reveals that on average only about a third of artworks with an identical set of artist-size-subject descriptions end up being priced in the same range. Diversity of prices for what appears to be rather similar artworks[5] is self-explanatory. Subject functions in much the same way as size – a useful descriptive factor for an artwork but rarely an important valuation driver on its own.

5. The actual images of several of the series included in Exhibit 3.8 can be found in the color insert, Chapter 4.

Exhibit 3.8 - Valuation ranges of artworks with identical artist, size and subject factors

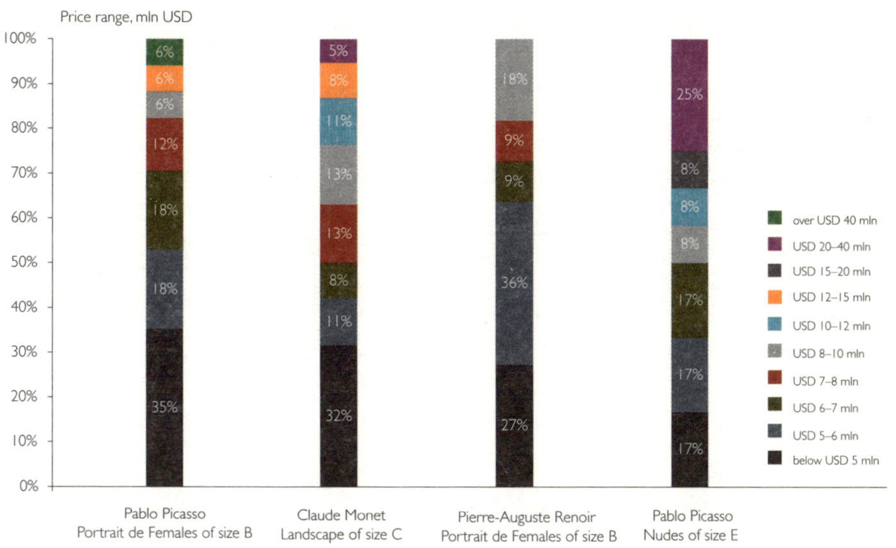

The most frequent combinations of size and subject

Pablo Picasso

- Portrait de Females of size B – 17 works
- Nudes of size E – 12 works
- Portrait de Females of size E – 10 works

Pierre-Auguste Renoir

- Portrait de Females of size B – 11 works
- Portrait de Females of size C – 4 works
- Nudes of size C – 3 works

Claude Monet

- Landscapes of size B – 16 works
- Landscapes of size C – 38 works
- Landscapes of size D – 23 works

Source: www.skatepress.com

3.4.4 Historical period and artist maturity

In Chapter 2, we analyzed the distribution of valuation averages and specifically of investment returns for artworks created in different historical periods (see Exhibit 2.3). The data experiments conducted in this chapter demonstrate that descriptive valuation drivers such as artist, size and subject hardly help in establishing accurate and reliable valuation ranges for works of art. Adding further descriptive valuation drivers makes little practical sense, as significant paintings rarely enter the market with, for example, identical artist, subject, size and year of make factors. There are some data samples available that can be considered as having more than three descriptive factors that match, which supports building a reliable valuation range for an artwork in theory.

For artworks included in Skate's Top 1000, the year 1888 turns out to be the most productive, with 3.6% (or 36) of the Top 1000 masterpieces being created then. More than half of them (19) happen to be landscapes. Exhibit 3.9 shows their distribution by price, and as we have previously seen with different combinations of valuation drivers, matching two descriptive factors (this time year of make and subject) does not at all help to establish valuation ranges for comparable artworks.

These 19 landscapes painted in 1888 contain four C-size landscapes by van Gogh, which are shown in Exhibit 3.10.

Meticulous research allowed us to sample artworks in such a way that when four of the descriptive valuation factors matched,[6] the data began to make some sense. It is quite clear from Exhibit 3.10 that C-size van Gogh landscapes from 1888 commanded a valuation level of about USD 18.5 million (hammer price, i.e. before buyer's premium) in the late 1980s, and that the price fell by almost half 15 years down the road to about USD 10 million in 2003-2004. These are nominal as-reported prices, with the present values adjusted for inflation, which suggests that the true value of these artworks declined by about two-thirds over the same period once the purchasing parity of the dollar in 1987-1989 and 2003-2004 is taken into account.

Not only does this data give us a fairly good indication of how comparable paintings by van Gogh could be valued today, it also reminds us

6. In fact, there are even five factors – artist name, size, subject, year of creation (period) and artist maturity (obviously van Gogh was of the same age and artistic maturity when he painted his works in 1888). Artist maturity is an interesting factor on a standalone basis when compared without taking into account the artist's name in the data series. Samples using this valuation factor are shown in Chapter 5 (section 5.3).

Exhibit 3.9 – Valuation ranges of artworks with identical year of make and subject factors

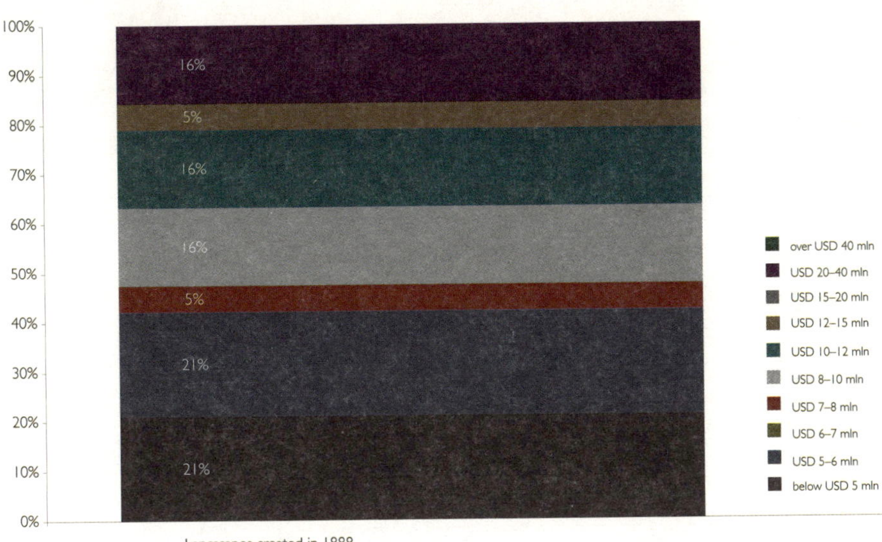

Source: www.skatepress.com

of the massive volatility of art prices and the significant devaluation risks carried by the most expensive masterpieces.

In practical terms, however, it is rather difficult to build peer groups of comparable artworks that match in four or more descriptive factors to take valuation snapshots on the basis of recently recorded prices. The peer group data in Exhibit 3.10 demonstrates that even if one manages to create an accurate peer group, the artwork comparables will carry price tags reported over a period of time, thus making a valuation based on these records largely irrelevant to today's market conditions. Unlike the peer group data used for analogue-based valuation of traditional assets (when market prices are taken for the same trading day for all assets in the group), the diffuse dates on which the art sales occurred diminish the usefulness of the peer group data for the comparable artworks.

Exhibit 3.10 – van Gogh peer group: C-size landscapes painted in 1888[7]

	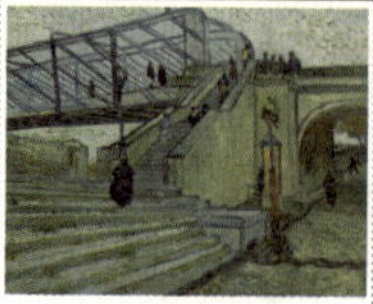	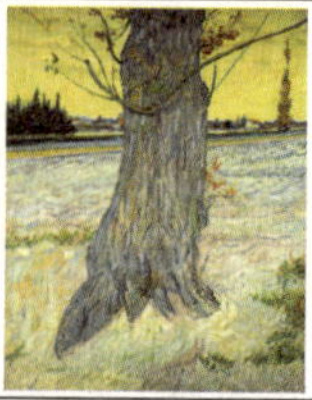	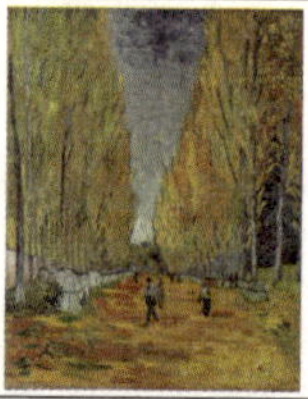	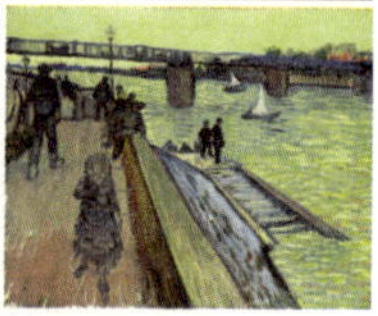
Artist	Vincent van Gogh	Vincent van Gogh	Vincent van Gogh	Vincent van Gogh
Title	*Le pont de Trinquetaille*	*Le vieil If*	*L'allée des Alyscamps*	*Le pont de Trinquetaille*
Year of creation	1888	1888	1888	1888
Year of sale	1987	1989	2003	2004
Low estimate			12,000,000	12,000,000
High estimate			18,000,000	18,000,000
Premium price	20,367,091	20,350,000	11,767,500	11,207,500
Hammer price	18,515,537	18,500,000	10,500,000	10,000,000
Present value	33,099,581	29,814,535	11,574,154	10,623,037
Repeat sale:				
Previous price, USD				15,402,500
ERR, %				(8.57%)
Holding period, years				5 years

All prices are in USD
Source: www.skatepress.com

7. The actual images of these artworks are presented in the color insert in Chapter 4. Exhibit 3.10 summarizes the descriptive valuation factors of this van Gogh series.

3.5. Conclusion

Tangible, fact-based valuation drivers offer little help in determining accurate price ranges for artwork valuation purposes. Relying on various combinations of artist name, painting size, subject, year of make and artist maturity factors yields no accuracy in estimating artworks' value when three or fewer drivers are used. Data series that sample art with four matching criteria are very rare and include artworks with prices recorded at public sales so distant from each other in time that no sensible valuation can be derived on that basis.
All of these conclusions bring us to the key intangible valuation factors – provenance and irrational premium. Whether an artwork qualifies for either or both of these factors always involves a judgment call, and no single rule exists that answers this question for every artwork and every party to a transaction.

With this conclusion, we have traveled full-circle and are now face-to-face with the third party we met earlier in this chapter, namely, the art expert. As we see it, based on the data we have discussed above, the ability to determine which artworks possess these intangible valuation factors and essentially sense the emotional or intellectual attachments of the buyers and the sellers is a unique skill confined to art experts and dealers. These experts, more than any objective data about artworks' descriptive valuation factors and previously established public price records, ultimately determine the value of art assets.

Chapter 4
Valuing the World's Most Significant Masterpieces – Skate's Art Asset Pricing Model (AAPM)

In this chapter, we will examine several practical approaches to valuing significant artworks. The valuation methods and algorithms presented in this chapter are most suitable for works of art priced in the USD 3-25 million range. For various reasons, wealthy investors and institutions seeking to deploy significant capital into art assets will find it relatively difficult to make investments in works of art priced at less than USD 3 million. In particular, due to the art market infrastructure's shortcomings (e.g. its low level of transparency), more room exists for price manipulation and fraud with large volumes in the market's less expensive segments. This reality naturally makes the market for the works of living artists a fundamentally attractive proposition, as theoretically authenticity is easier to check and there are far more options to promote contemporary art using the artists themselves. In Chapter 6, we will cover the specifics of how to value the art created by living artists.

4.1. The segment over USD 25 million – where the rational valuation approach stops

On three notable occasions over the past several years, public sales of artworks have been made at mind-boggling prices. The resulting discussion as to what determines the value of art has been extremely relevant and of genuine interest to a broad audience. In May 2004, Picasso's Garçon à la Pipe was sold at a public auction for USD 104.2 million, a price that remains the all-time price record for a public auction sale in nominal terms. This transaction, however, failed to beat the real terms price record set by the sale of van Gogh's Portrait du Dr. Gachet in May 1990, which to this day remains the most expensive work of art in real terms that has been sold at a public auction.[1]

In May 2006, in another phenomenal sale confirming the strength of the market for Picasso's works, Dora Maar au Chat captured the second spot in Skate's Top 1000 after being sold for USD 95.2 million. In Skate's Art Valuation Letter, we commented on the May 2006 auctions, writing, "There seems to be no end in sight to Picasso's dominance. Out of 10 new additions to Skate's Top 600 that were recorded this week, six came from Picasso. In most of the cases Picasso's paintings were sold well over the top range of the estimates, and out of the four repeat sales recorded this week, Picasso's Sylvette produced the highest annualized ERR (15.43%). As of today, Pablo Picasso stands head and shoulders above the rest of the world's most valuable artists with the combined market value of his works from Skate's Top 1000 equal to USD 1.6 billion, or almost twice the market value of the second most valuable artist (Claude Monet with a market cap of USD 872 million). In fact, Picasso has contributed over 17% of the total value of Skate's Top 1000 most valuable paintings."

As we will see later in this chapter, a challenge to Picasso's price leadership appeared just several weeks after the Dora Maar au Chat sale, but before we revert to that event, it is worth seeing the "faces" of the world's most valuable art as they appeared following the Spring 2006 auction season (Exhibit 4.1).

As we will see in Chapter 5, rich people are getting richer, and they are tending to spend more on art in absolute terms. While there seems to be no shortage of extremely wealthy art investors who are driven by an irrational passion for a work of art and are thus happy to spend tens of millions of dollars on a given piece, these very same investors may be increasingly unhappy with the transaction costs the oligopolistic market structure imposes on them (see Chapter 1 for a discussion of commission levels and Exhibit 4.1 above for the buyer's premiums paid on the world's three most expensive artworks).

1. There is a fascinating book written by Cynthia Saltzman, *Portrait du Dr. Gachet: The Story of a van Gogh Masterpiece, Money, Politics, Collectors, Greed, and Loss* (Penguin, 1998), which gives the story of the artwork and the process of auction bidding that resulted in Japanese paper magnate Ryoei Saito's offering the all-time highest price for a work of art (in real terms) ever paid at an auction.

Exhibit 4.1 – The world's three most valuable paintings

Skate's Top 1000			
	1st	**2nd**	**3rd**
Artist	Pablo Picasso	Pablo Picasso	Vincent van Gogh
Title	*Garçon à la Pipe*	*Dora Maar au Chat*	*Portrait du Dr. Gachet*
Year of creation	1905	1941	1890
Subject	Male Portrait	Female Portrait	Male Portrait
Year of sale	2004	2006	1990
Low estimate		> 50,000,000	40,000,000
High estimate			50,000,000
*Premium price**	104,168,000	95,216,000	82,500,000
Buyer's premium pait	11,167,554	10,216,000	7,500,000
Present value	99,787,364	85,167,901	117,782,508

All prices are in USD
* Consistently used in all Skate's ratings, the premium price is the same as the price in nominal terms and is the artwork auction price that includes the buyer's premium (i.e. commission paid by a buyer to an auction house, which is listed separately in the buyer's premium line). The present value is the same as the price in real terms and is the hammer price (premium price less buyer's premium), which is adjusted for inflation (all data are calculated as of May 7, 2006 in Exhibit 4.1)
Pablo Picasso, Garçon à la Pipe © Succession Picasso/VBK, Vienna 2006, © Buenos Dias/Bridgeman Art Library
Vincent van Gogh, Portrait du Dr. Gachet © Christie's Images Limited
Source: www.skatepress.com

One trend that we will increasingly see in the future is the public announcement of big ticket art transactions completed outside the auction market. Potential investors who neither doubt an artwork's authenticity nor envision export restrictions and are comfortable disclosing their identity will be tempted to make over-the-counter ("OTC") transactions that are publicly announced. Many trades involving significant artworks are already quietly conducted in this manner with the assistance of art dealers, art experts, private bankers and major art shows. We anticipate that the need to establish new benchmarks and increase the number of public price records as a way to defend new valuation levels for significant artworks will make it an accepted practice to publicize artist price records achieved on OTC trades.

One recent notable example of this practice came on the heels of the banner sale of Picasso's Dora Maar au Chat described above. As widely reported in the global media in June 2006, American billionaire Ronald Lauder (the son of Estee and Joseph Lauder, a Jewish couple with roots in the Austro-Hungarian empire and best known for the Estee Lauder cosmetics firm that Mrs. Lauder founded with her husband in 1946) bought Gustav Klimt's iconic portrait of Adele Bloch-Bauer for USD 135 million on the OTC market. With Mr. Lauder's purchase, the Golden Adele portrait catapulted into the slot reserved for the word's most expensive work of art in both real and nominal terms, and it did so in an unprecedented setting, namely, a public transaction conducted outside the auction market. Mr. Lauder, an art connoisseur with his own gallery – the five-year old Neue Galerie in Manhattan that is devoted entirely to German and Austrian fine and decorative arts – and art research capabilities (somewhat of a qualified institutional investor in terms of the financial world), was so confident of the artwork's authenticity, its cultural importance and the strength of its context value that he had no need to rely on the services of a professional auction house to provide assurances of authenticity and provenance. Lauder's family history and his interest in turn-of-the-century Austrian and German art and charity initiatives formed the basis for the apparently unlimited irrationality premium he was prepared to pay to associate his name with Klimt's arguably most significant work of art[2] available for private investment.

Incidentally, the same irrational, emotional context apparently drove Ryoei Saito's decision to pay USD 82.5 million for Portrait du Dr. Gachet. Afterward, Mr. Saito reportedly said he bought the painting because "he saw himself" in the image of van Gogh's doctor.[3]

The consistent appearance of irrationally priced art transactions in recent years, which has had the effect of pricing artworks well

2. Adele Bauer, a member of a wealthy Jewish family in Vienna, entered a pre-arranged marriage with Ferdinand Bloch, a local banker. Introduced to Klimt shortly before her marriage, Adele was widely believed to have had a 12-year long affair with Klimt, making the subject of Golden Adele essentially identical to that of Picasso's Dora Maar au Chat. Well before the Lauder purchase, the image of Adele was a well-known symbol often used in Klimt-focused research publications (including Frank Whitford's book *Klimt*, published by Thames & Hudson in 1990 and used as a source for background information on Adele Bauer).

3. Saltzman, *Portrait du Dr. Gachet: The Story of a van Gogh Masterpiece, Money, Politics, Collectors, Greed, and Loss*, pg. 324.

outside the highest limit of ranges implied by their respective peer groups, has led to the creation of a new peer group of artworks priced over USD 25 million. There are currently 44 works in Skate's Top 1000.

Based on statistical data compiled by Skate Press, no single artwork purchased for more than USD 27 million has been sold more than once on the global art market in the last 25 years. As we saw in Chapter 2, the highest priced masterpiece that has been subject to a repeat sale is Picasso's Le Miroir, which was initially purchased for USD 26.4 million. After a six-year holding period, it was returned to the market where it realized an annualized return of -6.27%. The next repeat sale entry by initial purchase value, Monet's Dans La Prairie, had been purchased for USD 24.3 million. It generated a -4.87% annualized investment return over a holding period of 11 years.

It seems obvious that artworks costing over USD 25 million are unlikely to be purchased by museums, as they are simply beyond the budgets of most institutions. Generally, the acquirers are persons who intend to retain them for the long-term, often for the rest of their lives. From a financial point of view, the price that such art investors pay is irrelevant, as anything over USD 25 million is largely due to the irrational premium an investor is paying. Statistically there is no floor to support art valuation above this price level. When and if such paintings ever return to the market, their prices are likely to be determined by the ability of their sellers to find new individual investors with the same or even more powerful irrational, emotional drivers, as well as adequate financial means, to support prices that meet or exceed the original price paid.

4.2. Skate's Art Asset Pricing Model – masterpiece price as the equation linking an artwork's fair value with the irrationality premium and provenance factor

In Chapter 2, we introduced Skate's Masterpieces Peer Group (Skate's Top 1000) as our fundamental approach to valuing the world's most expensive art based on an analogue (multiples) valuation approach widely used in capital markets. This peer group, which we think qualifies as an important and very useful resource, is published in Schedule A.

In Chapter 3, we covered a number of descriptive valuation drivers, including size, artist name and artwork subject to see which particular ratios and multiples should be used to value Skate's Top 1000 artworks with a greater degree of accuracy. The key takeaway from Chapter 3 is that no particular descriptive valuation driver suffices on a standalone basis. Rather, in our opinion, it is only possible to achieve acceptable precision in predicting valuation and measuring historical investment returns if one can construct a narrow peer group of artworks having four or more identical descriptive valuation drivers.

Unfortunately for the finance world, though a great joy for art lovers and collectors, significant artworks are not produced in identical series, meaning that every important artwork is different. This condition makes it extremely difficult to find an accurate peer group where many descriptive valuation factors match with those of similar Skate's Top 1000 masterpieces.

The inability of art to be standardized as an investment object provides only a partial answer to the question of why valuing significant art is everything but a clear, undisputable and verifiable algorithm. The key reason why art valuation is a tricky exercise lies in two intangible valuation drivers – provenance and irrational premium – which we briefly covered in section 3.5 of this book and will consider further in this chapter.

Fully understanding and accepting the additional intangible uniqueness that its ownership history bestows on any particular artwork and the emotional and cultural context in which buy and sell decisions are made is very important, and thinking through the financial implications of intangible art valuation can help greatly in creating a fairly straightforward and structured approach to art valuation. This approach defines Skate's Art Asset Pricing Model.

Provenance provides a good starting point. From a rational and psychological point of view, the provenance factor used in art valuation has two utilities. One is to give a verifiable public certification of an artwork's authenticity. In an environment where public records of important artworks and their authenticity attributes are largely non-existent (covered in detail in Chapter 1), listing an artwork's ownership history with the support of literature, witnesses, heirs and prior owners (artwork provenance) provides a substitute for authenticity assurance and a much needed complementary proof to certifications from art experts. The second utility of provenance lies in stirring the emotional appeal of an artwork, which may move potential buyers – who for one reason or another on a personal level are sensitive to the prior ownership story – accept a greater price. This second utility is captured by irrational premium, which in essence is the extent to which such emotional appeal converts into valuation differences that apply to buyers rather than to artworks or provenance themselves. Different buyers will assign different values to the very same artwork with obviously the same provenance depending on their subjective judgments as to the importance of the provenance history. Hence, we view the provenance factor as essentially nothing more than a discount rate that reflects the degree of forgery, ownership title conflict and export restriction risks that all result from an artwork's prior ownership history (including how visible and where the work resided and whether its whereabouts were known at all times).

Irrational premium, as we have demonstrated previously, is not specific to a painting, and it is not necessarily specific to a collector either. Rather, it is more of an impulse valuation driver that captures the aesthetical appeal of a particular artwork to a particular buyer at a given point in time. Whether Mr. Lauder would pay a similar irrational premium for van Gogh's Portrait du Dr Gachet as he paid for Klimt's Golden Adele is difficult to say, but the most likely answer is "no." Golden Adele was dear to Mr. Lauder's heart for a particular set of reasons captured in its ownership history (including the story of its Holocaust-era expropriation), cultural significance and the historical context of its subject, none of which exists with Portrait du Dr Gachet sixteen years ago, this occasion would not have offered the opportunity to measure the irrational premium appetites of two collectors and then apply them universally to other artworks of interest to them. Just as each painting is unique, so too is the presence and degree of a collector's irrational appetite when considering a particular painting.

Our discussion of tangible valuation drivers[4] started in Chapter 3 and continued with an analysis of the intangible valuation factors above.

4. Tangible valuation drivers are objective fact-based descriptive factors that include size, artist name, subject, period, artist maturity and year of creation for a given work of art.

We are now able to formulate a fairly simple model that can be applied in practice when determining a value and an estimated price range for a significant artwork.

Skate's Art Asset Pricing Model

P = (FV + IP) x PF, where

P *(price)* – an artwork's target price

FV *(fair value)* – the fair value of an artwork estimated on the basis of Skate's Masterpieces Peer Group, which appears as a price range defined using a narrower comparables group resulting from highly accurate similarity among descriptive factors (a good example of such narrow peer group is presented in Exhibit 3.10)

IP *(irrational premium)* – an expert estimate of how much a particular buyer is prepared to pay for a particular work of art

PF *(provenance factor)* – a discount rate that varies from 0 to 1 and reflects the risk of forgery, export restrictions and/or ownership title conflicts

The practical valuation algorithm suggested by Skate's AAPM is the following, which applies with greatest accuracy to artworks priced in the USD 3-25 million range:

1) The artwork that is being valued has to be attributed first with the entire set of descriptions assembled (artist name, year of creation, period, artist maturity at the time of artwork creation, subject, size, cultural context, and ownership history). For important masterpieces, such research is very easy to access by simply obtaining auction houses' catalogue notes, which contain all of this information. These catalogue notes are one of the most important value propositions of major auction houses and normally contain the entire set of descriptive information and provenance details necessary to move forward with the valuation. If this information is not immediately available, it must be researched and prepared before any meaningful artwork valuation can be made.

2) In using Skate's Masterpieces Peer Group and the tangible (descriptive) valuation factors, the artwork must be placed in a peer group of comparable artworks. These works are created by the same artist and ideally in the same genre and year, are of the

same size and so forth. For less expensive artworks (less than USD 3 million), market professionals use automated databases such as Artprice and Artnet, which contain a large number of price records for artworks in all price categories. See examples of such narrow peer groups in Exhibit 3.10 and the exhibits appearing further in this chapter.

3) Assembling and analyzing the peer group for the artwork will result in the price range for the fair value (FV), which is supported by reference to analogue sales recorded for similar artworks in the past.

4) Irrational premium should be set as zero for the seller's expectation management purposes. A market intermediary or a direct seller, using the auction process and having knowledge of the psychology and purchasing power of the buyer, should then try to achieve a maximum possible irrational premium, the determination of which is the core competence of professional auctioneers and art dealers.

5) The provenance factor should reflect the risk that the artwork in question is a forgery or possesses unclear ownership title or travel restrictions. This very powerful valuation driver is remarkably simple to use. For example, by setting it to 0.5 to encapsulate various risks surrounding an artwork, one reduces the target value of this asset by half. Clearly, setting the provenance factor necessitates a judgment call that both transaction parties have to agree upon, but it nevertheless allows enough attention to be paid to this fundamental risk element of art investing.

Skate's AAPM has practical utility for several reasons. First, Skate's AAPM offers a solid basis for a well-grounded discussion of reserve price with an artwork's seller. Essentially, the reserve price should be equal to the artwork's fair value multiplied by the provenance factor, with the irrational premium set to zero. In this way, the seller understands the rationale for the minimum accepted price and understands that any price paid on top of this minimum reflects the product of an intermediary's skill in finding buyers with the greatest emotional attachment to a particular artwork. In real life, sellers often rely on the historical cost (without ownership costs capitalized) to determine the reserve price for a sale. The logic of "I paid USD 20 million for an artwork and want to sell for at least the same price" is not always helpful if it is not supported by a peer group fair value range. This logic leads to many big ticket lots going unsold at major auctions.

Second, Skate's AAPM provides scientific proof for the strong investment case offered by contemporary art, specifically works of living artists. Provided the living artist maintains a rational mindset and wants to support the market for his or her art, it should be much easier to check the authenticity of such artworks and keep the provenance factor at 1. On the contrary, the more time that has passed since the artwork's creation, the more difficult it becomes to recover the details of its ownership history and render buyers comfortable with the various risks associated with its purchase. Hence, artworks created beyond the memory of living generations, particularly from before World War II, carry on average a lower provenance factor (i.e., their value is always discounted as a result of the risks associated with a longer and murkier history).

Third, we purposely left a certain contradiction in Skate's AAPM. The fair value is calculated on the basis of public records for transactions with artworks of comparable descriptive valuation factors, but those transactions are made with irrational premium (paid by other buyers for similar artworks) included in the price. As every new transaction happens in the context of public knowledge of prior deals and irrational premium is very much momentum and buyer specific, we believe it is acceptable to allow "double counting" of irrational premiums in the price. These irrational premiums are first averaged in the fair value calculation for other deals, with the irrational premium specific to the artwork being valued for its sale to a particular buyer taking place afterwards. From a financial point of view, once the irrational premium is subjectively paid, it is capitalized in the overall art price levels and stays there as a part of the objective market price until a new publicly disclosed trade conducts a sort of "impairment test" to this intangible art asset value component.

As the art market price discovery happens in fairly illiquid environment and is a thin line that connects the few and scattered dots of public price records, it is in the best interest of art market intermediaries to keep most transactions experiencing significant negative returns (deals where a seller disposes of an artwork at a major loss) out of the public eye to avoid the build-up of objective evidence showing how quickly and significantly irrational premiums can be wiped out of the art asset price.

Finally, Skate's AAPM does not take into account the ownership costs that a buyer will incur upon acquiring an artwork, nor does it reflect the personal tax situation of the buyer, specifically the VAT requirement and future capital gains taxes that might apply when and if the work is sold at a higher price in the future. In this context, a useful exercise to perform once a target valuation range is determined for a masterpiece is to estimate an expected holding period horizon and a threshold rate of return that would allow regaining both the original purchase price and the costs associated with the asset (buyer's premium, taxes, ownership costs like transport, insurance premium, storage and security).

We discussed the notion of threshold rate somewhat in Skate's Art Valuation Letter issued in the Spring of 2006. Analyzing the results of Q1 2006 of the Top 500 art market segment performance, we wrote:

"Skate's Top 500 threshold price, i.e. the auction price (with buyer's premium) of the 500th most expensive painting in nominal terms in our rating, has increased by 26.6% over the last four years, or 6.6% on an annualized basis, and currently stands slightly above USD 6.1 million. In other words, four years ago, a painting with a USD 4.8 million auction price could make it into the rating of the world's 500 most expensive artworks, whereas today even USD 6 million is not enough. However, this appreciation trend should not be misleading. With annual growth of 5-7% consistent over the last five years, Skate's Top 500 basket of the world's most significant art yields far less than mainstream investment markets and tends to provide a miserable investment return for individual paintings when they return to the market for one reason or another.[5] From Miro to Matisse, we have been observing and reporting in previous issues of the Art Valuation Letter small and often negative returns in the last 12 months against the backdrop of all record art prices, reflecting limited liquidity of the premium art market and the ridiculous level of transaction costs that kill already modest returns as art investors calculate their net results.

5. See Schedule C for an entire listing of repeat sales, including the 2006 sales of Miro and Matisse referenced here.

One striking fact is the dynamics of the buyer's premium (auction commission). Since 2002, the buyer's premium has increased from an average of 9.2% for the world's most significant art to 10.8%. In other words, at the current average growth rate of prices for world's most significant art, it can take four to six years for an art investor to simply recover the transaction costs (buyer's and seller's fees combined), thus naturally encouraging longer holding horizons."[6]

4.3. Measuring true market performance with Skate's AAPM

Another excellent way to use Skate's AAPM in practice is to measure true market performance for certain art market segments. The market of Roy Lichtenstein's works provides a good example, as several of them have recently been sold with public price records made available. Artworks coming from the same supply source often carry an identical provenance factor and many of the same tangible valuation drivers.

Exhibit 4.2 shows a narrow peer group of Liechtenstein's artworks that were recently sold. Having largely identical valuation drivers, this peer group was designed for Lichtenstein's Sinking Sun, which came to the market in 2006. The low and high estimates used in Exhibit 4.2 are those of the auction house and contradict the fair value ranges that would have been prepared for Lichtenstein's Sinking Sun had Skate's AAPM been used. Skate's Masterpieces Peer Group approach would not have justified the auction house's move to increase the lower price range by 50% just six months after the comparable public sale of Lichtenstein's work.

The auction house's attempt to push the Sinking Sun valuation beyond Lichtenstein's price record established six months prior to that by the sale of In the Car failed.[7] Sinking Sun sold well beyond the low level of the estimate range (a 22% discount to the low end of the pre-auction estimate), clearly finding a buyer at or just above a secret reserve price that the auction house and the seller reached prior to the auction. While failing to set a new price record for the artist, Sinking Sun nevertheless confirmed the strength of the current market for quality Lichtenstein works. Although art buyers were not prepared to accept a further push in valuations, they remained comfortable

6. These returns are before ownership costs are taken into consideration. With these costs added, an investor in Skate's Top 500 should generally feel lucky to exit whenever a positive net return is possible, with negative returns being the far more likely scenario.

7. For a detailed discussion of Lichtenstein artworks valuation please refer to Skate's Art Valuation Letter, Issue # 01-05-1-AWV dated October 11, 2005 (can be downloaded from www.skatepress.com, or accessed on Bloomberg at <KUNS> <GO>)

with the 8-digit price tag, which was unheard of for Lichtenstein's art until last year.

With most of Skate's AAPM valuation drivers being equal for Lichtenstein's works, the peer group in Exhibit 4.2 evidences (a) significant valuation step-up in the artist's works created in mid 1960s that was recorded between 2002 and 2005, but (b) no further appreciation from that new level as the market stands today.

Exhibit 4.2 – The three most valuable Roy Lichtenstein paintings

Skate's Top 1000			
	1st	2nd	3rd
Artist	Roy Lichtenstein	Roy Lichtenstein	Roy Lichtenstein
Title	*In the Car*	*Sinking Sun*	*Happy Tears*
Year of creation	1963	1964	1964
Year of sale	2005	2006	2002
Low estimate	12,000,000	15,000,000	5,000,000
High estimate	18,000,000	20,000,000	7,000,000
Premium price	16,256,000	15,696,000	7,159,500
Buyer's premium	1,756,000	1,696,000	659,500
Present value	14,888,917	14,027,654	7,274,407

All prices are in USD
Source: www.skatepress.com

The USD 8.5 mln gap between the 2nd and 3rd positions reflects Lichtenstein's valuation step-up between 2002 and 2005

Exhibit 4.3 – The Dora Maar peer group

	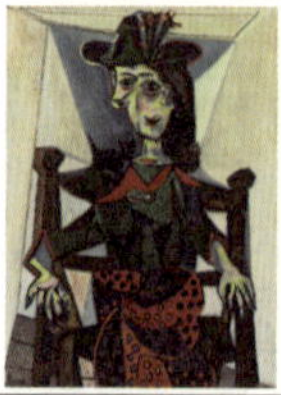	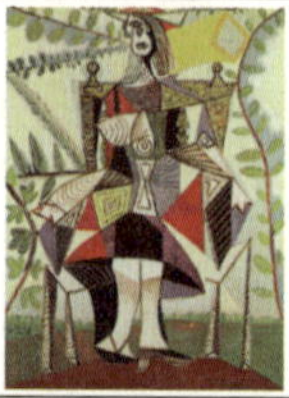	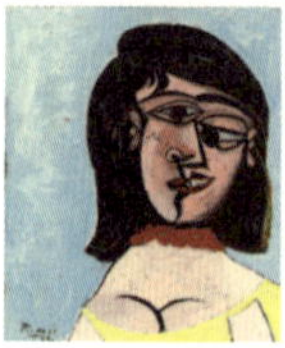	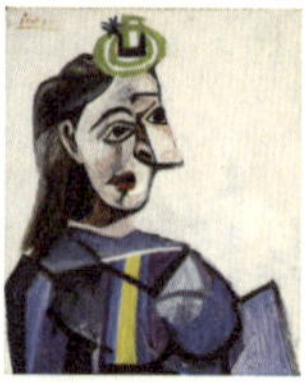	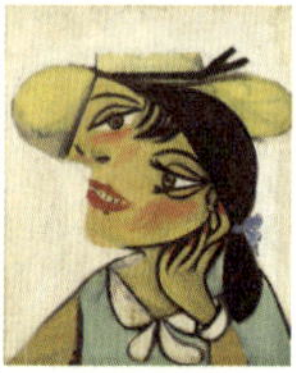
Artist	Pablo Picasso	Pablo Picasso	Pablo Picasso	Pablo Picasso	Pablo Picasso
Title	*Dora Maar au Chat*	*Femme assise dans un Jardin (Dora Maar)*	*Tete de Femme (Dora Maar)*	*Buste de Femme (Dora Maar)*	*Femme au chapeau de paille (Dora Maar)*
Auction house	Sotheby's	Sotheby's	Christie's	Christie's	Sotheby's
Location	New York	New York	New York	London	London
Year of sale	May 3, 2006	Nov. 10, 1999	May 2, 2006	Feb. 2, 2004	Jun. 26, 2001
Low estimate	50,000,000	40,000,000	5,000,000	4,540,501	3,956,479
High estimate	75,000,000	50,000,000	7,000,000	6,356,702	4,945,598
Premium price	95,216,000	49,502,500	5,616,000	5,094,896	4,046,206
Hammer price	85,000,000	45,000,000	5,000,000	4,542,318	3,672,915
Present value	85,167,901	54,251,337	5,009,877	4,949,712	4,186,710
Year of creation	1941	1938	1937	1942	1937
Size group	E	E	B	B	B
Changes in ownership	4 times	2 times	4 times	3 times	2 times
Most recent public appearance	1968	1997	1957	2003	1983
Exhibitions	3 times	9 times	2 times	6 times	3 times
Literature notes	1 time	6 times	2 times	n/a	2 times

Repeat sale					
Year of purchase				February 6, 2001	
Initial price				4,549,646	
ERR,%				(0.56%)	
Holding period				3 years	
Provenance	*Pierre Colle, Mr. and Mrs. Leigh B.Block, Berggruen & Cie*	*Mary Callery, Eleonore and Daniel Saidenberg*	*Bignou Gallery, Barney Collins, Stephen Hahn*	*Phoenix Assurance Company*	*Paloma Ruiz Picasso*

All prices are in USD
Source: www.skatepress.com

4.4. Irrational premium as the primary valuation driver for significant art

As we demonstrated in section 4.1, the irrational premium factor, which captures the subjective individual preferences and tastes of an art buyer, often becomes the overriding valuation driver, especially in the category of top-rated artworks. The artwork purchase decision is taken beyond the rational context, making it impossible to model art valuation universally.

Skate's AAPM formula suggests that the process of rational art valuation becomes irrelevant when the irrational premium driver significantly (i.e., by several times) exceeds the fair price established on the basis of peer group analysis.

The recent sale of Dora Maar au Chat offers an excellent example. When Rustam Tariko, a freshly minted Russian millionaire,[8] purchased this Picasso masterpiece for a stunning price of USD 85 million (with a buyer's commission of over USD 10.2 million on top of that), his irrational passion to own this artwork was obviously the principal driving factor. As we can see in Exhibit 4.3, this image, one of Picasso's many muses, fits nicely in the peer group of other Dora images. The only difference is that the price bears no resemblance

8. Rustam Tariko made his fortune on Russian Standard vodka, and ironically a bank of the same name specialized in providing consumer loans to Russian customers who had never before had access to such financial products. Mr. Tariko's identity was widely reported in the media, including The New York Post and Bloomberg.

to the Dora fair price that we have determined on the basis of these comparables.

It is particularly striking that just one day before the Russian tycoon's acquisition, a Dora Maar painted by Picasso four years before the one purchased by Mr. Tariko (and in a format half the size of Dora Maar au Chat) fetched a much (indeed 17 times) lesser amount. While calculating an exact breakdown of each tangible and intangible factor's significance is difficult, it is rather obvious that, based on our findings in Chapter 3, the painting's size and year of creation alone could not command this difference. The provenance factor discount is equalized due to authenticity guarantees provided by auction houses, thus leaving the subjective irrational premium as the factor largely responsible for the USD 80 million valuation step-up achieved by Dora Maar au Chat in one day.

The power of irrational premium is not limited to the world's most valuable art. As we move down Skate's Top 1000, we see even more examples of phenomenal price differences between fairly comparable artworks. These differences can be explained in no other way than by attributing them to the subjective judgments of buyers concerning how valuable those particular works are to them.

Exhibit 4.4 focuses on what is perhaps the most "standard product" within Skate's Top 1000. There are as many as 24 Claude Monet's Nymphéas in the value rating, with the six most comparable being presented in this exhibit.

All of Monet's top priced Nymphéas are visually similar and are mostly of a D-size. Their dates of creation span two years, and their provenance is similar. Despite these similarities, the works experienced a wide price range of USD 6.5 million to USD 19 million (by hammer price) over a time difference in public price records not exceeding six years. The only consistency is in effective returns, with every single painting in the sampling experiencing a negative effective rate of return based on a repeat sale.

We can offer no explanation for this wide valuation range other than the irrational premium professionally generated during the auction process and eventually paid by individual buyers.

Exhibit 4.4 – The Nymphéas peer group

	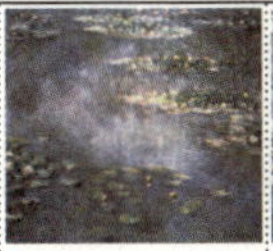	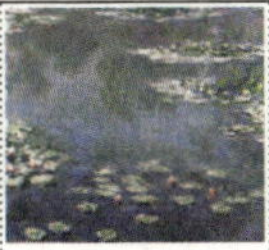	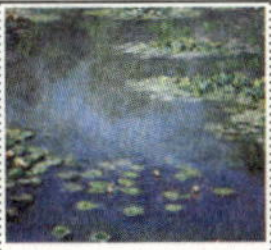	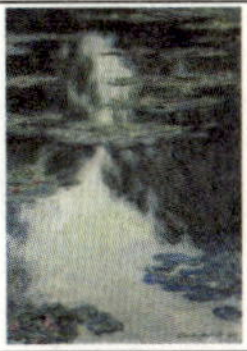	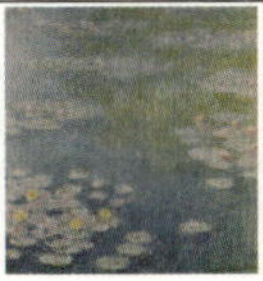	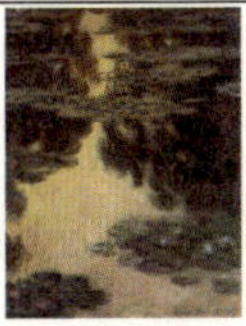
Artist	Claude Monet	Claude Monet	Claude Monet	Claude Monet	Claude Monet	Claude Monet
Title	*Nymphéas*	*Nymphéas*	*Nymphéas*	*Nymphéas*	*Nymphéas*	*Nymphéas*
Auction house	Christie's	Sotheby's	Sotheby's	Christie's	Sotheby's	Sotheby's
Location	New York	London	New York	New York	New York	New York
Year of sale	May 8 2000	Jun. 24, 2002	Nov. 5, 2002	May 2, 2006	Nov. 5, 2003	May 10, 2001
Low estimate	20,000,000	14,970,060	16,000,000	10,000,000	10,000,000	7,000,000
High estimate	25,000,000	22,455,090	20,000,000	15,000,000	15,000,000	10,000,000
Premium price	20,906,000	20,182,111	18,709,500	11,216,000	10,424,000	7,155,750
Hammer price	19,000,000	18,338,737	17,000,000	10,000,000	9,300,446	6,499,773
Present value	22,478,717	20,683,323	19,025,372	10,019,753	10,227,971	7,421,519
Year of creation	1906	1906	1906	1907	1908	1907
Size group	D	D	D	C	D	C
Year of first sale	1909	1910	1909	1923	1909	1918
Year of last sale		1940	1999 (r.s.)	1968	1988 (r.s.)	1990 (r.s.)
Changes in ownership	4 times	4 times	8 times	8 times	8 times	10 times
Artist's family holding period	3 years	4 years	3 years	16 years	1 year	11 years
Most recent public appearance	1974	1925	1910	1968	1986	1999
Exhibitions	13 times	10 times	2 times	2 times	2 times	14 times
Literature notes	n/a	6 times	5 times	5 times	11 times	10 times

Repeat sale						
Year of purchase			Nov. 8, 1999		Nov. 29, 1988	May 17, 1990
Initial price			22,522,500		10,505,051	9,680,000
ERR,%			(9.46%)		(0.91%)	(3.69%)
Holding period			3 years		15 years	11 years
Provenance	*Galerie Durand-Ruel*	*Durand-Ruel*	*Durand-Ruel, Arthur Tooth and Sons Ltd, Knoedler & Co*	*Bernheim-Jeune, Acquavella Galleries, Aristotle Onassis*	*Bernheim-Jeune, Dr. Guggen-heim*	*Durand-Ruel, Bernheim-Jeune, The Detroit Institute of Arts, Malbin Collection*

All prices are in USD
Source: www.skatepress.com

Monet's Nymphéas also offer a striking example of the practical usefulness of Skate's Masterpieces Peer Group analysis, which seeks to sample a peer group for valuation purposes on the basis of objective factors. Exhibit 4.5 presents all of Monet's paintings depicting nymphéas and priced above Skate's Top 1000 threshold (entrance) price. This sampling offers a broad range of artworks across the entire value rating, with the top price in the 67th position and bottom price in the 959th spot. A brief examination of size group and year of creation, two descriptive fact based valuation factors in addition to artist name and genre (subject), allows us to narrow the peer group to a set of Monet's masterpieces with four identical features – Monet's Nymphéas of the D-size painted in 1906 (see Exhibit 4.4) or the even less accurately defined sampling of Monet's Nymphéas of the F-size completed between 1916 and 1919, for example. The valuation range derived from such narrow peer groups is far more precise and allows for a much more accurate estimate than we would have achieved if identical ownership history had been included instead of one of the simpler descriptive valuation drivers like year of creation or size.

Mathematically, the supremacy of simple descriptive valuation factors over far more refined valuation drivers like provenance is easy to explain by returning to the definition of provenance we gave earlier in the chapter. When provenance is treated as a discount rate reflecting risk of forgery, export restrictions and ownership title disputes, analyzing differences in provenance offers no assistance in improving the objective valuation range of artworks. The only utility of a provenance discussion is that it can be exploited to cause a greater irrational premium in the eyes of a potential buyer excited by something related to the painting itself. Skate's data demonstrate that differences in irrational premiums accepted by art buyers for various Nymphéas largely explain the wide variety of prices that these Monet's artworks have commanded.

Exhibit 4.5 – The Nymphéas broad peer group

Top 1000 rank	*Title*	*Year of creation*	*Auction date*	*Hammer price, USD*	*Purchase price, USD*	*Size group*	*Repeat sale ERR,%*
67	Nymphéas	1906	May 8, 2000	19,000,000	20,906,000	D	
73	Nymphéas	1906	Jun. 24, 2002	18,338,737	20,182,111	D	
79	Nymphéas	1906	Nov. 5,2002	17,000,000	18,709,500	D	(9.46%)
98	Le bassin aux nym-phéas	1917 - 1919	May 6, 2004	15,000,446	16,808,000	E	
138	Nymphéas	1907	Nov. 1, 2005	12,500,000	14,016,000	E	(0.20%)
152	Nymphéas	1905	Nov. 13, 1996	12,000,000	13,202,500	D	
199	Nymphéas, temps gris	1907 -	May 2, 2006	10,000,000	11,216,000	C	
226	Nymphéas	1908	Nov. 5, 2003	9,300,446	10,424,000	D	(0.91%)
241	Nymphéas	1916 - 1919	May 9, 2001	9,000,000	9,906,000	F	
246	Le bassin aux nym-phéas	1917-1919	Nov. 16, 1998	9,000,000	9,902,500	E	

260	Nymphéas	1907	Nov. 13, 1990	8,600,000	9,460,000	D	
283	Le bassin aux nym-phéas	1917 - 1919	Nov. 28, 1989	8,109,794	8,920,774	E	
324	Nymphéas	1908	May 10, 2000	7,599,773	8,365,750	D	9.06%
363	Le bassin aux Nym-phéas	1917-1920	Feb. 5, 2001	7,047,676	7,758,443	E	
365	Nymphéas	1914-1917	Jun. 21, 2004	6,895,877	7,730,882	F	
368	Nymphéas	1914-1917	Nov. 15, 1989	7,000,000	7,700,000	F	
422	Nymphéas	1907	May 10, 2001	6,499,773	7,155,750	C	(3.69%)
455	Le bassin aux nym-phéas	1917-1919	May 8, 2000	6,200,000	6,826,000	F	
572	Nymphéas	1914-1917	Nov. 13, 1997	5,250,000	5,777,500	E	
587	Nymphéas	1914-1917	May 15, 1990	5,200,000	5,720,000	E	
719	Nymphéas	1908	Nov. 12, 1996	4,600,000	5,062,500	D	
757	Nymphéas	1908	Jun. 28, 1999	4,430,966	4,876,563	D	(5.05%)
907	Nymphéas, Reflets de Saule	1920	Nov. 14, 1990	4,000,000	4,400,000	F	
959	Nymphéas	1914-1917	Nov. 4, 2003	3,700,000	4,151,500	F	

4.5. The masterpieces market segment – when collecting ambition is a routine trade-off for competitive investment returns

While Skate's AAPM offers some interesting valuation discussion topics concerning the notion of an artwork's fair price, it clearly fails to accurately predict the actual market price. The problem is in the irrational premium component of Skate's Art Asset Pricing Model. Not only does irrational premium vary from one art buyer to another, it is not consistent for any one individual either, as art buyers normally apply different irrational premiums to different works of art depending on their subjective aesthetic appeals, personal relevance and context. As we have seen in this chapter, the market price for significant artworks is largely driven by the subjective irrational premium a buyer is prepared to pay. This clear and simple fact explains the basis for the dominance of auction houses in the art market infrastructure. The auction process allows the irrational motives of buyers to be exploited and played against one another in the most efficient way possible.

It is no wonder that people and institutions choosing to pay millions of dollars for works of art almost never make money, even before transaction and ownership costs are considered. This sad feature of the premium segment of the art investment market is demonstrated in Schedule C, which details all the repeat sales of artworks in Skate's rating of the world's 1000 most expensive artworks.

Some investments in the masterpieces segment actually do yield positive returns, however. In the last 26 years, the transaction with the highest realized effective rate of return was Cézanne's Carrière de Bibémus, which yielded a 28% annualized ERR. When art market liquidity risk and transaction and ownership costs are taken into account, however, even this rate of return is clearly unacceptable.

In this context, every economic analysis of art asset prices that tries to establish a correlation between art prices and macroeconomic growth rates and stock market performance has a limited value when done statistically, as there are issues with the quality of data and the comparability of artworks. As seen in Schedule C and Chapter 2, the true returns of the premium art market segment consistently lag behind those of the stock and bond markets. What any published index of art prices does in reality is to capture the dynamics of irrational premiums paid by art investors and not true investment returns on significant art assets, as there are limited liquidity and repeat sales. These irrational premium dynamics can indeed be nicely correlated with economic growth when speaking about art sold to "new money" like that seen in the growth of the Russian and Asian art market segments.

Our review of Skate's Top 1000 yields a very clear message: the premium segment of the art investment market is definitely not for investors seeking to achieve investment returns adequate for the underlying risks in the art asset class. Instead, this segment is a playground for personal and institutional egos and ambitions, with the competition of irrational premiums carefully managed by auction houses and other professional market intermediaries seeking to control quality art supply and price level disclosures.

4.6. Case studies of successful art investment strategies

While achieving significant positive returns in the premium art market segment is difficult, there are case studies of successful art investment strategies to be found.

As we saw previously in this chapter, Cézanne's Carrière de Bibémus so far is the highest yielding artwork in Skate's Top 1000 on the basis of actual rates of returns. Exhibit 4.6 compares this masterpiece with other B-size landscapes by Cézanne. Interestingly, out of the five other paintings, only two had recorded public repeat sales in recent years and none scored an annualized return comparable to that of Carrière de Bibémus.

The reason why one particular Cézanne landscape provided a rewarding investment has to do with timing, the critical factor of any investment strategy. It turns out that an investor purchased Carrière de Bibémus just a few years before art prices peaked in late 1980s and held it for a very short three-year period, selling it back in a quickly appreciating market in 1989. During that time, Cézanne achieved a firm valuation step-up similar to the one demonstrated earlier in this chapter with Liechtenstein's Exhibit 4.2. Neither descriptive valua-

Exhibit 4.6 – The Cézanne B-size landscapes peer group

Artist	Paul Cézanne	Paul Cézanne	Paul Cézanne	Paul Cézanne	Paul Cézanne	Paul Cézanne
Title	*Les toits de l'Estaque*	*Les grands arbres au Jas de Bouffan*	*La Côte Du Galet, À Pontoise*	*Le Jas de Bouffan*	*CARRIERE DE BIBEMUS*	*Environs de Gardanne*
Auction house	Christie's	Christie's	Phillips	Sotheby's	Sotheby's	Phillips
Location	New York, 12 May 1997	New York, 4 May 2005	New York, 6 Nov 2000	New York, 12 Nov 1990	New York, 15 Nov 1989	New York, 11 May 2000
Year of sale	1997	2005	2000	1990	1989	2000
Low estimate	8,000,000	12,000,000	8,000,000	7,000,000	6,000,000	6,000,000
High estimate	10,000,000	16,000,000	10,000,000	9,000,000	8,000,000	8,000,000
Premium price	12,652,500	11,776,000	8,527,500	7,150,000	6,600,000	5,062,500
Hammer price	11,500,000	10,500,000	7,750,000	6,500,000	6,000,000	4,596,818
Present value	14,574,329	10,959,105	9,032,022	9,856,876	9,669,579	5,438,451
Year of creation	1883-1885	1885-1887	1879-1881	1885-1887	1898	1886-1890
Size group	B	B	B	B	B	B
Repeat sale:						
Previous price		7,954,930	11,002,500		3,190,000	
ERR, %		3.00%	(8.76%)		27.75%	
Holding period, years		9	4		3	

All prices are in USD
Source: www.skatepress.com

tion drivers nor the provenance factor would justify such a striking difference in Cézanne's investment returns within the peer group in Exhibit 4.6. Making art investments just before a certain artist will be re-valued upwards by the market seems to be a far more successful investment strategy than carefully choosing artworks from a group of similar peers on the basis of cultural context and ownership history nuances.

Another example of such an investment strategy is represented by the Twombly peer-group in Exhibit 4.7, where the timing for both buy and sell decisions with respect to Untitled (New York City) seems to be extremely propitious in helping to generate an annualized return of about 20% over a 20-year holding period.[9] The painting was acquired well before Twombly migrated to the masterpieces multimillion dollar league in the late 1990s and was sold at what appears to be a peak price to date (the auction house estimates shown in Exhibit 4.7 suggest that the auction house tried to push valuation even further but was forced to sell at the reserve price below the estimate range after the art market apparently resisted any further appreciation of Twombly).

9. If by art investment market standards such returns are considered successful, they are still unlikely to be competitive in comparison to mainstream investment market returns when transaction, ownership costs and taxes are take into account and a premium for liquidity risk is demanded.

Exhibit 4.7 – The Twombly peer group

Artist	Cy Twombly	Cy Twombly	Cy Twombly
Title	*Untitled (New York City)*	*Untitled*	*Untitled*
Auction house	Sotheby's	Sotheby's	Sotheby's
Location	New York	New York	New York
Year of sale	November 9, 2005	November 12, 2002	May 8, 1990
Low estimate	8,000,000	4,000,000	5,000,000

High estimate	10,000,000	6,000,000	6,000,000
Premium price	8,696,000	5,619,500	5,500,000
Hammer price	7,750,000	5,100,000	5,000,000
Present value	7,957,869	5,707,612	7,852,167
Year of creation	1968	1970	1971
Size group	F	F	G
Changes in ownership	5 times	1 time	2 times
Most recent public appearance	1994	n/a	n/a
Exhibitions	9 times	n/a	n/a
Literature notes	2 times	1 time	1 time
Repeat sale			
Year of purchase	May 6 1986		
Initial price	220,000		
ERR	19.92%		
Holding period	20 years		
Provenance	*Mr. and Mrs. Victor W. Ganz, Leo Castelli Gallery, Karsten Greve*	*Acquired by the present owner directly from the artist in 1972*	*Gian Enzo Sperone*

All prices are in USD
Source: www.skatepress.com

4.7. Art valuation: ground principles

This chapter concludes our research into art valuation. Skate's extensive research of the premium segment of the art investment market,[10] as summarized in this and previous chapters, allows us to make the following conclusions:

- Art valuation is driven by both tangible and objective elements (descriptive factors) like artist name, artwork size, genre and year of creation, as well as intangible factors like provenance and the irrational premium applicable to a specific buyer.

- Skate's Masterpieces Peer Group analysis, which creates a group of comparable artworks that have public price records and is selected on the basis of identical descriptive factors, offers a useful valuation tool to establish a price range for significant artworks. The breadth of this range, normally starting from 25%, is often quite similar to auction house estimates published before important auctions.

- For valuation purposes, provenance should be stripped of cultural and emotional aspects of ownership history, which are instead captured by the irrational premium, and considered purely as the discount rate reflecting risks of forgery, export restrictions and ownership title conflicts.

- Should art deals be made on a purely rational basis, the target price of an artwork should be defined simply as the mean derived from Skate's Masterpieces Peer Group analysis and discounted for the provenance factor (i.e., reduced for the probability of a question regarding an artwork's specific authenticity and other related risks).[11]

- As demonstrated by several examples in this chapter, the price of important masterpieces in reality is largely driven by an irrational, passion-to-own behavior on the part of art collectors. Resulting art prices include significant irrational premiums paid for cultural connotations, historical context and aesthetic pleasures that are impossible to quantify universally. Irrational premium is not only unique to an individual buyer, but it also varies signifi-

10. Measured with Skate's Top 1000 value rating of the world's most expensive art based on public price records.

11. Equation introduced earlier in the chapter and referred to as Skate's Art Asset Pricing Model.

cantly for each buyer depending on the artwork whose purchase he or she is considering.

• The ability to exploit the irrational premium capacity of a potential art buyer characterizes the core competence of art market professionals and offers an objective premise for the long-term viability of the auction houses' business model.

• Driven by the irrational behavior patterns of art buyers, the premium segment of the art market rarely offers positive investment returns, and its returns are generally not competitive to those of mainstream investment markets.

• There is money to be made by art investors, however, but to do so investors must focus on less expensive art (the segment below USD 3 million per work seems to offer the most upside potential) and make timing a key component of their investment strategy. Investing in art produced by living artists seems to be a sensible strategy, as it provides for maximum possible provenance factor (1) and allows more options in value-enhancing strategies using the charisma of the living artist himself.

On the basis of these conclusions, we believe it is sensible to argue that the art investment market is not suitable for professional institutional investors for a variety of reasons, including the inability to deploy significant amounts of capital in a cost-efficient manner or conduct transactions in a transparent, cost-efficient and verifiable manner.

The Artworks

Vincent van Gogh

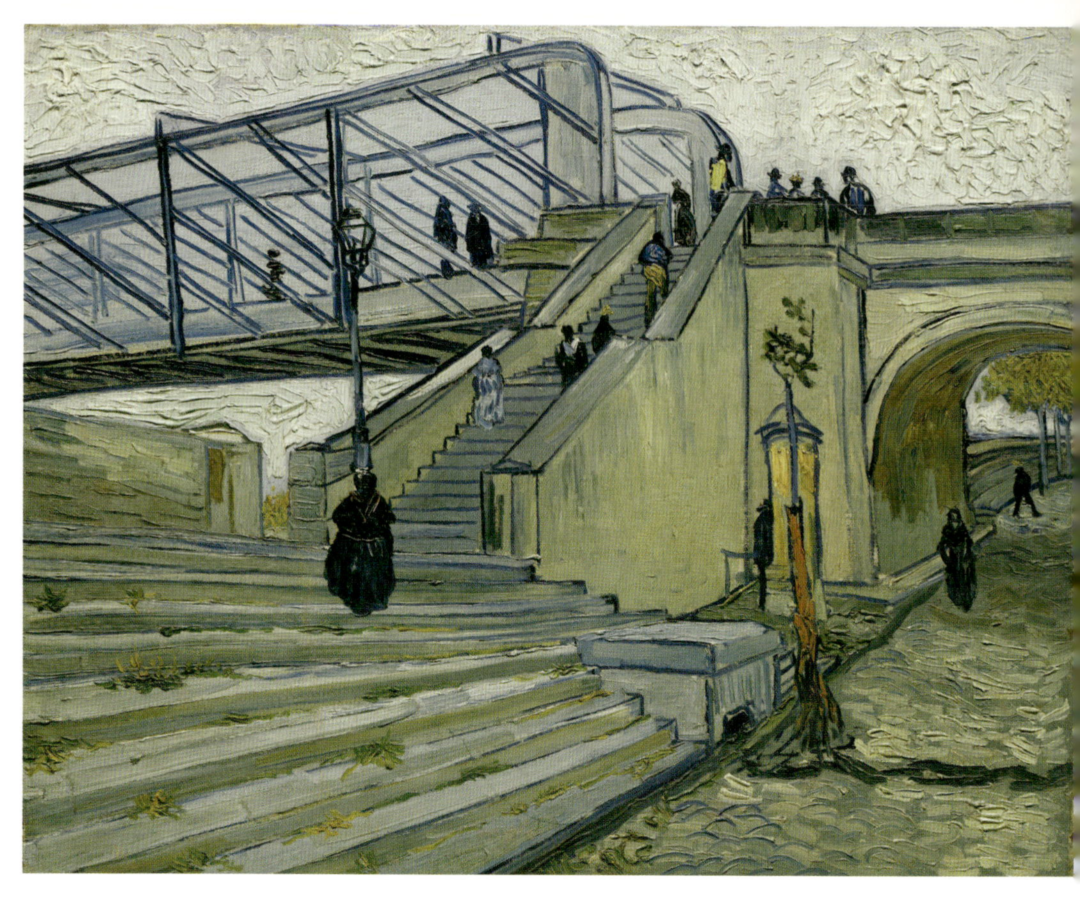

Vincent van Gogh, "Le pont de Trinquetaille", 1888, © Christie's Images Limited

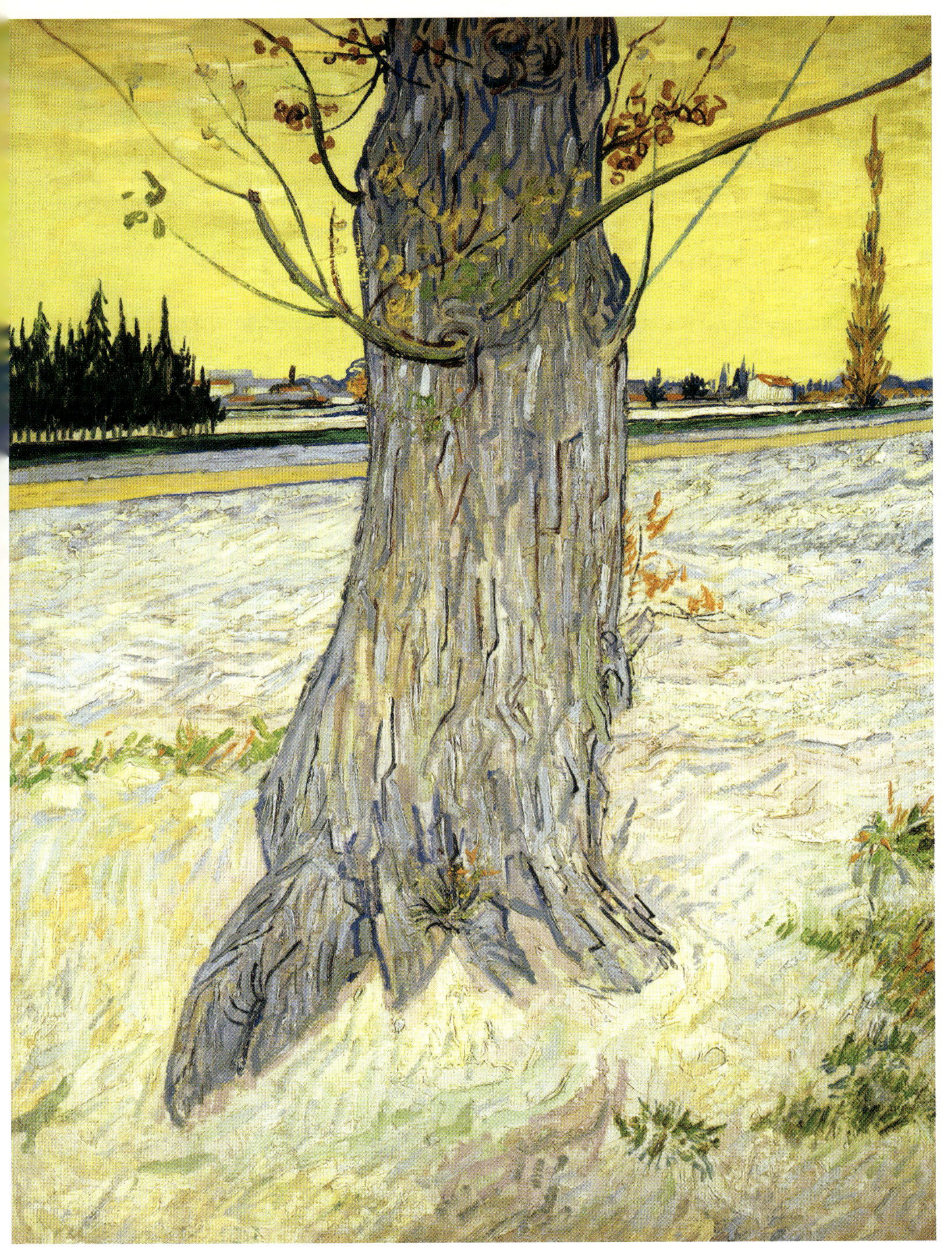

Vincent van Gogh, "Le vieil If", 1888, © Christie's Images Limited

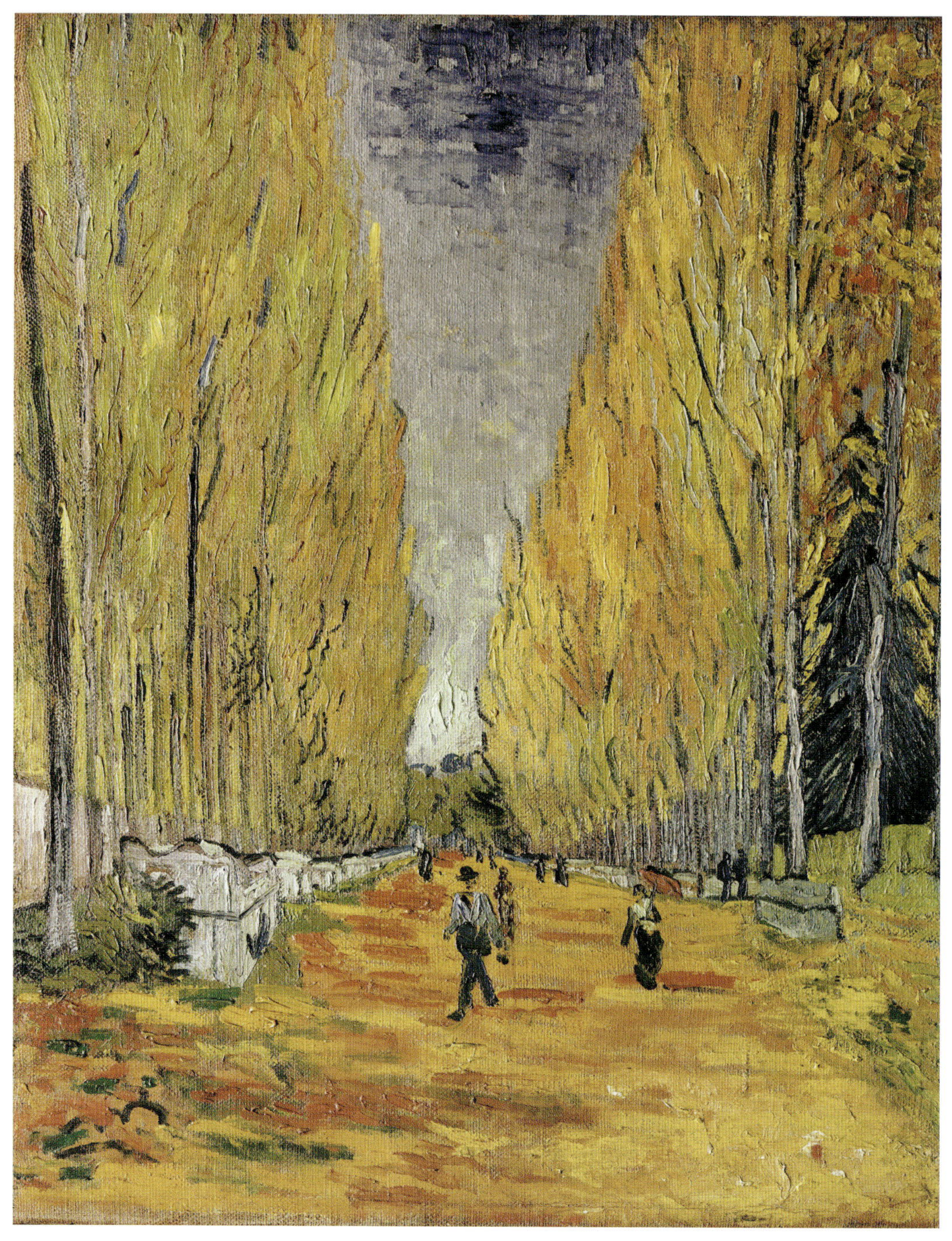

Vincent van Gogh, "L'allée des Alyscamps", 1888, © Christie's Images Limited

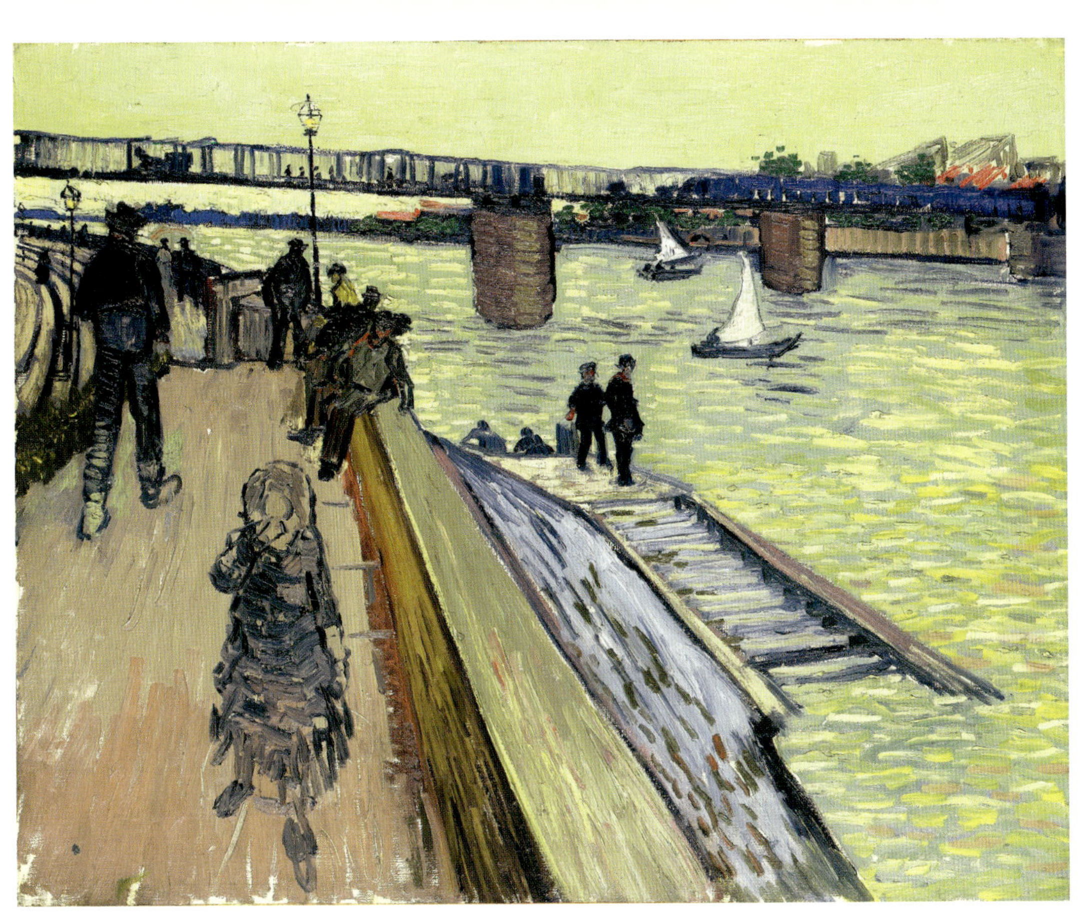

Vincent van Gogh, "Le pont de Trinquetaille", 1888, © Christie's Images Limited

Roy Lichtenstein

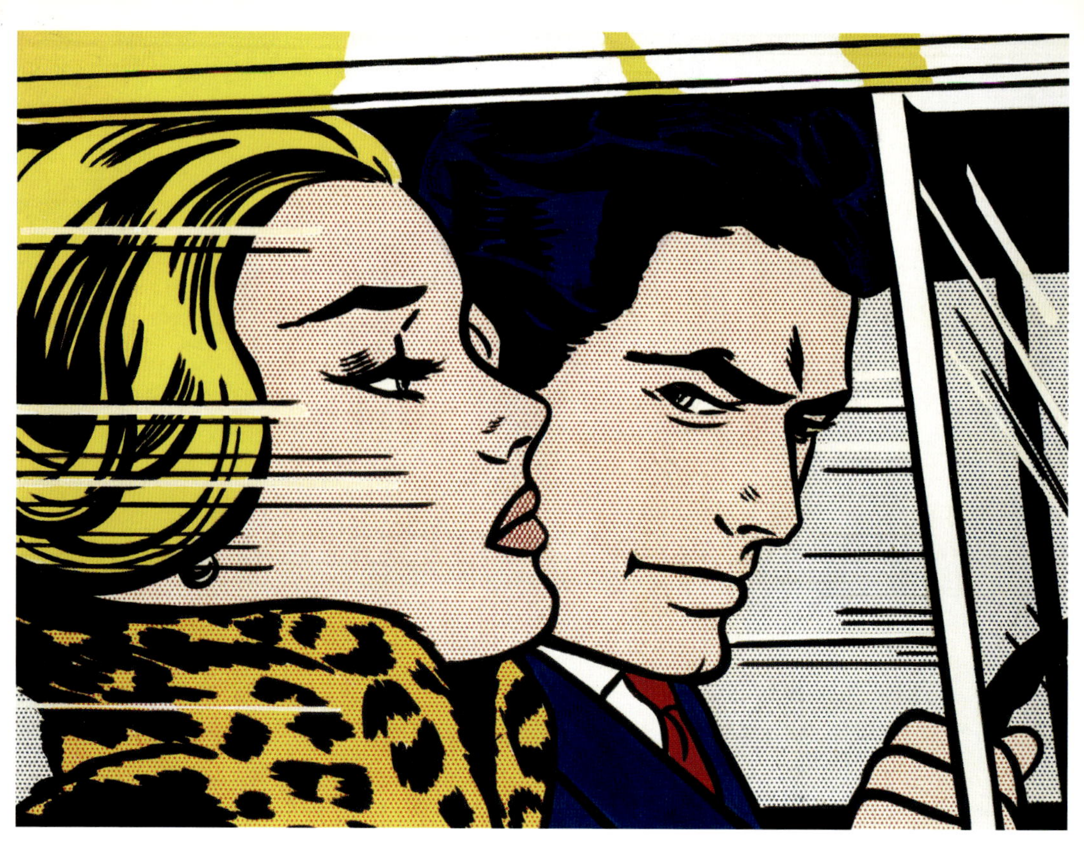

Roy Lichtenstein, "In the car", 1963/© Estate of Roy Lichtenstein/VBK, Vienna 2006, © Christie's Images Limited

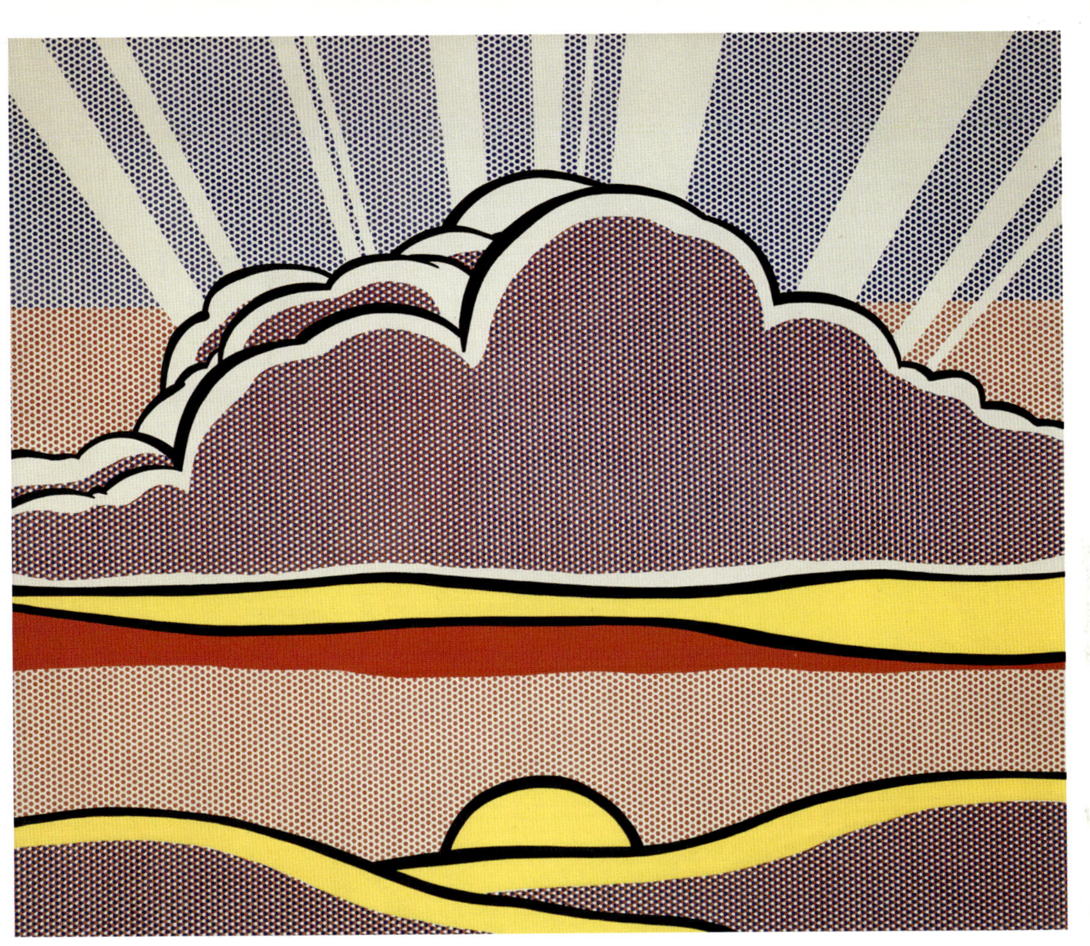

Roy Lichtenstein, "Sinking sun", 1964/© Estate of Roy Lichtenstein/VBK, Vienna 2006, © akg-images

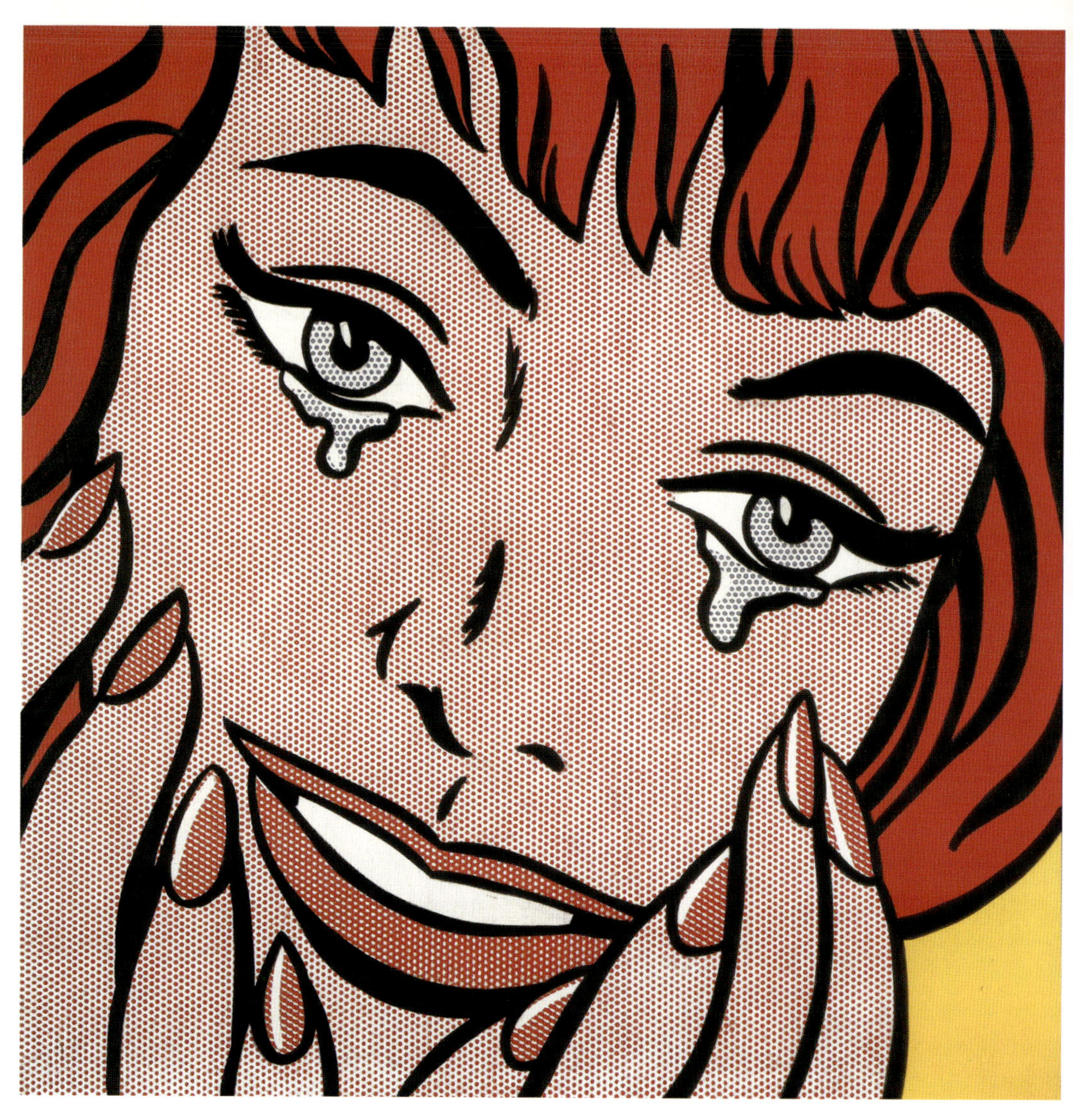

Roy Lichtenstein, "Happy tears", 1964/© Estate of Roy Lichtenstein/VBK, Vienna 2006, © Christie's Images Limited

Pablo Picasso

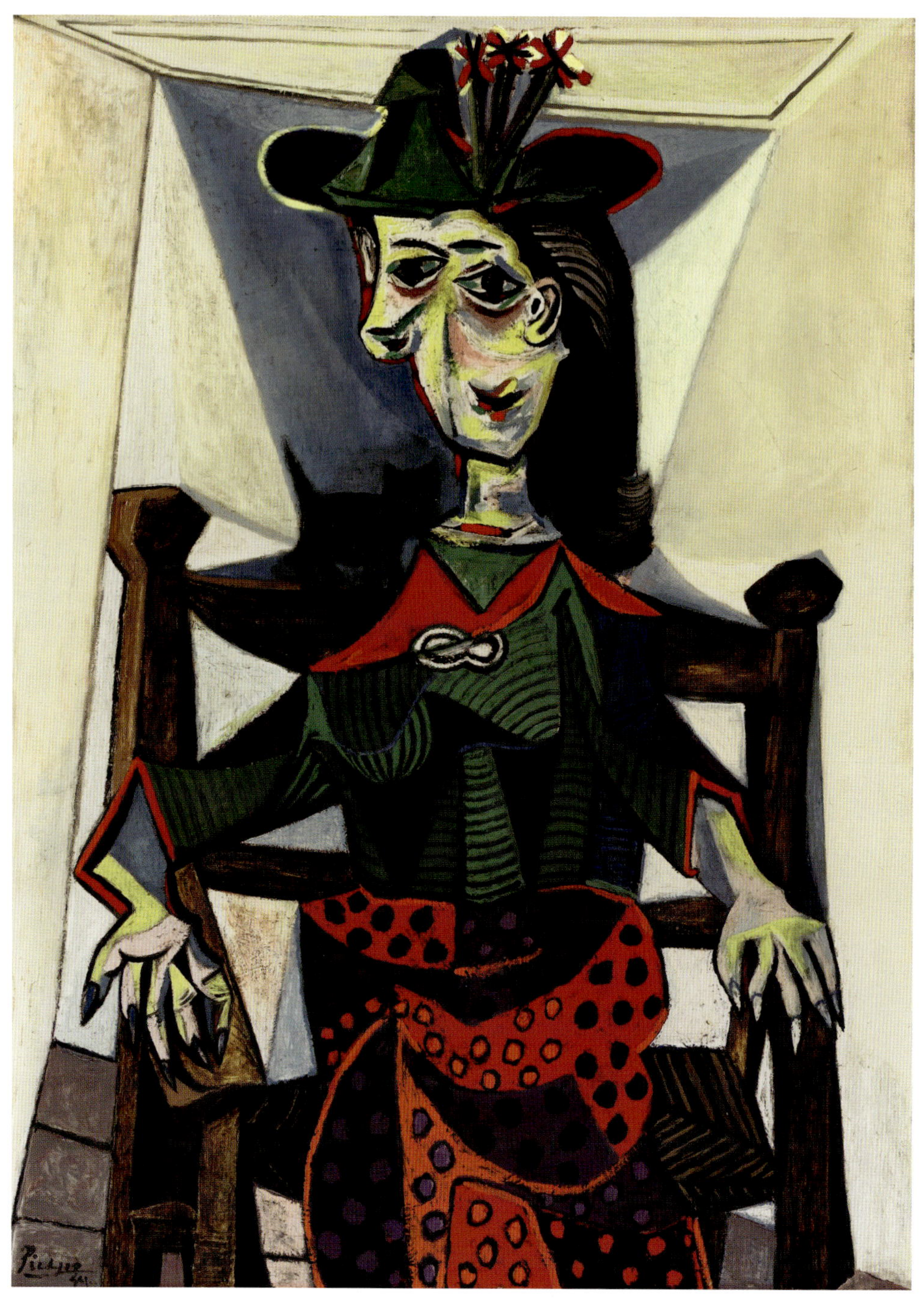

Pablo Picasso, "Dora Maar au Chat", 1941/© Succession Picasso/VBK, Vienna 2006

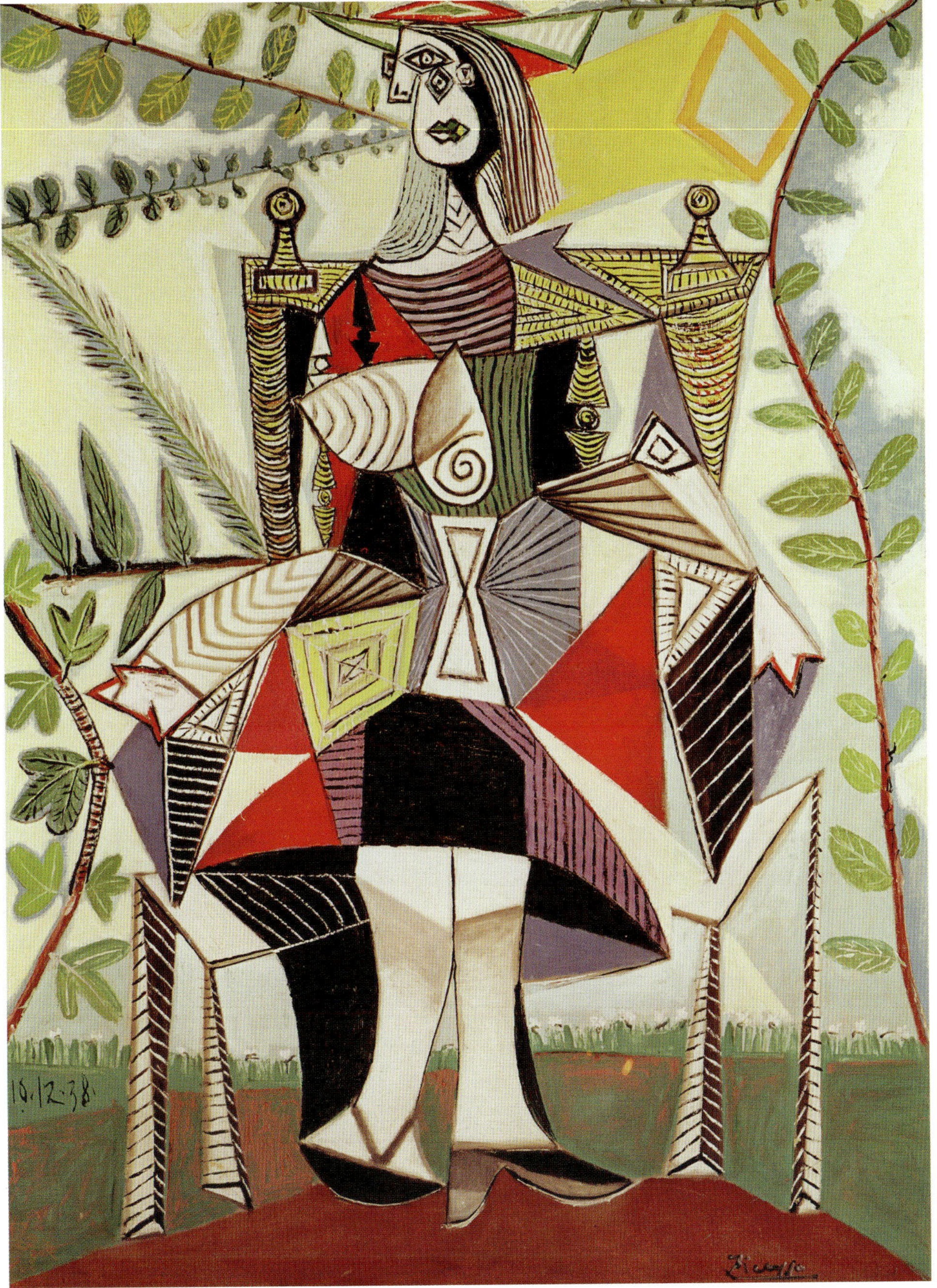

Pablo Picasso, "Femme assise dans un Jardin", 1938/© Succession Picasso/VBK, Vienna 2006
© Private Collection/Giraudon/The Bridgeman Art Library

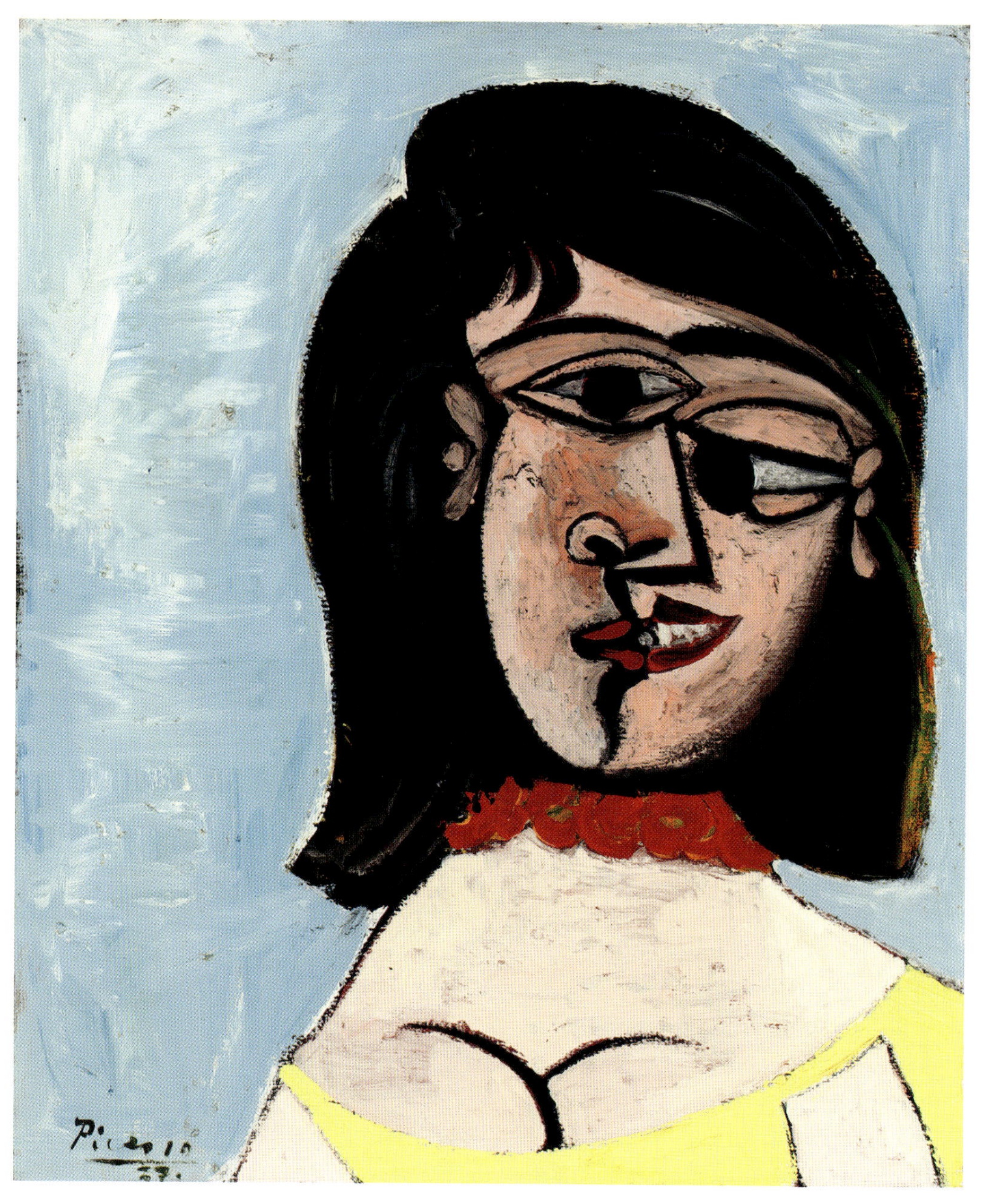

Pablo Picasso, "Tête de Femme" (Dora Maar), 1937/© Succession Picasso/VBK, Vienna 2006, © Christie's Images Limited

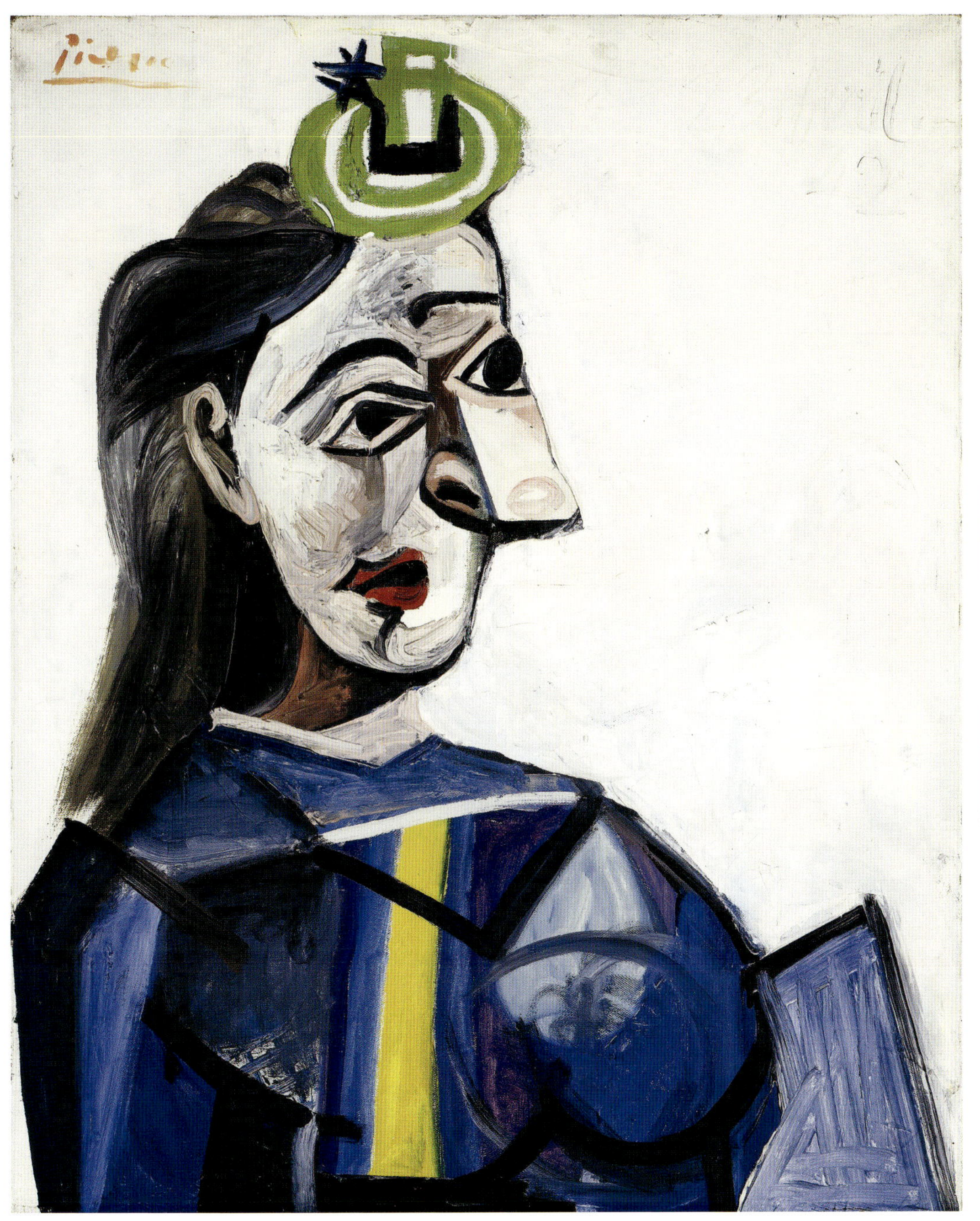

Pablo Picasso, "Buste de femme" (Dora Maar), 1942/© Succession Picasso/VBK, Vienna 2006, © Christie's Images Limited

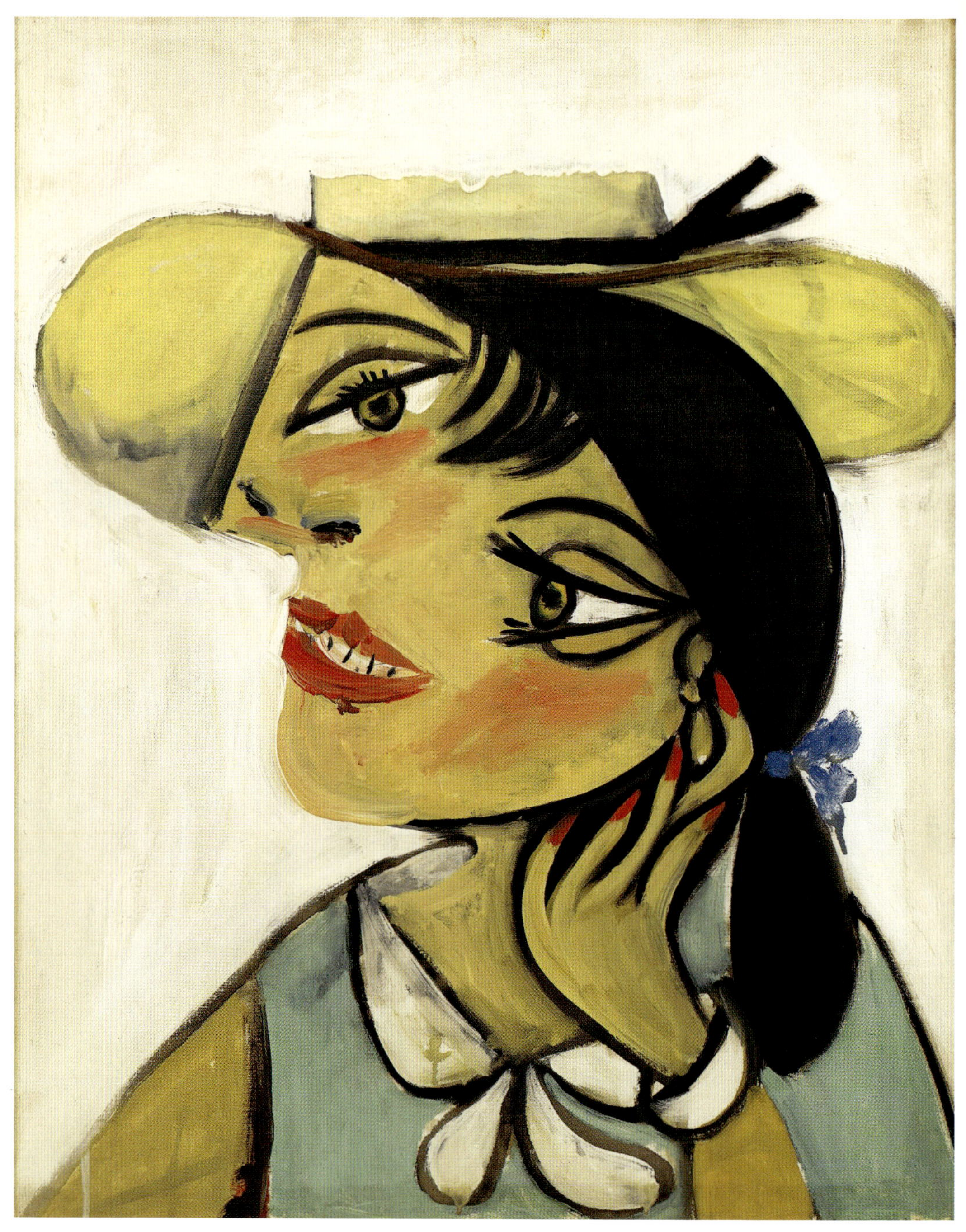

Pablo Picasso, "Femme au chapeau de paille", 1937/© Succession Picasso/VBK, Vienna 2006

Claude Monet

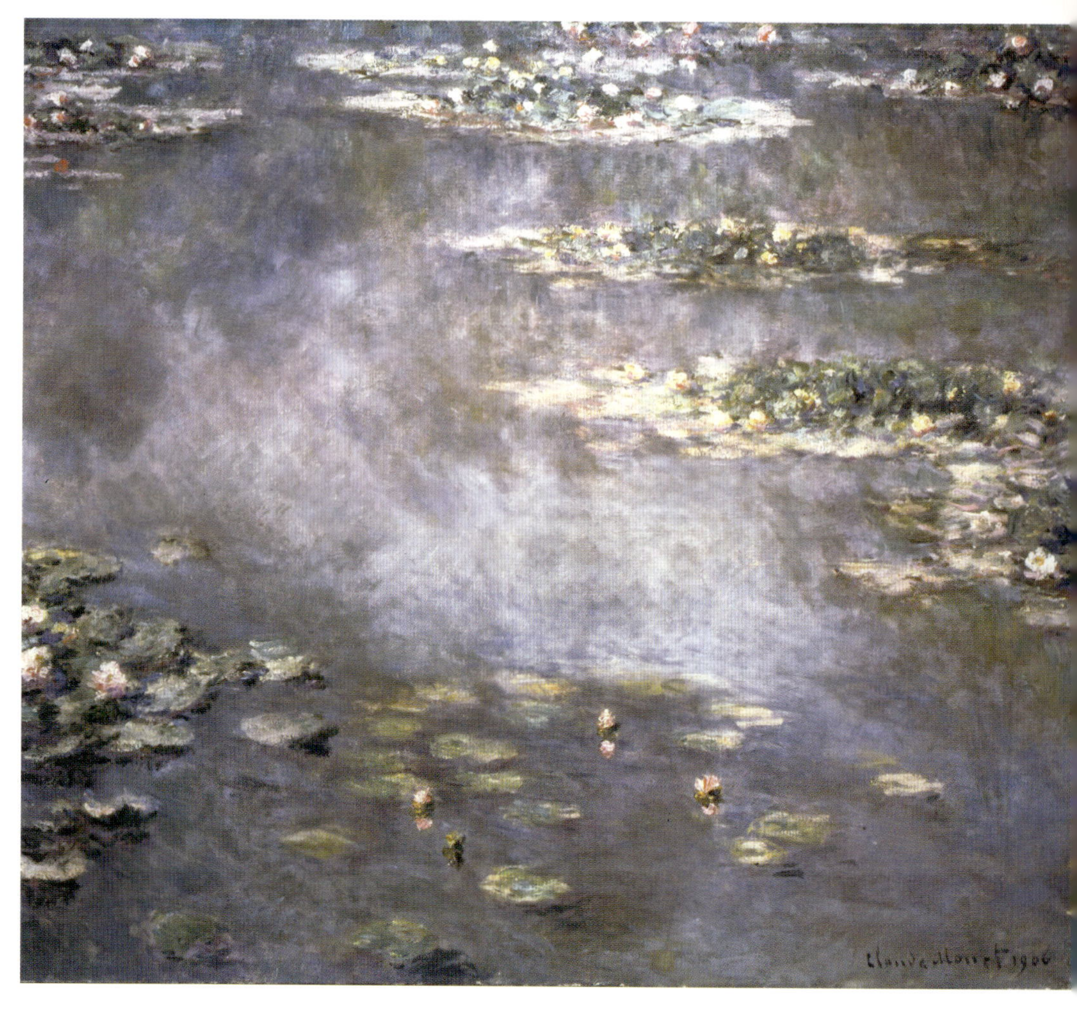

Claude Monet, "Nymphéas", 1906, © Christie's Images Limited

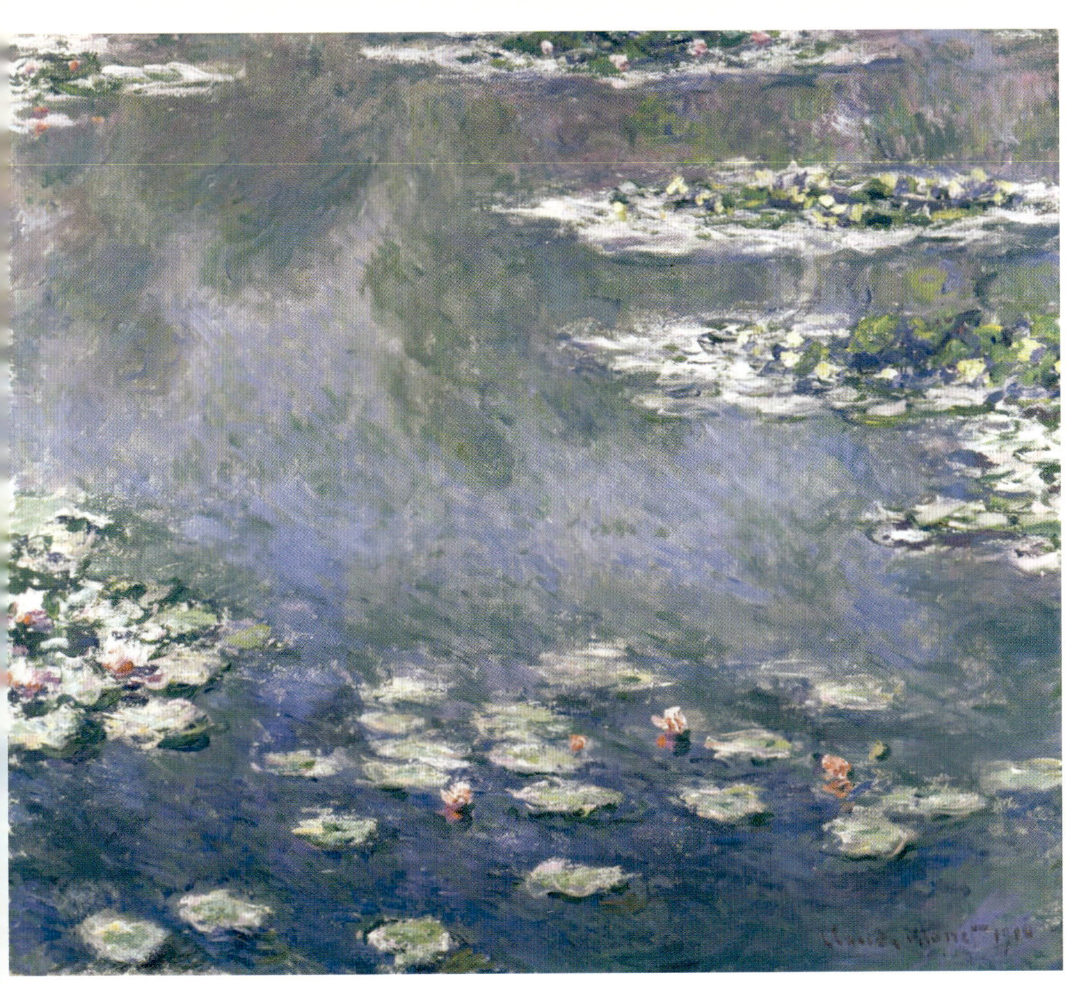

Claude Monet, "Nymphéas", 1906

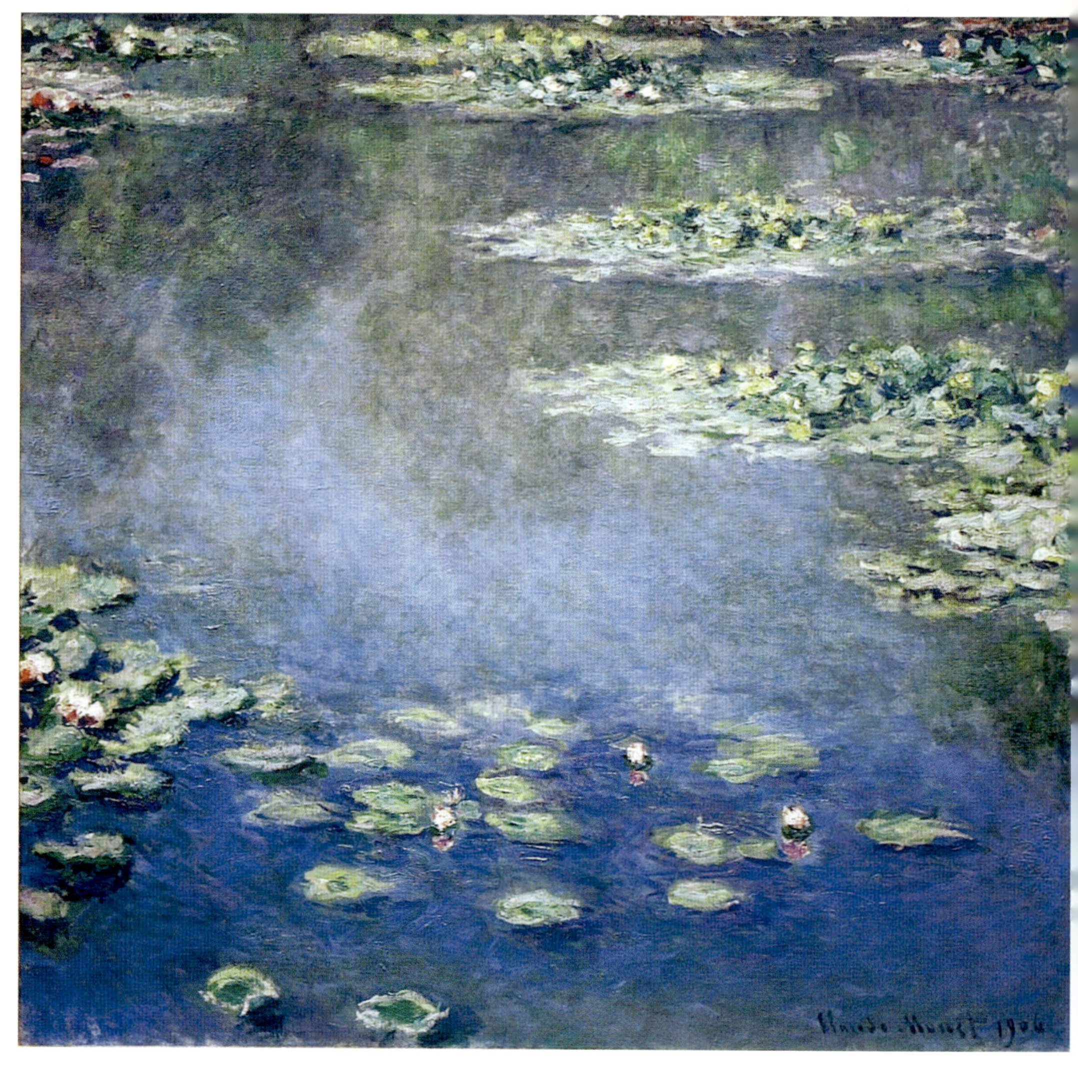

Claude Monet, "Nymphéas", 1906

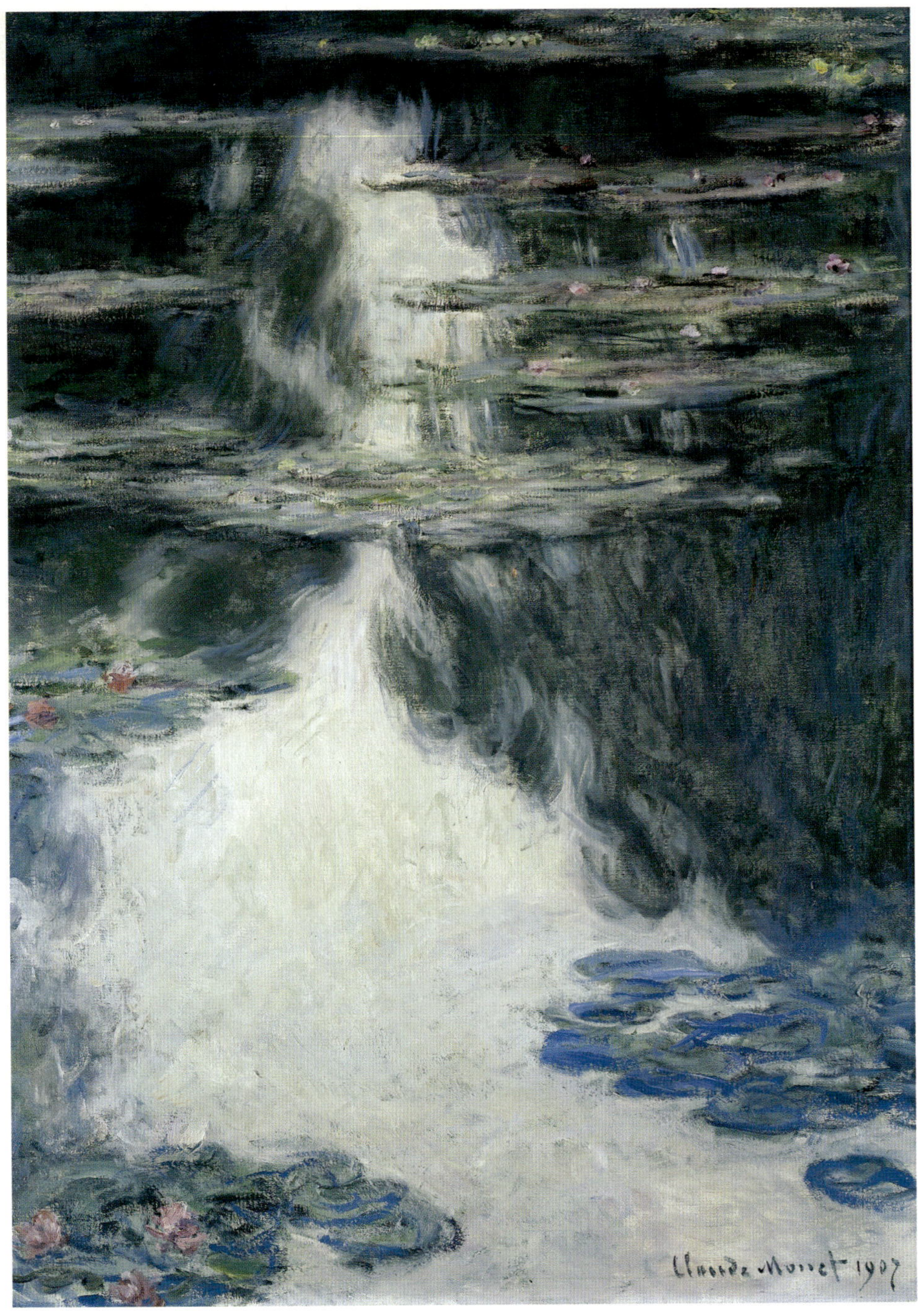

Claude Monet, "Nymphéas", 1907, © Christie's Images Limited

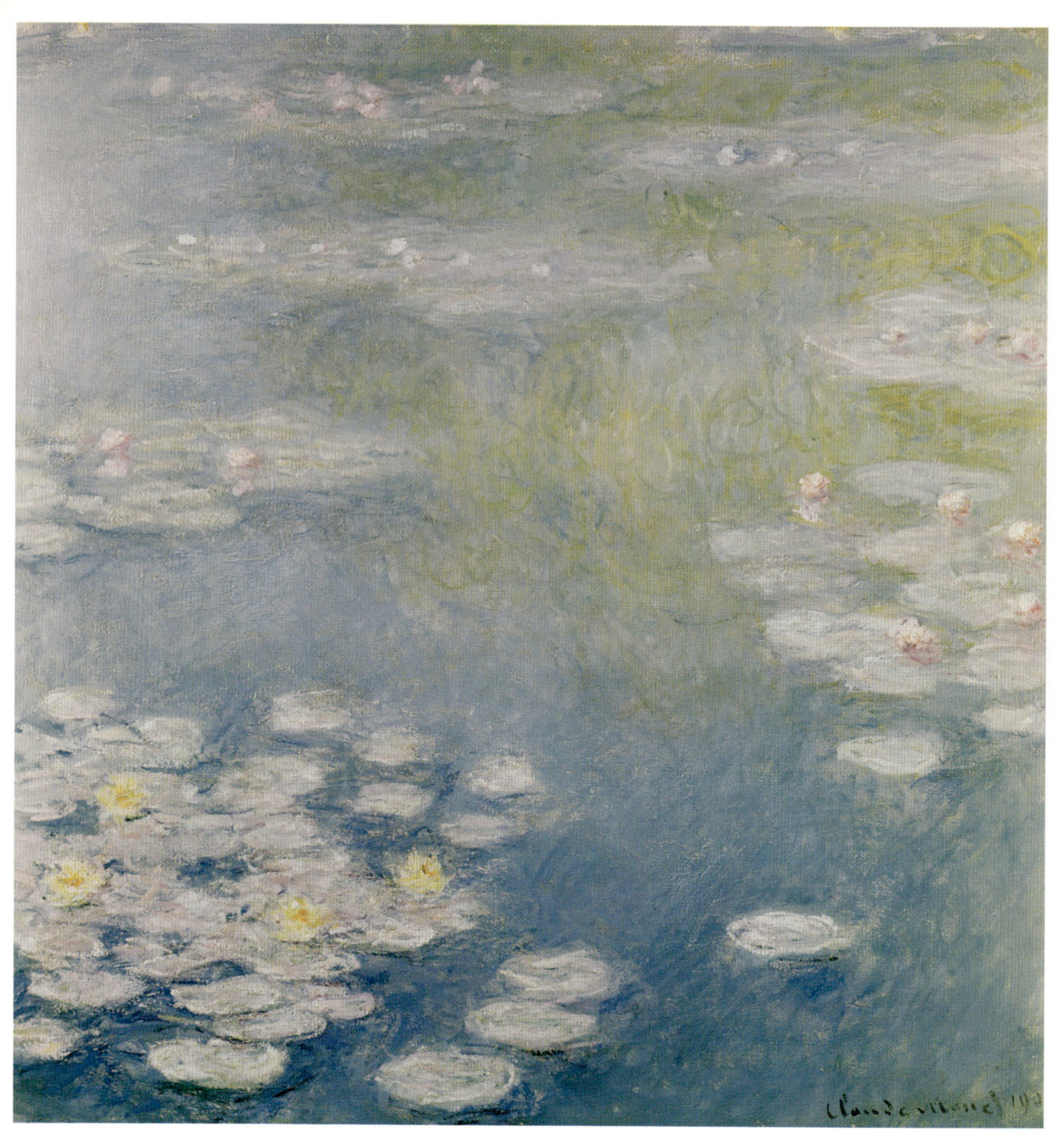

Claude Monet, "Nymphéas", 1908, © Private Collection/The Bridgeman Art Library

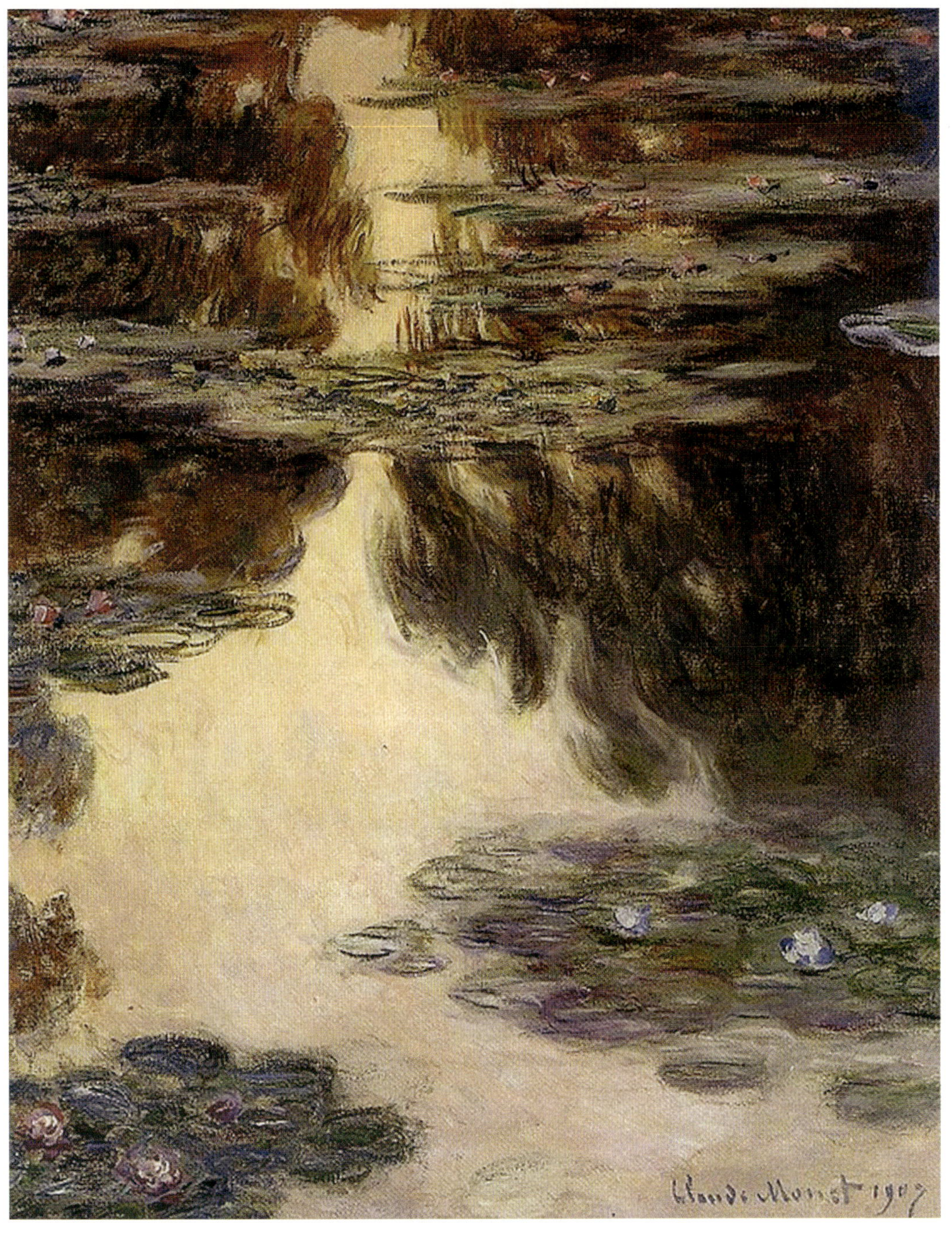

Claude Monet, "Nymphéas", 1907

Paul Cézanne

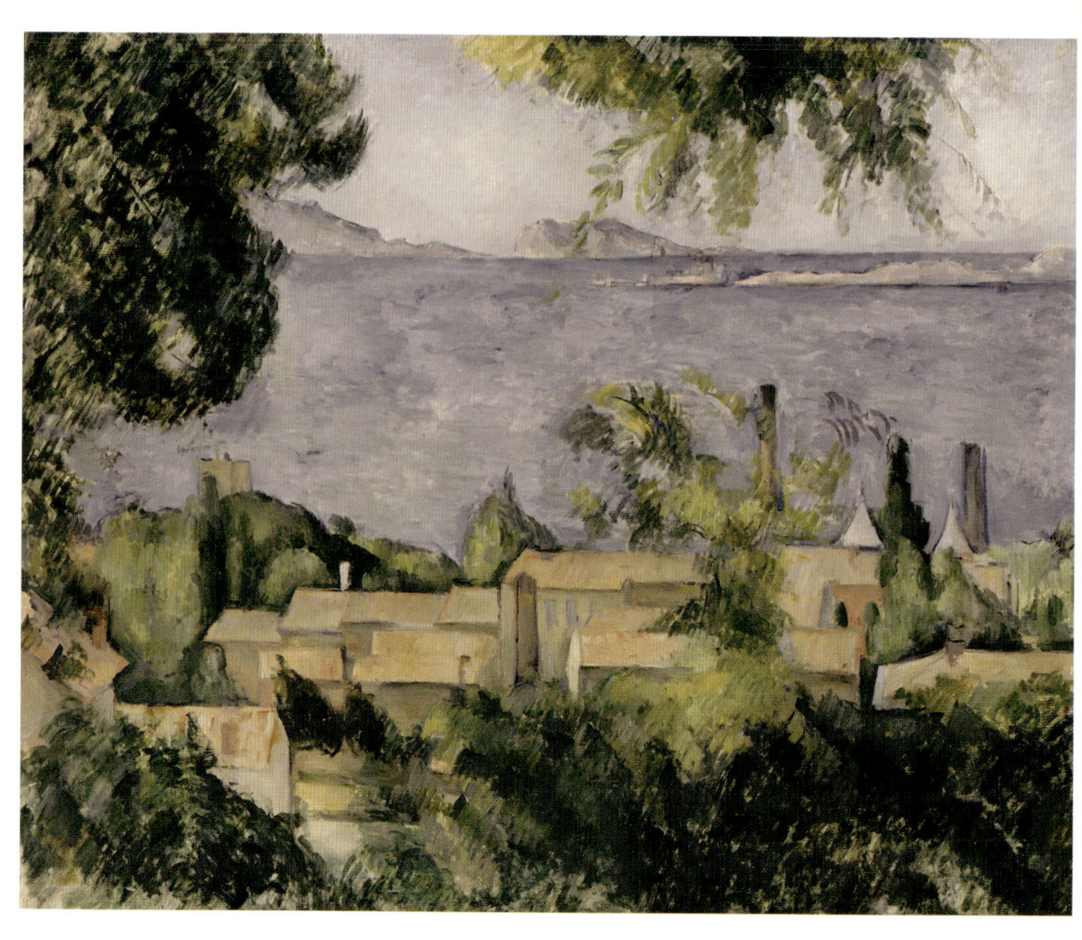

Paul Cézanne, "Les toits de l'Estaque", 1883-1885, © Christie's Images Limited

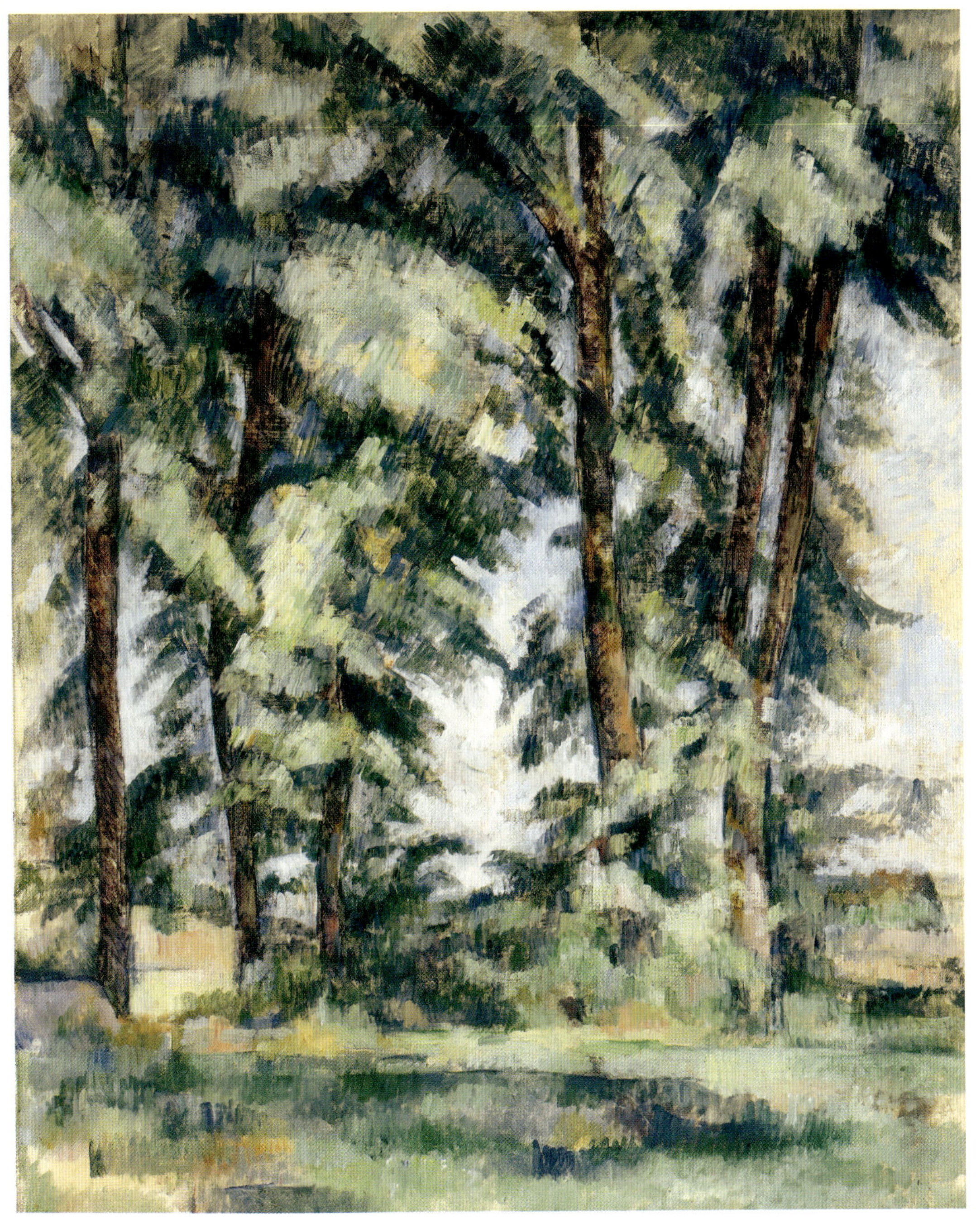

Paul Cézanne, "Les grands arbres au Jas de Bouffan", 1885-1887, © Christie's Images Limited

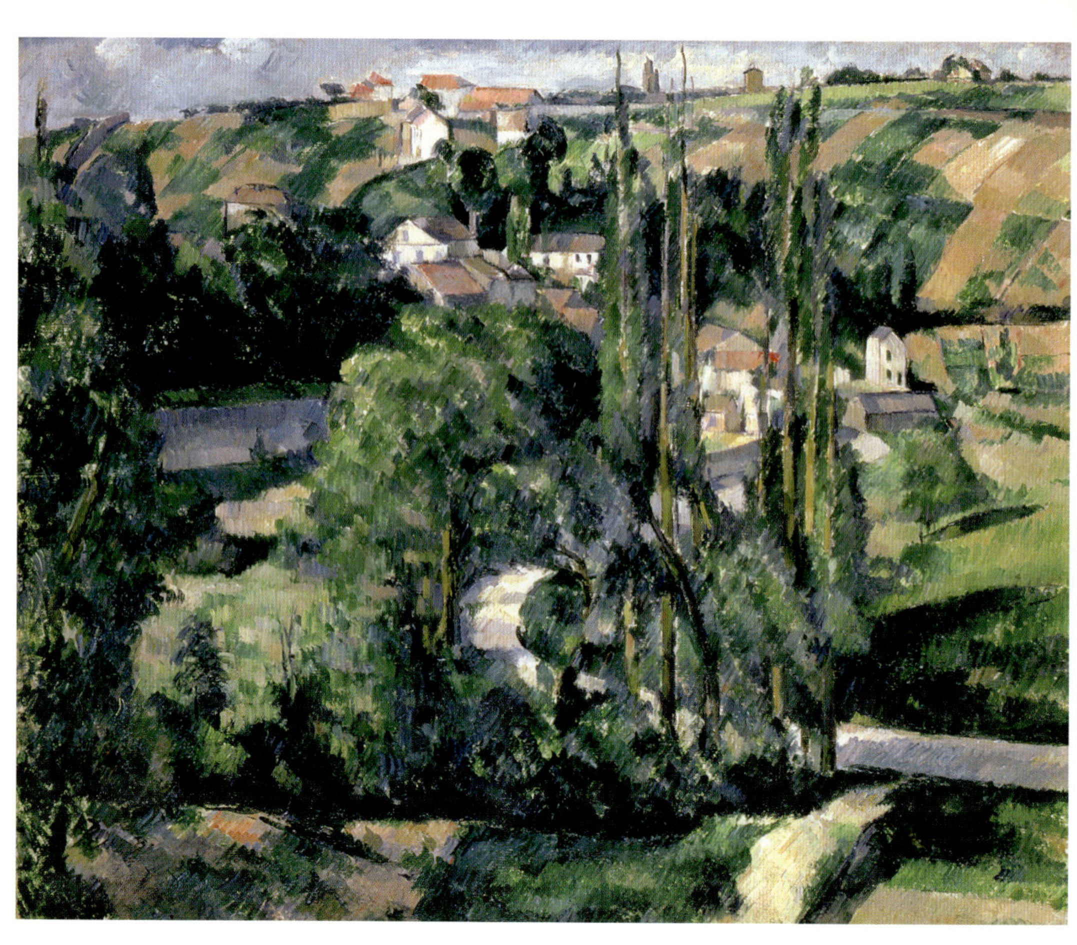

Paul Cézanne, "La Côte Du Galet, À Pontoise", 1879-1881, © Buenos Dias/Bridgeman Art Library

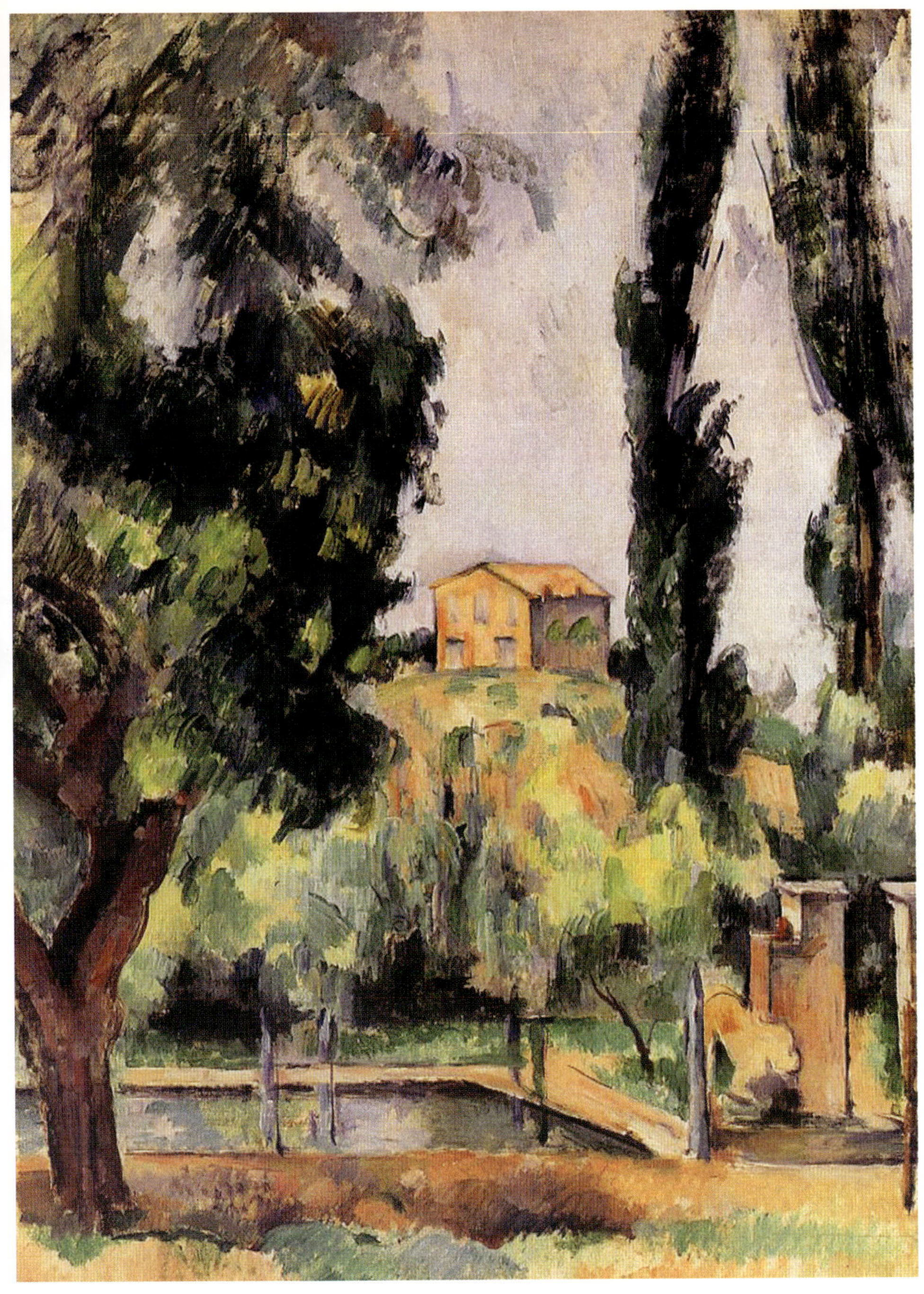

Paul Cézanne, "Le Jas de Bouffan", 1885-1887

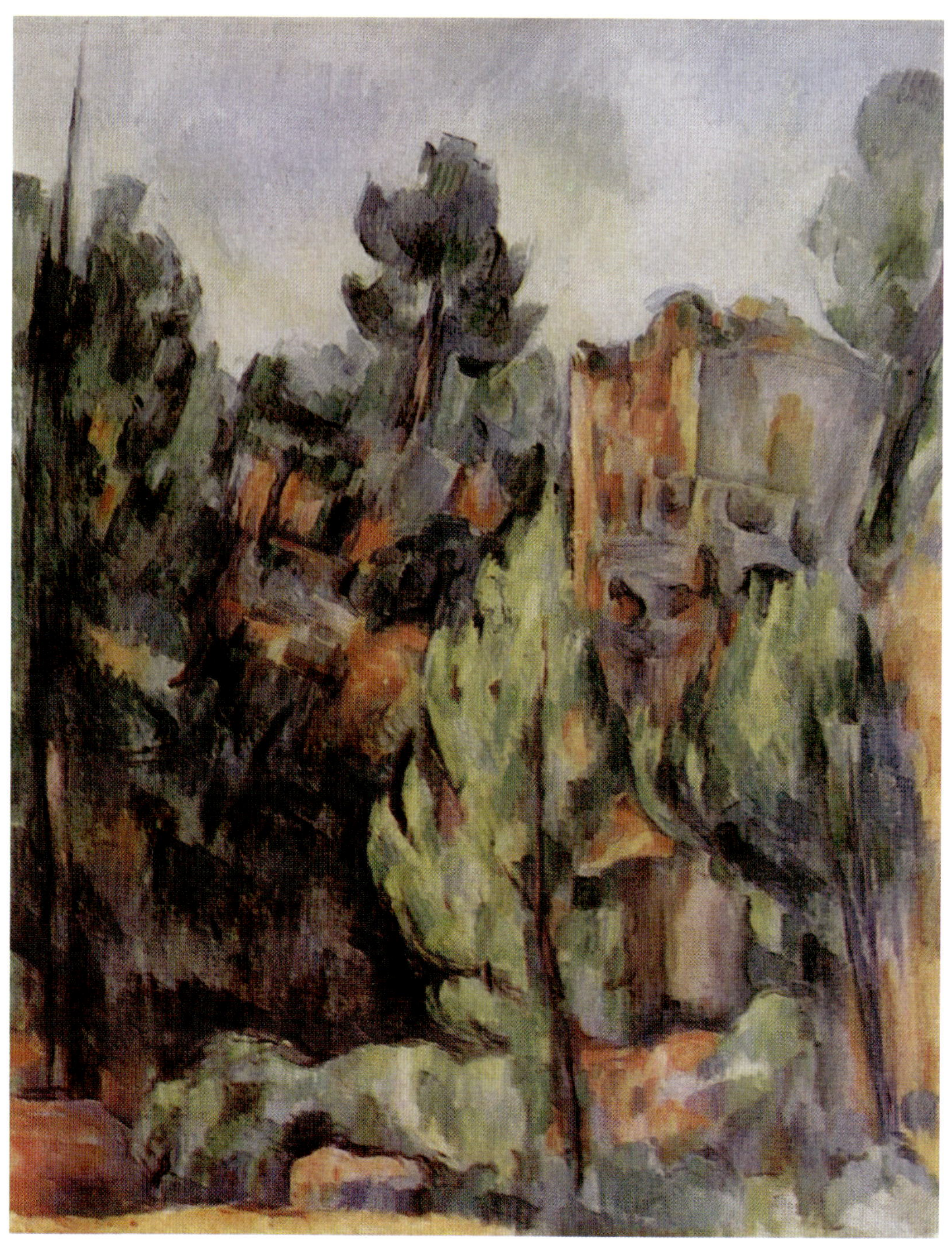

Paul Cézanne, "Carriere de Bibemus", 1898

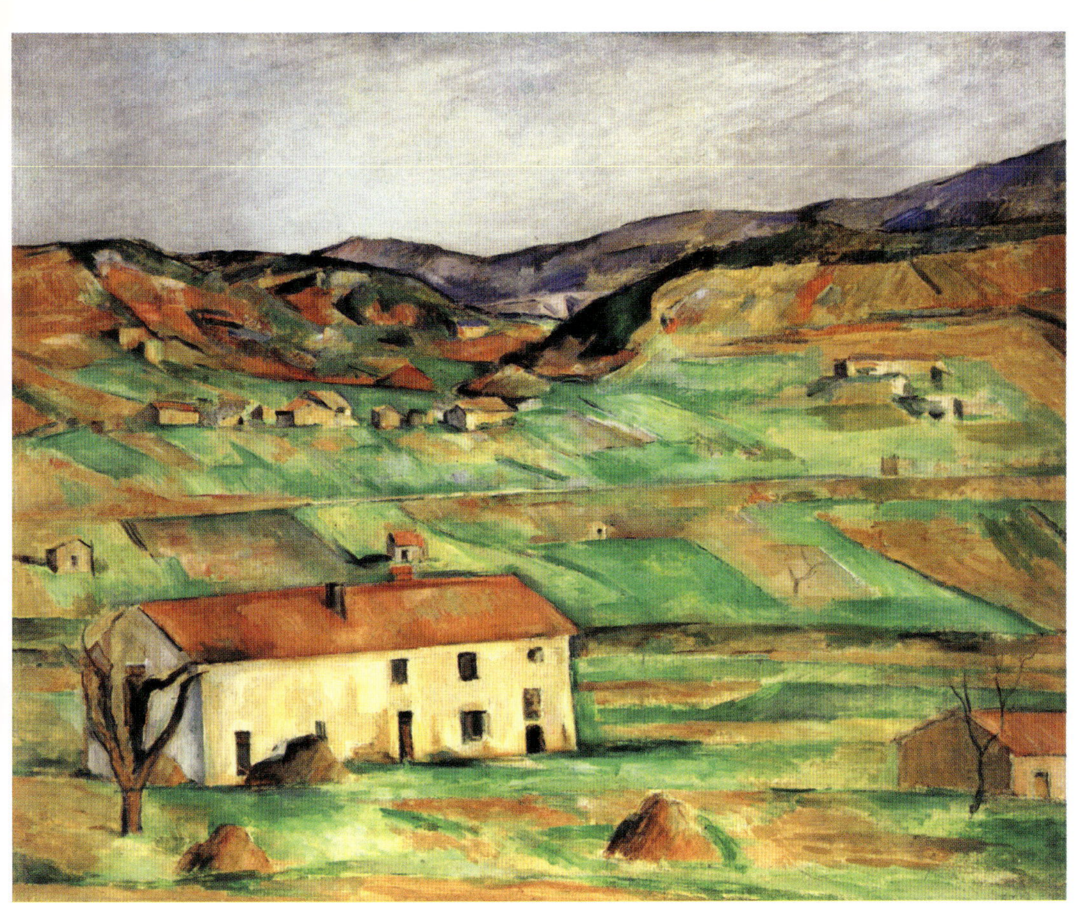

Paul Cézanne, "Environs de Gardanne", 1886-1890

Chapter 5
Strategies for Investing in the Art Market

Art is frequently treated as an alternative investment class by investors, the media and even investment professionals. While in the previous four chapters we have demonstrated that the premium art market segment is hardly suitable for professional investments and has many features that make rational and transparent investing impossible, an increasing amount of capital is nevertheless flowing into art assets.

5.1. As the rich get richer the art market will continue to grow and become more liquid

The exact volume of art purchases is difficult to measure. We have provided some estimates in the first chapter already[1], and Exhibits 5.1 and 5.2 give us a particularly good idea as to the prevailing trend, namely, that a consistently increasing amount of funds will be available for art investments.

These capital inflows are driven less by attractive returns than by the increasingly larger amounts of capital available to high net worth individuals ("HNWI")[2] around the world. According to the World Wealth Report, one of the most respected publications tracking the accumulation and allocation of wealth by HNWI around the world (published by Merrill Lynch and Capgemini) the total capital available to HNWI is expected to grow from an already astonishing USD 33.3 trillion in 2005 to USD 44.6 trillion in 2010 (Exhibit 5.1), an in-

1. An interesting estimate of the UK market is provided by the Artquest, a program funded jointly by Arts Council England and the University of the Arts London. "The UK has the largest art and antiques market in Europe. It is second only to the USA in the world with a 25% global share; a turnover in 2002 of £4.2 billion," http://www.artquest.org.uk/artlaw/patrons/market-forart.htm

2. High net worth individuals are defined as individuals holding no less than USD 1 million in financial (liquid) assets. There were 8.7 million people around the world in 2005 who met this criterion. Source: Merrill Lynch and Capgemini World Wealth Report, 2006, page 4.

Exhibit 5.1 – HNWI financial wealth forecast by region

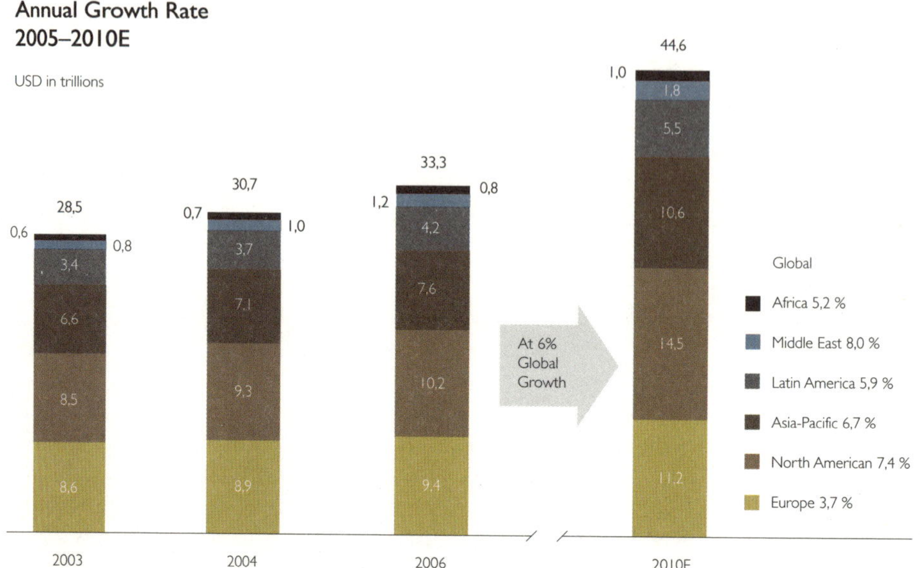

Source: World Wealth Report, 2006, by Merrill Lunch

crease of one third over just five years. The rich are indeed getting richer very quickly.

According to Exhibit 5.2, 20% of HNWI assets in 2005 were allocated to alternative investments. Clearly, most of these funds were invested in private equity, hedge funds and structured products and commodities (including precious metals). Assuming, however, that just 0.1% of HNWI investments go into what Merrill Lynch and Capgemini refer to as "investments of passion," USD 6.7 billion ends up being allocated to fine art and collectibles. In reality, the amount allocated is far greater. As we saw in Chapter 1, the combined value of the world's 1000 most valuable works of art (Skate's Top 1000) currently stands

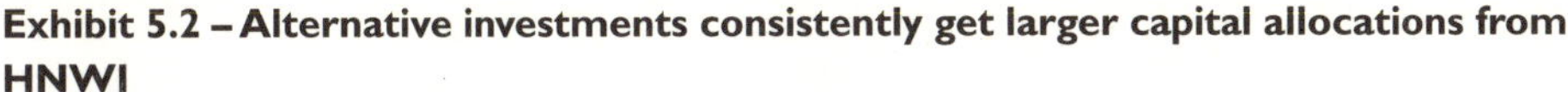

Exhibit 5.2 – Alternative investments consistently get larger capital allocations from HNWI

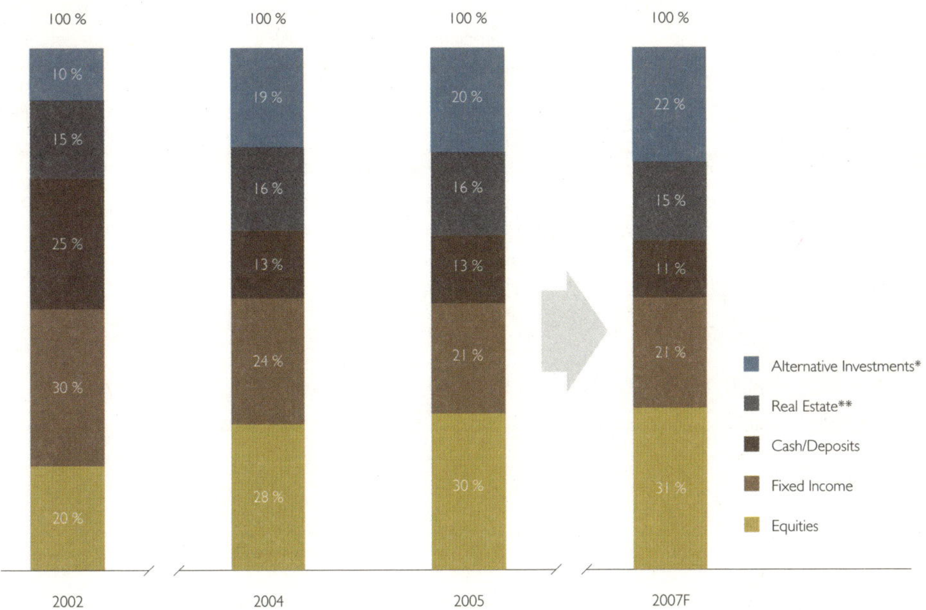

Note: 2004 numbers have been restated due to a change in methodology: To improve accuracy, regional data has been weighed to reflect the financial wealth of that region; results were then accepted to create a more representative global figure.
*Includes: Structured products, hedge funds, managed funds, foreign currency, commodities (inlcuding precious metals), private equity and investments of passion (fine art&collectables)
**Includes: Direct real-estate investments and REITS
Source: Capgemini/Merril Lynch Relationship Manager Surveys, March 2003, April 2005, March 2006

at USD 9.3 billion, and while of course a significant percentage of art is held by institutions[3] and museums, HNWI hold far more than USD 6.7 billion in art assets. We estimate that investments of passion contribute to at least 0.3% of HNWI allocations to alternative investments (or 0.06% of total assets), which implies at least USD 20 billion.

Going a step forward, if we take the forecasts by Merrill Lynch and Capgemini for HNWI asset growth and increased allocation to alternative investments and assume that 0.3% of allocated capital will go into fine arts and collectibles, at least USD 9.4 billion in new capital should flow into the art market between 2006-2010 at a rate of approximately USD 1.9 billion per year. Incidentally, this forecasted

3. Corporate collections are perhaps the dominant forms of institutional investments into significant art. Two major examples are the collections of Japanese insurance group Sompo (http://www.sompo-japan.co.jp/museum/english/info/index.html) and Deutsche Bank (http://www.community.db.com/art/)

annual inflow of fresh funds corresponds to about one third of the auction market's annual turnover (USD 5.8 billion in 2005, see Chapter 1). Assuming there is no increase in HNWI allocations to art investments and the number of art buyers and sellers remains stable, in the coming five years HNWI should provide a powerful source of additional liquidity to the global art market.

We see two principal sources of supply to satisfy this increase in demand. One source is the art carefully assembled and groomed through the rational art investment strategies described further in this chapter. The other comes from Sotheby's elegant "4D concept," which explains the reasons why significant art enters the market.

Exhibit 5.3 – Sotheby's "4D-Concept" – Principal reasons for the sale of significant artworks

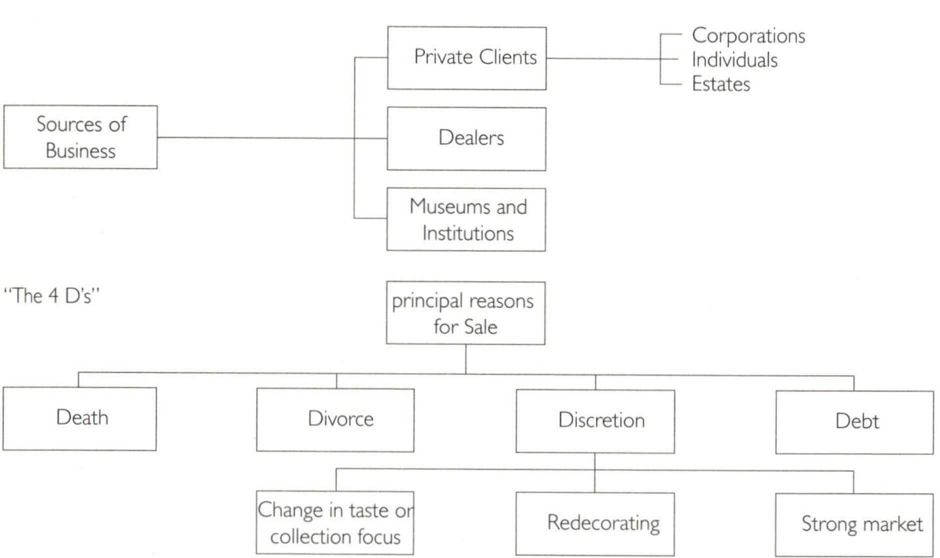

5.2. Art investment strategies

With disappointing returns the norm in the art market's premium segment, are there actually any art investment strategies suitable for rational investors? We believe that there are. First, the rational investor can make private equity-styled investments into art, and second, the investor can acquire securities that in one way or another track the performance of the art market (the latter is covered in section 5.4).

Rational investing in art requires the approach and discipline of private equity investing. Art assets, like securities in privately held companies, are generally illiquid and yield solid returns only when bought at very reasonable price levels. As the investor must seek a competitive investment return that not only compensates for the higher risk in comparison to more liquid assets but also covers the significant ownership and transaction costs, it becomes clear that the threshold rate of return on art investments should be over 35-40% on an annualized basis. In fact, none of the repeat sales of Skate's Top 1000 masterpieces has generated effective returns at this level in the last 20 years.

When a private equity approach to art investing is taken, rational return-oriented investors should plan on being closely involved with "managing" their art assets in the same way private equity investors participate in their investment companies. In order to achieve adequate returns on art investments, simply purchasing art with good appreciation potential is not enough; investments also have to be actively managed for this appreciation potential to materialize. In private equity language – there are many ideas, but the ability to execute is key to achieving a significant valuation step-up between making and exiting an investment. In other words, there is plenty of interesting art available on the market, but quality art investment management is critical to making good art appreciate over the holding horizon. Less financially savvy readers should think about the power of compounding. For example, setting a 40% threshold annualized rate of return for a USD 1 million art investment in order to adequately compensate for higher risks, as well as the transaction and ownership costs, one should expect to receive USD 3.8 million at the end of a 7-year investment cycle, with the art portfolio growing by 21% annually (the effect of compounding a 21% rate over the 7-year period yields a 40% annualized rate of return). From a rational investor's standpoint, a four-fold increase in a work's price during a 7-year holding period should not be taken as a sign of fantastic investment returns but rather seen as minimally acceptable rates of return that compensate for art assets' idiosyncratic risks and various costs.

The preceding review of target returns demonstrates once again that rational art investors should look for art investments below Skate's Top 1000 value threshold (around USD 4 million as of September 2006). As we saw in Exhibit 2.1, historically the average growth of the Top 100, Top 300 and Top 500 artworks portfolio prices is within 5-6% on an annual basis, with none of the repeat sales in Skate's Top 1000 generating more than a 27% annualized effective rate of return over the last 20 years. How to select and enhance the value of art in the lower price category is the key question for rational art investors. In the next chapter we will cover some tips.

5.3. A private equity approach to art investing

Continuing our focus on certain private equity-styled considerations that relate to investing in art, we note that two compelling principles underlie a rational return-focused art investment strategy: (1) diversification is essential, and (2) investment in art assets begins but definitely does not end with an artwork's purchase. The first rule is rather obvious. Art is a high-risk investment class, and putting together a diverse portfolio of art assets (a collection) comprised of artworks from different cultural contexts, periods and provenance backgrounds helps to reduce the investment risk.

The second rule arises from the notion that an art asset itself usually does not generate any positive cash flow (loaning to exhibitions and licensing the image for reproduction rarely generate any income for the art asset holder, as they are considered promotional opportunities for artworks). Hence, once investors acquire title to an artwork, they incur two general types of expenses – ownership costs and value enhancement costs, the latter of which we will cover in greater detail further.
From a financial point of view, ownership costs are difficult to capitalize. As we saw in Chapter 3, the accounting view of art investments is that a masterpiece's depreciation is matched by its ownership costs,

or a work of art does not fall in accounting value as long as it is being insured, stored and protected properly. In other words, ownership expenses, including restoration expenses when applicable, are essentially the way to keep a significant work of art from depreciating. An investment into an artwork is therefore like a venture capital investment in a start-up where there is little visibility as to when this business would move to positive cash flows. Instead, an investor is not only expected to pay a price for an artwork but also to write checks from time to time in order to cover ownership expenses.

The rational private equity approach can only justify such investments when there is a clear exit strategy that allows a loss-making asset to be sold to another buyer at a premium sufficient to generate an adequate rate of return (the example in section 3.2 suggests that the "premium" can actually mean selling an art asset at several times its initial price depending on the holding horizon and the threshold rate of return applied by the investor). A classic business-like approach to enhancing an asset's value that suggests measures like developing unique competitive advantages, growth in sales and discipline in costs obviously does not apply to art investments. So exactly which art investment strategies should be applied to achieve a decent chance to exit an artwork at a significant valuation step-up over the original purchase price?

The answers are fairly straightforward. An artwork must be able to travel up the value chain by possessing the ability to be compared in a high-value peer group, with its story carrying enough components to stir an irrational premium from prospective buyers.

An artwork value enhancement strategy must be designed to fundamentally render a given artwork somehow comparable to works in a certain peer group, which suggests a valuation range that would yield an investor a suitable return upon exit. A good example strategy being employed in the international art market is the promotion of Austrian and German impressionists. Following very high-profile exhibitions and major auctions of works by Gustav Klimt and Egon Schiele, which eventually established previously unheard of prices for Austrian art, we can expect art market insiders to follow up with more Austrian names and place them in the context of Klimt and Schiele valuations on the basis of their cultural relevance and comparable artistic training, context and historical circumstances. When auction catalogue notes or reviews by art critics emphasize parallels between artworks of less well-known artists and those artists who already command valuation levels in Skate's Top 1000, what we see is often little more than a well calculated attempt to place artworks and their creators in valuation peer groups that justify high prices.

An enhancement effort only helps drive valuations to new price levels if the related art story contains enough convincing factual data (often emphasizing social and cultural context, history and ownership) to support a higher priced peer group, thereby encouraging more investors to consider paying higher irrational premiums for such art. A critical skill for any value enhancement strategy is the ability to conduct thorough art research and produce credible knowledge that allows art assets to be classified into peer groups priced at significant premiums to the prices currently paid for artworks. This knowledge, when assembled and communicated to the art market properly, is capable not only of capturing higher irrational premiums assigned to a given artwork but also of allowing starting offer prices to be set at higher levels on the basis of a more favorable (higher-priced) valuation range.

In addition to an artwork's purchase price and ownership costs, a successful art investment process should allocate certain capital to value-enhancing research for related works of art, as well as public communication efforts to feed this new knowledge to the market, which will in turn allow artworks to be firmly perceived in a peer group of higher valued masterpieces. Here is where the role of established art museums and art experts is critical, as their endorsement of value-enhancing research is essential to create necessary new perceptions of an artwork in the art investing public. This endorsement often comes through bundling works of less well-known artists with masterpieces from a target peer group into a joint exhibition, as well as managing a news flow necessary to initiate press reviews of an exhibition. Sponsorship of exhibitions organized by major museums (by owners of artworks bundled and promoted with more well-known masterpieces that are often already part of a museum collection) – including publishing catalogues and covering travel and insurance costs if exhibitions go on the road – can often be the way to softly improve the chances of quicker endorsement of new peer groups for related artworks from major museums and art critics.

The success of the value-enhancement strategy for an art asset depends not only on the quality of the research and the ability to publicly communicate new, value adding knowledge about artworks but also on several intrinsic artwork qualities that can objectively be taken into account and used in the same way private equity funds use screening criteria to select investment targets. Our research of Skate's Top 1000 most valuable artworks suggests three art specific qualities (screening criteria for selection of artworks for rational investment strategies):

1) Artist maturity

More than a third of the artworks that rank as the world's most valuable masterpieces today were created by artists between 30-44 years old. In contrast, less than 5% of these masterpieces were created by artists younger than 25. The age range over 75 seems to be the least productive, with only 4.5% of the world's most valuable artworks created by artists in this age group.

Exhibit 5.4 – Ages at which artists created the world's most valuable masterpieces based on Skate's Top 1000

Artist maturity	*Number of works in the Top 1000*
<20	6
20 – 24	41
25 – 29	85
30 – 34	117
35 – 39	116
40 – 44	109
45 – 49	93
50 – 54	99
55 – 59	74
60 – 64	53
65 – 69	38
70 – 74	41
75 – 79	23
>80	22
unknown	83

Source: www.skatepress.com

A rational approach to art investment should clearly give preference to artworks produced at the height of an artist's productivity and professional maturity or to "special situation" ages that can be then played out in the value-enhancement strategy (painted during major world crises, a work believed to be an artist's last, etc.).

2) Large number of works but limited and tightly controlled free float with artist taking leadership in "product category"

Skate's rating of the top 1000 artworks is populated by 171 artists representing 17 different nationalities. Approximately one third of the artists have four or more works in Skate's Top 1000. Those artists capture nearly 90% of the total value of Skate's Top 1000 artworks.

A winning rational art investment strategy must focus on identifying artists who can emerge as one of three or four leaders in a class of their own, whether it be a national group, period, genre or some other compelling class. For example, we anticipate that some of the most successful art investment strategies in the coming decade will result from investing in "products" like artworks by the most valuable female artist (there are currently only seven in Skate's Top 1000, which suggests a certain scarcity value premium), Chinese and Indian artists, and artworks with the most references in new media (e.g. movies and the Internet, including comics images).

As its ultimate objective, an art investment strategy that uses significant capital (millions of dollars) has to produce a big hit. An artist has to become the world champion (or runner up) in very well defined categories with a clear customer base (buyers to whom such artists can appeal and generate significant irrational premiums) and with a significant but well controlled supply of art. The most valuable artists (see Schedule B) had very productive careers, and their artistic heritage is measured with hundreds and even thousands of artworks. At the same time, it is better that the free float of an artist picked for one's art investment strategy be limited. In ideal circumstances, an artist's works should be housed in the best museums and corporate collections around the world, with very little chance of appearing in the open market in the near future, including times when prices are expected to increase. Controlling the supply of artworks in the market is a critical element of a successful art investment strategy. The illiquid nature of the art market and its reliance on a limited number of public price records for the price discovery process create the risk that chaotic supply and price fluctuations will allow third party sellers to harvest most of an investor's value enhancement efforts even before valuations reach target levels.

3) Potentially strong "equity story"

The ability to present a strong and compelling "equity story" is perhaps the key screening criterion. For the art world this means the cultural story of relevance to a large enough number of prospective buyers capable of paying significant irrational premiums once this "equity story" is articulated, supported by evidence and fed to the market. In general, the richer the ownership history of an artwork, the stronger the basis for the "equity story," which makes the artwork more suitable for a successful rational art investment approach.

The role of the first customers illustrates one more striking parallel between venture capital investments into early pre-revenue start up companies and rational high-return focused investments in risky art assets. Just as early stage endorsement of a start-up's products and services by the first reputable customers almost guarantees a valuation step-up for the enterprise, for artworks and artists this very same role is played by purchases made by major museums and the best known private and corporate collectors. In fact, long-established reputable collectors, whether corporate trusts or families, have the ability to take essential and often irreversible steps in implementing value enhancement strategies for certain art assets once the fact of their purchases becomes publicly known.[4] Lining up the support of important and reputable art buyers for one's art investment strategy is an extremely important element of successful art investing, similar to private equity funds' ability to hook entrepreneurs with prospective first customers for a yet untested product.

4. Prices paid in such transactions normally remain confidential, providing additional insight into why price transparency runs counter to the interests of many of art market participants. Such "endorsement" deals are often made at relatively low prices to make it financially appealing for "name-lending" buyers to buy into art whose value is being "pumped." Disclosing low transaction prices at this stage is in the interests of neither sellers promoting related art nor major buyers. When artworks from the same series enter a major public market the new and much higher price level does not seem contradictive to prices paid a few years ago by "endorsement" buyers.

5.4. Buying exposure to the art market through art funds and art stocks

Investing in art assets can actually generate significant returns, but it requires a "private-equity" styled approach that includes hands-on involvement. Investments are needed after purchase of art assets, as well as considerable focus on research, public communication and other essential steps aimed at enhancing the value of portfolio artworks. Simply purchasing art and then sitting back and enjoying the acquisition will unlikely generate significant returns; in fact, ownership costs will make such investments look more expensive by the day. Furthermore, the art market's poor liquidity and exorbitant transaction costs will most likely make passive art investments loss makers in the event that one is forced to sell quickly (see Exhibit 5.3).

Individuals and professional asset managers might consider a standard alternative to investing in actual assets. Are there any securities backed by art? At the end of the day, many people believe that the growth in oil prices or the Chinese economic miracle offer great investment opportunities, although very few actually buy crude oil or establish business in China. Purchasing oil stocks and Chinese companies (and mutual funds with investments in such stocks) is a far more conventional strategy for most investors interested in building such exposure. Why should art be any different?

Art is both different and similar at the same time. It is different in the sense that collective forms of investing in art apparently do not work, or at least they have not worked to date. There have been quite a few attempts to establish mutual funds to invest in art assets, but none has enjoyed credible and lasting success. We have already examined some of the fundamental reasons why such investing has not worked. The joy of ownership (captured in irrational premiums paid for the world's most significant art assets) is one powerful reason why art investors prefer physical possession of art to investing in what should be a more cost efficient and better managed art fund vehicle. Another reason is the high degree of subjectivity involved in pricing art assets. Investors in art funds are effectively asked to trust an art fund manager's subjective judgment, which is difficult for many investors to accept. Finally, it is very difficult to ensure that collective forms of art investing are managed without abuse, as the art market's lack of transparency makes it extremely difficult to audit the performance of art funds with any degree of objectivity or efficiency.

For rational investors seeking exposure to the art market without actually buying art assets, there are two investment strategies to consider. One strategy is investing in art stocks, which is covered below. Another involves a new generation of art funds that we believe will become available to art investors in the near future. These are described in section 5.5.

As of July 15, 2006, there were six companies that could be classified as having art stocks on the basis that most of their revenues and profits are generated from providing products and services related to the art market (see Exhibit 5.5).[5] The art stocks segment turns out to be tiny. With a combined market capitalization of only USD 1.9 billion (as of July 15, 2006) it is dominated by a single company – Sotheby's. This company contributes to almost 85% of the segment's total market capitalization and can accurately be considered a good proxy for the art stocks market. The fact that there are very few publicly-traded art businesses is a sure sign that art business skills are very much artisan in nature. The difficulty in expanding these businesses and their dependency on key individuals is such that transformation into lasting enterprises capable of continuing without the involvement of their charismatic founders is unlikely. We already covered the example of Christie's in Chapter 1. Another example can be seen in the Thomas Kinkade Company, which was intended to commercialize Thomas Kinkade's artworks by being the sole exclusive licensee of all Thomas Kinkade works that could be sold in the form of decorative products, merchandise and actual art through multiple distribution channels in the United States. The Thomas Kinkade Company was de-listed from the New York Stock Exchange in December 2004.

5. Interestingly, when *Skate's Art Investment Handbook* was published first time in November 2005 (published in Russian by Alpina Business Books, subsidiary of Sanoma-Independent Media), there were two more art stocks at that time, Artemis and Partridge art galleries. Partridge has since been de-listed, and because no official financial information exists on Artemis since 2003, we have removed this company from our list of art stocks.

Exhibit 5.5 – Art Stocks (publicly traded companies in the art sector)[6]

Name	Sotheby's Holding Inc	Artprice S.A	Artnet AG	Art in Motion Income Fund	Finarte Casa D'aste	Art'e S.p.A.
Ticker	BID	PRC	AYD	AIM-UN	FCD	ART
Exchange	NYSE	Euronext Paris	Frankfurt, XETRA	Toronto Stock Exchange	Milan, Berlin	Milan
Employees	1,443	37	42	450	n/a	n/a
2005 sales*	513,508	4,153	7,709	58,074	16,259	52,356
2005 profit*	61,602	2,831	1,364	(22,016)	(3,438)	835
2004 profit*	86,679	(1,814)	(645)	13,034	764	(5,998)
MCAP**	1,586	149	55	21	32	30
YTD performance	38%	32%	17%	-100%	-31%	-33%
P/E as of Jul. 15, 2006	25.7	52.6	40.4	neg	neg	35.9
P/E as of Dec. 31, 2005	18.1	40.3	33.6	neg	neg	53.6
P/E as of Dec. 31, 2004	13.0	neg	neg	2.7	100.2	neg

* All values are in thsd USD
** mln USD

Tracking art stocks for over five years, we have learned that investors generally feel comfortable with the auction and information business models. All other art market related business models remain untested in stock investors' minds, including publicly traded art dealers and art media companies active in event management or promotion of certain artists' works.

To compare the performance of art stocks and the stock market benchmark (the S&P 500 is used for this purpose), Skate Press has

6. For more information about each of the Art Stocks business models, current prices and returns as well for independent equity research please visit www.skatepress.com.

established the Skate's Art Stocks Index, which is the market cap weighted USD index of all art stocks. The comparative performance of Sotheby's share price, Skate's Art Stock Index and the S&P 500 benchmark is shown in Exhibit 5.6. Covering the 5-year period ending on July 15, 2006, this chart confirms that Sotheby's shares can be safely used as the proxy for the art stocks market. As we see in Exhibit 5.6, art stocks experienced a mixed fortune when compared to overall stock market performance in the last five years. While recently they have been significantly outperforming the S&P 500, only several years ago they were doing far worse than the market. The significant volatility of the art stocks market is fairly representative of art prices' volatility in general, as well as the art market's poor level of transparency.

Exhibit 5.6 – 5-year performance chart – Sotheby's share price, Skate's Art Stocks and the S&P 500

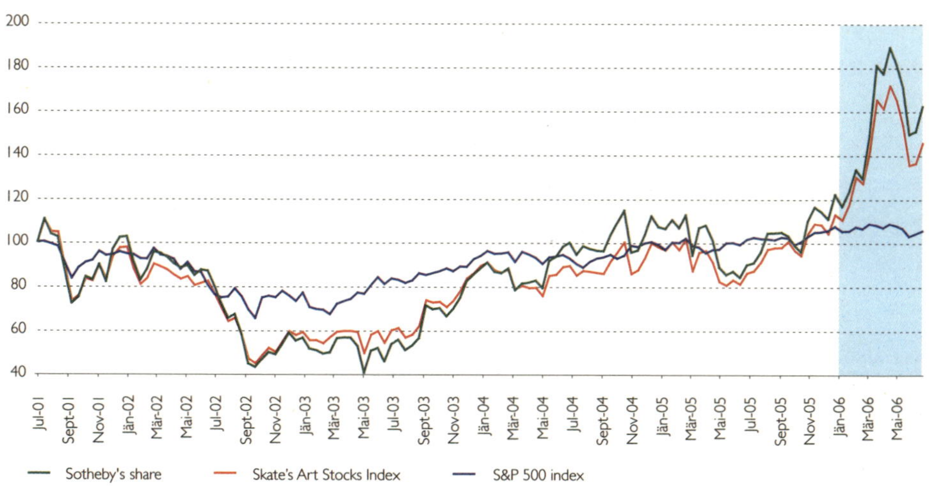

Source: www.skatepress.com, Bloomberg

Ironically, Wall Street rarely covers Sotheby's as a benchmark for the art market, and in most cases investment banking analysts place Sotheby's into the category of luxury goods. Exhibit 5.7 examines the performance of Sotheby's versus luxury goods majors (tracked with Skate's proprietary index) and tells the story of fairly independent share price dynamics demonstrated by Sotheby's.

Skate's Luxury Majors Index fairly accurately and consistently tracks the development of Exhibit 5.1, which depicts the growth of assets in possession of HNWI. Sotheby's stock offers more volatility but potentially greater returns, particularly when the art market experiences boom phases.

In summary, building exposure to the art market without investing in art assets is actually possible. While there are only a limited number of stocks available and while one should exercise caution when picking art stocks for an investment portfolio, Sotheby's seems to be a fairly accurate art market benchmark.[7]

Exhibit 5.7 – 3-years performance chart – Sotheby's share price versus Skate's Luxury Majors

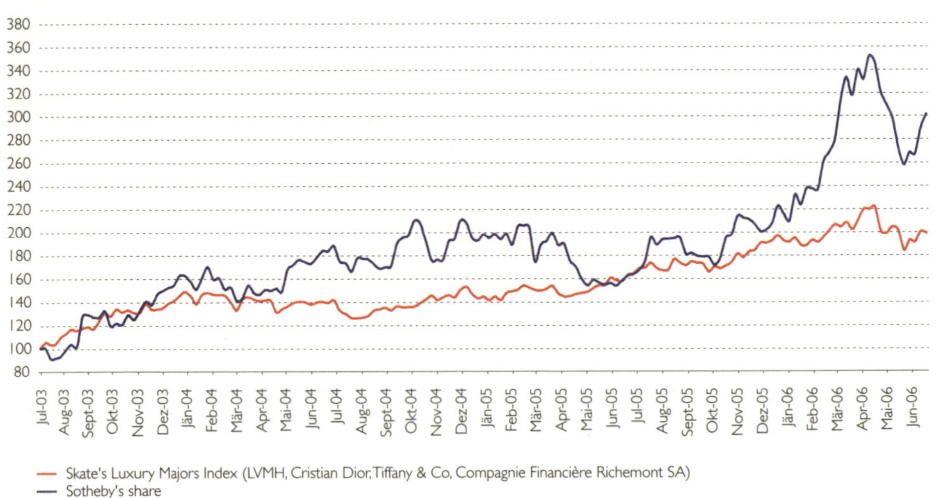

Source: www.skatepress.com, Bloomberg

5.5. A summary of art investment strategies

The art investment market is not experiencing any shortage in new capital flows. A strong increase in capital available to HNWI around the world and their growing interest in alternative investments is likely to provide a solid foundation for future demand for art investments.

The irrational approach to art investing that makes investors more interested in owning works of art than achieving adequate investment returns is widespread in the art market's premium segment. Rational art investment strategies aimed at achieving returns should be focused on less pricey segments. These strategies are best carried out when styled around private equity discipline that requires not only a thorough investment screening process but also continuous hands-on involvement with artworks after investment decisions are made.

Buying exposure to the art market is also possible through the purchase of publicly-traded securities in companies that derive most of their revenue and earnings from serving the art market (art stocks). The concept of art funds, however, seems to have been doomed from the beginning, as the subjective nature of art investment decisions, a lack of transparency and accountability, and the absence of a joy-of-ownership element do not help to build enough confidence and interest on the part of investors.

While Chapter 6 looks at what the future will likely hold for the art investment market, one prediction belongs to this chapter. We believe that a new generation of art funds will be designed and introduced to the investment market in the near future, and unlike existing art funds, these new collective investment vehicles will start from already well established and "branded" collections of significant art, which instead of being sold at auction houses can be securitized into investment fund units and sold in private placement to HNWI around the world. In this way, the subjectivity of art investment decisions is gone, as investors would already know what art the investment fund holds. Such funds can also have a finite life and gradually sell off artworks at optimal valuations, distributing the proceeds from art sales to unit holders. The unit holders could be offered a priority to

7. For more information about each of the Art Stocks business models, current prices and returns as well for independent equity research please visit www.skatepress.com.

bid for artworks in the fund's collection before they are tendered on the open market and be awarded such works provided that their bid is the highest. This would allow them to lock a certain threshold rate of return on a work of art from the fund's collection.

This new form of art investment fund is likely to develop as an alternative to the oligopoly driven auction market that currently controls sales of large collections. For art sellers, the rationale to support this new class of art funds is a reduction in transaction costs, the ability to remain in physical control of their art (on the basis of custody agreements with an art fund) for a longer period of time and, in cases of large collections, the ability to quickly sell an ownership interest in significant art without depressing art market prices.

Chapter 6
The Art Market by 2020

Limited liquidity, low transparency, and modest returns in the highest priced segment accompanied by an increasing inflow of new funds and investors are the key features of today's art investment market. This chapter summarizes the key future trends in this market as we currently see them.

6.1. Producing contemporary art will become a well structured media business

Every art market participant today seems to agree that contemporary art is a serious business with its own unique forces. Hundreds of museums around the world devote formidable resources to collections of living artists, and curators of corporate collections busily source quality art directly from artists' studios. Dozens of art shows, thousands of art galleries and hundreds of thousands of collectors are buying and selling contemporary art across the globe.

Interior design, corporate collections, limited state and municipal funding, as well as personal hobbies (often elevated to the format of private museums) provide perhaps the most important demand drivers in the contemporary art market. A vigorous and growing contemporary market exists as each year investors and intermediaries who trade art for a living end-up contributing at least several hundred million dollars of capital to the market for the works of living artists.

Those buying contemporary art to decorate the walls of their new house or to publish a fancy catalogue bearing a corporate logo more often than not cherish the hope that their art will appreciate in the near future. Based on the data that we have already seen, such appreciation may prove unlikely for higher-priced works.

Exhibit 6.1 – Living artists in Skate's Top 1000

Rank	*Artist*	*Works in Top 1000*	*Total value, USD*	*Average price, USD*	*Nationality*	*Year of birth*	*Weighted average ERR**
19	Jasper Johns	14	95,354,500	6,811,036	American	1930	-1.10%
30	Lucian Freud	9	57,007,692	6,334,188	British	1922	
39	Cy Twombly	7	42,079,500	6,011,357	American	1928	-7.29%
61	Jeff Koons	4	20,999,250	5,249,813	American	1955	
78	Gerhard Richter	3	15,150,412	5,050,137	German	1932	
88	Robert Rauschenberg	2	13,642,500	6,821,250	American	1925	1.12%
102	Bruce Nauman	1	9,906,000	9,906,000	American	1941	
105	Robert Ryman	1	9,648,000	9,648,000	American	1930	
108	Frank Stella	2	9,435,500	4,717,750	American	1936	
141	David Hockney	1	5,378,348	5,378,348	British	1937	
151	Chuck Close	1	4,832,000	4,832,000	American	1940	
165	Andrew Wyeth	1	4,384,000	4,384,000	American	1917	

*The effective rate of return (ERR), annualized in USD, is based on repeat sales of artworks of a particular artist and is limited to artworks that were already in Skate's Top 1000 when originally purchased.
Source: www.skatepress.com

As of September 1, 2006, living artists' works accounted for 4.6% of the total number of artworks in Skate's Top 1000. The combined value of this segment was close to USD 300 million in nominal prices (see Exhibit 6.1). Jasper Johns, the most valuable living artist, ranked 19th in Skate's list of the most valuable artists, ahead of names like Chagall, Mondrian and Giacometti.

From a fundamental art valuation perspective, the works of living artists possess two distinct features that other art assets generally do not share. First, unless the artist has a reputation for sloppiness in record keeping, authenticity checks are simple and straightforward (the provenance multiple is equal to 1 as per Skate's Art Asset Pricing Model described in Chapter 4). This condition clearly makes contemporary art more attractive for investment. Second, living artists can increase the supply of their works on the market. Applying the principles of the stock market, one can view the possibility of increased supply as bad news, positing that the value of existing artworks can be diluted as an artist produces more works, something that often happens in practice when dealers and galleries fail to manage a productive artist from a valuation point of view. Of course, an artist can and should have reasons for his creativity aside from enhancing the market value of his or her works, but as art valuation is the focus of this book, we have to examine supply and demand drivers from a pure valuation standpoint. Having an artist available to produce more works can be good news as well, however. In situations when an artist is professionally "produced" and marketed by an experienced gallery owner or other art market professional, the value of his or her works can increase despite the increase in supply. Increasing supply also helps to broaden the market and improve liquidity once certain price floors are firmly established for a given artist's works.

As we discussed previously, an artist's name, while clearly important, is not the sole decisive art valuation driver. When a successful and widely recognized artist is alive, getting him or her to produce art in a relevant, value-enhancing context and placing his or her works into the ownership of reputable collectors and museums perhaps has more of an impact on eventual art valuation dynamics than the artist's name itself. Art production, mastered by the most successful dealers and galleries, is all about trading in perception and brands, understanding cultural context, identifying topics of interest and arousing the aid (and perhaps the patronage) of opinion leaders, all in an effort to stir the hype. In essence, art production is nothing more than another form of media business.

Between now and 2020, the art producing media segment will definitely become more official, more structured and less pretentious. Just as creating and marketing books, music, computer games and movies became a well-structured corporate industry where both major players and rather small private initiatives have been able to thrive, the same will inevitably occur within the world of contemporary art. In the end, corporate players will emerge who specialize in producing and marketing contemporary art, and these players, unlike some of the art world's traditionally more pretentious elements, will not be shy about turning art promotion into a professional business.

6.2. Consolidation of the dealer business and the emergence of art investment banks

It is truly amazing that the art investment market, with its USD 5 billion in annual turnover, has no single professional "art investment bank." Some valid reasons exist for such a bank's absence, however. As demonstrated earlier in this book, art investment decisions, particularly those involving works in the higher price range, rest largely on individual cultural contexts and the emotional aspirations of investors. Given that investors' interests tend to be local and confined to national cultures, little value would be added by a hypothetical global art investment bank. The great degree of irrationality encompassing art investment decisions also limits the ability to commercialize the professional rational investment advice that traditional investment banks offer.

That being said, a market does exist for the services of art brokerage, art asset management and the creation and execution of large-scale art investment and disposal strategies. Auction houses and small businesses – art galleries, art dealers and individual art experts – currently meet the demand for these services. The arrival of significant new capital to the art market on the one hand and the irresistible emergence of a rational line of thinking as far as art investing is concerned on the other will generate substantial demand for cost-efficient professional art investment advice based on traditional finance principles with a global view. This demand will only increase in the future.

Traditional galleries and dealers – beset with conflicts of interest and possessing a core competence that explores and exploits irrational motives among buyers and sellers – will find themselves poorly positioned to capture the demand for this new money-driven rational art investment service. Private banks that largely treat art as a marginal asset class and at best try to provide basic facilitation and expert introduction service will definitely choose to stay away from a focused art investment advisory model. These banks are also largely unwilling to serve clients with less than USD 5 million in liquid assets. The inability of art asset owners to leverage their collections and the exorbitant commission levels of major auction houses clearly leave room for specialized art investment advisory service and art investment product providers. The business models of these specialized services and product providers will offer reduced art ownership costs, provide access to global art, and match lenders and borrowers against art assets, and thus foster a more transparent and rational approach to art investing.

6.3. Sarbanes-Oxley for the museum industry

In recent years the media have highlighted the changing roles of museums, with many people arguing that the museum's role as a "sacred depositary" of artworks accumulated over the years should be recast into one of a more dynamic media-like institution capable of promoting cultural education to younger generations in a language they find understandable.

From the perspective of art investment, this development illustrates just one of many changes that state-funded museums and collections must make. Museums serve the art market both as an extremely important source of demand (and to a far less extent supply) and as a determinant of price trends. Museums play a major role in driving public opinion and bestowing acceptance and recognition to the names of artists and collectors. As Cynthia Freeland elegantly stated, "museums are the primary contemporary institutions upholding classical standards of artistic value."[1]

As we have seen in previous chapters, irrational premium and provenance drive valuation in a powerful way, particularly for the world's most significant art. Museums, or to be more precise their curators, determine exhibition schedules and sources of artworks for major exhibitions and tours (which in turn drives the schedule of catalogue publication), thus in large part determining how many people will see artworks, and thus significantly influencing provenance multi-

1. Cynthia Freeland, *Art Theory: A Very Short Introduction* (Oxford University Press, 2001), pg. 69. The book also contains an excellent chapter titled "Museums' Changing Purposes" (pg. 68), which is recommended as supplementary reading.

ples and irrationality premiums for individual works of art. In simple terms, curators at large museums can add meaningful value to certain private collections, individual paintings or artist names simply by affixing the name of their institution to the collection, painting or artist. This credibility resource makes a huge difference, as it allows a museum-enhanced[2] work of art to be propelled into the league of the world's most valuable masterpieces. Giving the "right" prior exhibition and literature story to an artwork before it is auctioned and pressing the right emotional buttons in potential buyers who look at an artwork as a museum quality asset can have a serious effect on an artwork's valuation. Many of the most expensive artworks that constitute a peer group of their own (e.g. those priced over USD 25 million each and described in section 4.1) have been part of "road shows" that for several years toured the world with major museums' collections provided to them on loan before being auctioned and sold at mind-boggling prices.

The hundreds of millions of dollars that museums spend each year purchasing art in a market lacking price and commission transparency further enhances the museum curator's ability to influence prices. The absence of price and commission transparency obviously gives the parties who run museums and major art foundations ample opportunity to abuse their market power, and at times misconduct occurs. In recent years, there have unfortunately been a number of reports of very public and high-profile scandals involving abuse of museum curator's market power worldwide.[3]

What the art investment market needs is a set of national laws or self-regulating best practice controls that will subject the museum industry to stringent rules establishing a universal system of internal controls. These changes could be somewhat similar to the sweeping changes in corporate governance introduced across the global stock markets following the adoption of the Sarbanes-Oxley Act in the United States after the Enron fallout.

While museums are clearly very different from public companies, as institutions they nevertheless face similar issues. First, their credibility and reputation is a major asset that should be protected. Governance abuses and dishonest and unethical behavior among managers is one such credibility risk. Establishing firm internal control

2. A museum does not need to buy a work of art to enhance its value; simply allowing it to be exhibited in the museum or taking it on loan for a tour or use of its image on the front page of a museum-branded exhibition catalogue will have an effect on an artwork's value.

3. One example concerns Marion True, a former curator at the J. Paul Getty Museum, and Robert Hecht, an American dealer, both of whom have been indicted on charges of trafficking in objects illegally obtained in Italy through use of a complex of offshore companies. See a report by Hugh Eakin and Elisabetta Povoleddo's report, "Antiquities Trial in Rome Focuses on a London Dealer," *The New York Times*, March 30, 2006.

policies for what museum curators and directors can and cannot do and what their public reporting requirements are, as well as a system for internal audits are the immediate and unquestionable responsibility of art museum owners and financial backers. Second, financial disclosure should be made an accepted practice at major art museums and foundations. Disclosing prices of art transactions, commissions paid, names of key intermediaries used and the overall state of public museum finances should be a mandatory practice. Such disclosure will not only contribute to improving museums' internal controls, but it will also bring more transparency to the global art investment market in general. Finally, introduction of independent third-party auditing of finances at museums and public art foundations should become mandatory. Unlike standard financial audits, third-party audits would involve a specific set of procedures aimed at identifying major failures in internal controls for such essential decisions as art procurements, exhibition content and budget planning, as well as the verification of reported financial indicators. These audits should also verify that there are no conflicts of interest involving museum curators and managers or that disclosure of potential conflicts is adequate.

It is our view that the museum industry worldwide should adopt more regulation of this kind. Given the important role of museums in the art investment markets of so many countries (and considering the increasingly global drift and breadth of the overall art market), greater financial and ethical discipline and fuller disclosure requirements will go a long way in helping to make the art market, both on a local country and a global level, more transparent and attractive for investors.

6.4. Deals exceeding USD 25 million leave virtually no hope for positive investment returns during the life of the buyer

Eye-catching stories of artworks selling for exorbitant prices appear consistently in recent history. Back in 1958, the art market was shocked by the GBP 220,000 that well known entrepreneur and collector Paul Mellon paid for Cézanne's Garçon au Gilet Rouge. Then five times as expensive as any previous painting's sale, this sale was recorded at an auction where seven impressionist and modern artworks from the Goldschmidt family's collection were sold. Was the price paid by Mr. Mellon at that time economically justified?

Today, 48 years later, one can certainly say that yes, Mellon made a sound investment that would definitely preserve capital and allow for a reasonable (in this case, a likely excellent) economic return if a proper exit time were to be chosen. Adjusting that auction price to inflation, Garçon au Gilet Rouge today would stand at USD 4.2 million in real terms, which would place it near the bottom of Skate's Top 1000 and definitely far below the price range for important Cézanne works as they are valued today (for Cézanne's artworks current valuations please refer to Schedule A and to the color insert in Chapter 4).

It is unknown whether the buyers of Picasso's Garçon à la Pipe and Klimt's Golden Adele will have to wait 30-50 years before achieving a positive return on their investments (should they choose to exit at all). Skate's statistics show, however, that the holding horizons for such masterpieces will most certainly exceed 20 years to avoid negative returns, which will most likely push an economically justified exit beyond the lifetime of those who currently own the most highly valued artworks.[4]

In Chapter 4, we provided fascinating examples of purchase decisions by Ryoei Saito and Ronald Lauder, which gave the art world new price records. We also provided data that allow one to assume there could be more Saitos and Lauders coming to the market with their own irrational agendas concerning art purchases that will continue to capture the public's attention with headline-grabbing prices. The fact that some people choose to pay USD 30 million or USD 130 million for a painting does not necessarily mean these are fair price levels for any particular work of art in the future or that a particular artwork will sell again at a comparable price. Clearly, those who managed to buy impressionist paintings in the 1950s at one tenth or even one half of what Paul Mellon paid for Garçon au Gilet Rouge did considerably better in terms of annualized returns on their investments, although without nearly the level of publicity surrounding them.

4. A quote by Ryoei Saito is quite revealing in this regard. He went on record at one point saying, "I am telling the people around me to put the paintings into my coffin and burn them with me when I die" – quoted in Saltzman's *Portrait du Dr. Gachet: The Story of a van Gogh Masterpiece, Money, Politics, Collectors, Greed, and Loss*, pg. 324.

6.5. Increases in Russian and Asian investors will significantly broaden the global art market

When we consider multimillion dollar valuations for artworks, we cannot overemphasize how emotional and other subjective factors take center stage in determining prices paid for significant art. These factors naturally have a lot to do with national and historical consciousness.

In this context, the rapid increase in wealth seen in newly emerging economies, especially Russia, China and India, has clearly caught the attention of many participants in the art investment market. These participants are now seeking to cater to this freshly-minted class of wealthy art investors.

Sotheby's investors' presentation from May 2006 indicated that the growth in relatively new markets (naming specifically Russia and Asia) is one of the two key sources of the company's core auction business growth.

Exhibit 6.2 – The Russian art market

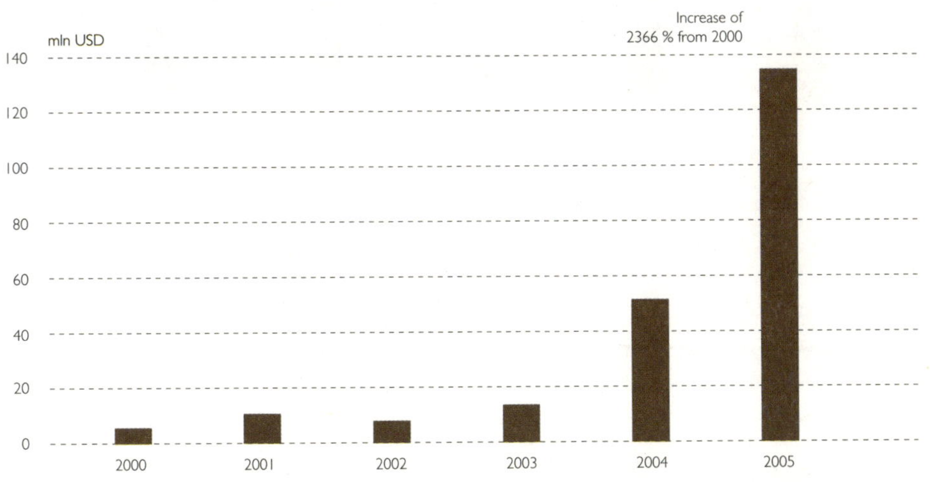

Source: Sotheby's investor briefing, May 2006

According to Sotheby's, Asian buyers have gone from representing 5% of the company's sales in 1998 to 9% in 2005, which is strongly correlated to the more than doubling of Asian art sales over the last several years. Exhibit 6.3 shows how the market for Russian art could grow over the next five years, given that its current volume stands approximately where the Asian art market's volume stood five years ago.

Exhibit 6.3 – Asian art sales

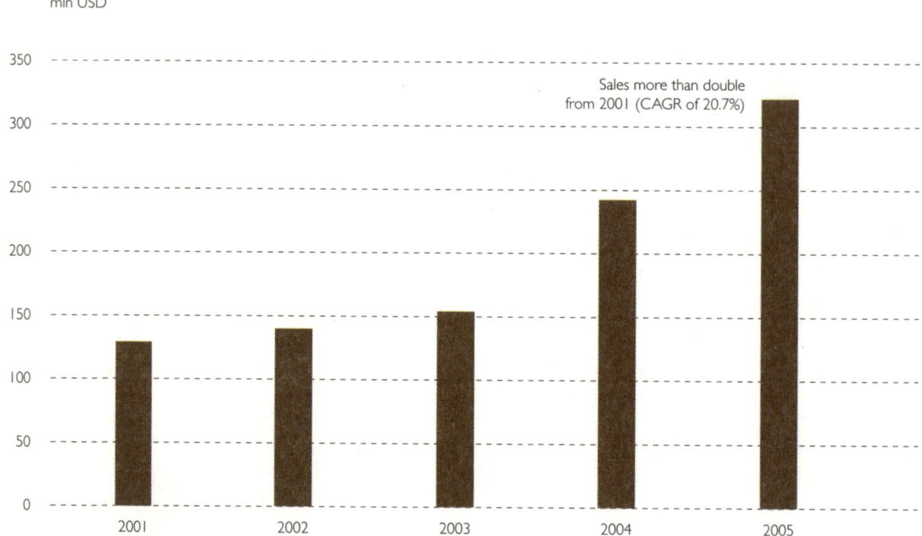

Note: Figures include all sales from Asian offices as well as sales of Chinese Paintings, Chinese Works of Art, Japanese, Korean and Indian Works of Art from New York and European offices.

Source: Sotheby's investor briefing, May 2006

Based on this data, which only reflect Sotheby's auction volumes, as well as data compiled by www.skatepress.com, we believe that five years from now Asian and Russian sales could contribute at least USD 1.5 billion to the art trade, capturing no less than 20% of the global art investment market turnover by 2010.

Epilogue

This book was finished in the airport lounge in St. Petersburg as I awaited a flight back home to Moscow. My trip had involved an especially long day with a local client, a diversified industrial and machinery plant with a nearly 200-year history and located a mere 20 minutes by boat from St. Petersburg's glorious Hermitage Museum.

My client's boardroom that day had been the site of an exciting presentation by a youthful CEO who was strongly supported by a new and capable management team. Exceptional share price performance (up 40% year-to-date) and 100% capacity utilization of a rolling steel plant were among the facts that generated the most excitement. Contributing to the upbeat atmosphere was the announcement of plans to launch a new tractor model in collaboration with a German partner. The company's board members left the meeting feeling proud that a once hopeless Soviet-era dinosaur had begun to experience such robust recovery.

Aside from feeling that the company was finally moving in the right direction, I was pleased to see a board willing to support the young management team. Hopefully with this support, my client can become a globally competitive company within the coming five to ten years. I hold every hope that the changes taking place at this company reflect what is happening in the Russian economy at large.

As I settled into the airport lounge for one final read of this manuscript, the magnificent Adele on the book's cover suddenly took on an entirely new meaning. The price paid for Golden Adele, combined with that paid for Garçon À La Pipe – roughly USD 235 million in total – represented my client's entire market capitalization. An entire factory with 8,000 employees had a value equal to that of just two paintings.

Comparisons like this one are hard to reconcile, but they do send a powerful message. Valuing the brushstroke of a genius at a price comparable to the value of a good size plant is actually very rational when one prioritizes the joy of ownership over the investment return. This is where the "portable utility" of an art asset comes to play. While art investors' businesses will forever be subject to the irritating impact of market forces and technological challenges, at the end of the day the owners of the world's most valuable masterpieces will always be able to enjoy their acquisitions in the comfort of their homes, in their own sponsored museums or, if they so choose, in their graves as well.

Acknowledgments

This book, the product of a team spread across many countries and united with a spirit of discovery, was a considerable pleasure to work on. Researching the world's art market and piecing together a puzzle of inconsistent data, incredible valuations and fascinating stories behind the most valuable artworks was truly an exciting endeavor.

First and foremost, I would like to thank the energetic Moscow-based research team of Skate Press that helped tremendously in putting this book together. Val Korinevsky was my sparring partner in designing Skate's Art Asset Pricing Model. Ivan Astafiev produced most of the data and charts used in the book. With a cold and guiding hand, Olesia Yakovenko managed our exciting editorial process and also conducted research for the most interesting peer groups and the stories surrounding the artworks. Adam Fuss has made it possible for our readers to experience this book in plain English.

Our colleagues in Vienna also contributed substantially to the effort. Maurizzio Poletto, a prodigy book artist, conceived the format and created the design for this edition. His partner design agency, Collettiva, and Markus Huber, managing director of the publisher, KunstAM GmbH, have been a tremendous help during many of the conceptual discussions about the book's content, as well as the production strategy.

On behalf of the entire team, I would like to thank our most valuable reviewers. Particularly instrumental were the directors of some of the world's most significant art banking practices at major private banks who for various reasons asked to remain anonymous; Dave Gray, the managing partner of PriceWaterhouseCoopers, who helped us to better understand accounting rules for art investments; Kevin Radell, the art market data and indices guru at Artnet; Michael Moriarty, my long-time New York based business partner and friend, and Anders Petterson of London-based ArtTactic Ltd, who provided, among other suggestions, specific and very insightful comments regarding the droit de suite (DDS) .

We particularly enjoyed receiving and discussing very inquisitive feedback from some of the art scholars whom we asked to review the manuscript. Christian Muschick of the Hochschule für Bankwirschaft (Germany) and Mary Scarvalone of Sotheby's Art Institute (UK) were especially helpful. Special thanks are also due to the librarians at Christie's who were so helpful when dealing with our requests and inquiries.

Finally, I want to thank Natasha, my wife and friend for over 10 years, who supported me during the weekends spent writing and editing this book at our beautiful and inspiring lake house that she created.

I hope you find this book to be worth at least the time you spent reading it. Should you have any thoughts or questions that you would like to share with me, I am available at skate@skatepress.com.
Thank you!

Sergey S. Skaterschikov

Schedule A

Skate's Masterpieces Peer Group (Top 1000 Works of Art by Market Value)

Rank	Artist	Title	Nominal value*, USD
not ranked	Gustav Klimt	The portrait of Adele Bloch-Bauer	135,000,000
1	Pablo Picasso	Garçon À La Pipe	104,168,000
2	Pablo Picasso	Dora Maar au chat	95,216,000
3	Vincent van Gogh	Portrait du Dr. Gachet	82,500,000
4	Pierre-Auguste Renoir	Au Moulin de la Galette	78,100,000
5	Sir Peter Paul Rubens	The Massacre of the Innocents	76,671,284
6	Vincent van Gogh	Portrait de l'artiste sans barbe	71,502,500
7	Paul Cézanne	Rideau, cruchon et compôtier	60,502,500
8	Pablo Picasso	Femme aux bras croisés	55,006,000
9	Vincent van Gogh	Irises	53,900,000
10	Pablo Picasso	Les Noces De Pierrette	51,650,000
11	Pablo Picasso	Femme assise dans un jardin	49,502,500
12	Pablo Picasso	Le rêve	48,402,500
13	Pablo Picasso	Self Portrait: Yo Picasso	47,850,000
14	Pablo Picasso	Nu au fauteuil noir	45,102,500
15	Pablo Picasso	Au Lapin Agile	40,700,000
16	Vincent van Gogh	L'Arlésienne, Madame Ginoux	40,336,000
17	Vincent van Gogh	Sunflowers	39,663,462
18	Paul Gauguin	Maternité (II)	39,208,000
19	Pablo Picasso	Acrobate et jeune Arlequin (+ pen & ink sketch, verso)	38,532,448
20	Paul Cézanne	La montagne Sainte-Victoire	38,502,500
21	Joseph Mallord William Turner	Giudecca, La Donna della Salute and San Giorgio	35,856,000
22	Georges Seurat	Paysage, l'Ile de la Grande-Jatte	35,202,500

Present value**, USD	Year of make	Year of sale	Subject***	Size group****
135,000,000	1907	2006	FemP	E
99,787,364	1905	2004	MaleP	D
85,167,901	1941 -	2006	FemP	E
117,782,508	1890	1990	MaleP	B
111,500,774	1876	1990	Othr	D
78,515,350	1609 - 1611	2002	Relgs	F
80,417,683	1889	1998	SelfP	A
67,145,006	1893 - 1894	1999	Slife	B
58,271,109	1901 - 1902	2000	FemP	B
86,153,380		1987	Lscape	C
77,684,517	1905	1989	Othr	F
54,251,337	1938	1999	FemP	E
55,279,257	1932	1997	FemP	E
71,293,619	1901	1989	SelfP	B
49,428,996	1932	1999	Nu	F
59,629,071	1905	1989	OthP	D
36,071,111	1890 -	2006	FemP	B
65,264,101	1889	1987	Slife	D
37,181,103	1899	2004	Nu	C
59,081,340	1905	1988	MaleP	D
39,959,788	1888 - 1890	2001	Lscape	C
32,222,333		2006	Lscape	C
39,066,185	1884	1999	Lscape	C

Rank	Artist	Title	Nominal value*, USD
23	Pablo Picasso	Le repos	34,736,000
24	Claude Monet	Bassin aux nymphéas et sentier au bord de l'eau	32,991,503
25	Canaletto	Venice, the Grand Canal, looking north-east from Palazzo Balbi to the Rialto Bridge	32,648,763
26	Pablo Picasso	Les femmes d'Alger (Version "O")	31,902,500
27	Amedeo Modigliani	Jeanne Hébuterne (Devant une porte)	31,368,000
28	Amedeo Modigliani	Jeanne hébuterne (Au chapeau)	30,285,632
29	Johannes (van Delft) Vermeer	A young woman seated at the virginals	29,934,771
30	Paul Cézanne	Bouilloire et fruits	29,466,721
31	Pablo Picasso	Angel Fernandez de soto	29,152,500
32	Gustav Klimt	Landhaus am Attersee	29,128,000
33	Rembrandt Harmensz van Rijn	Portrait of a lady in black costume and a cap and collar (Aeltje Pietersdr. Uylenburgh, wife of Johannes Cornelisz. Sylvius?)	28,676,151
34	Pablo Picasso	Nature morte aux tulipes	28,606,000
35	Paul Cézanne	Nature morte - Les grosses pommes	28,602,500
36	Andrea Mantegna	Descent into Limbo	28,568,000
37	Edgar Degas	Danseuse au repos (on joined sheet)	27,854,882
38	George Wesley Bellows	Polo crowd	27,702,500
39	Constantin Brancusi	Oiseau dans l'espace	27,456,000
40	Vincent van Gogh	Sous-bois	26,952,500
41	Amedeo Modigliani	Nu couché (Sur le côté gauche)	26,887,500
42	Edouard Manet	La rue Mosnier aux drapeaux	26,400,000

Present value**, USD	Year of make	Year of sale	Subject***	Size group****
31,061,235	1932	2006	OthP	F
37,331,114	1900	1998	Lscape	D
30,254,732		2005	Lscape	E
36,434,056	1955	1997	Nu	E
29,744,977	1919	2004	FemP	E
27,026,457	1919	2006	FemP	B
28,625,373	1670	2004	FemP	A
32,292,391	1888 - 1890	1999	Slife	B
35,327,530	1903	1995	MaleP	B
28,593,445	1914	2003	Lscape	E
30,392,757	1632	2000	FemP	B
30,760,350	1932	2000	Slife	E
36,583,911	1890 - 1894	1993	Slife	A
28,991,443	1490 - 1495	2003	Relgs	A
30,911,543	1879	1999	FemP	B
30,358,829	1910	1999	Othr	E
25,571,245	1922 - 1923	2005	S	-
32,363,607	1890	1995	Lscape	C
26,393,496	1917	2003	Nu	E
38,678,316	1878	1989	Lscape	C

Rank	Artist	Title	Nominal value*, USD
43	Vincent van Gogh	Autoportrait	26,400,000
44	Edouard Manet	Les courses au Bois de Boulogne	26,328,000
45	Pablo Picasso	Femme assise dans un fauteuil (Eva)	24,752,500
46	Pablo Picasso	Maternité	24,750,000
47	Claude Monet	Le portail (Soleil)	24,205,750
48	Paul Gauguin	Mata Mua (In Olden Times)	24,200,000
49	Pablo Picasso	Nu au collier	23,944,553
50	Pablo Picasso	Les Tuileries	23,821,899
51	David Smith	Cubi XXVIII	23,816,000
52	Gustav Klimt	Schloss Kammer am Attersee II	23,562,388
53	Pierre-Auguste Renoir	Dans les roses (Madame Léon Clapisson)	23,528,000
54	John Singer Sargent	Group with parasols (A siesta)	23,528,000
55	Paul Cézanne	Madame Cézanne au fauteuil jaune	23,102,500
56	Wassily Kandinsky	Fugue	22,990,000
57	Max Beckmann	Selbstbildnis mit Horn	22,555,750
58	Henri de Toulouse-Lautrec	La blanchisseuse	22,416,000
59	Mark Rothko	Homage to Matisse	22,416,000
60	Fernand Léger	La femme en rouge et vert	22,407,500
61	Egon Schiele	Herbstsonne	21,708,430
62	Paul Gauguin	Deux femmes or La chevelure fleurie	21,656,598
63	Charles Willson Peale	George Washington at Princeton	21,296,000
64	John Constable	The Lock (In its original gilt plaster and carved wood frame)	21,124,829

Present value**, USD	Year of make	Year of sale	Subject***	Size group****
37,690,402	1888	1990	SelfP	A
25,215,445	1872	2004	Othr	C
28,267,802	1913	1997	Nu	E
37,948,878	1901	1988	Fem&InfP	C
26,027,719	1892 - 1894	2000	Lscape	C
36,056,543	1892	1989	Lscape	C
24,541,019	1932	2002	Nu	C
33,826,463	1901	1990	Othr	B
21,819,965	1965	2005	S	-
26,891,884	1909	1997	Lscape	E
23,220,657	1882	2003	FemP	D
22,390,912	1905	2004	Othr	B
26,613,991	1888 - 1890	1997	FemP	C
32,822,059	1914	1990	A	E
23,406,887	1938	2001	SelfP	E
20,536,437	1886 - 1887	2005	FemP	C
20,536,437	1953 - 1954	2005	A	F
21,994,580	1914	2003	A	D
19,368,241	1914	2006	Slife	E
19,730,378	1902	2006	Nu	B
19,440,746	1779	2006	MaleP	F
29,122,352		1990	Lscape	E

Rank	Artist	Title	Nominal value*, USD
65	Egon Schiele	Krumauer Landschaft (Stadt und Fluss) (+ Kärntner Landschaft, unfinished, verso)	21,064,049
66	Piet Mondrian	New York/Boogie Woogie	21,008,000
67	Claude Monet	Nymphéas	20,906,000
68	Edouard Manet	Jeune fille dans un jardin	20,905,750
69	Pierre-Auguste Renoir	Baigneuse	20,902,500
70	Willem de Kooning	Interchange	20,680,000
71	Vincent van Gogh	Le pont de Trinquetaille	20,367,091
72	Vincent van Gogh	Le vieil If	20,350,000
73	Claude Monet	Nymphéas	20,182,111
74	Claude Monet	Londres, le Parlement, effet de soleil dans le brouillard	20,167,500
75	Canaletto	The Bucintoro at the Molo, Venice, on Ascension Day	20,084,329
76	Pablo Picasso	Le miroir	20,022,500
77	Pierre-Auguste Renoir	Jeune fille au Chat	19,965,000
78	Vincent van Gogh	La roubine du roi	19,802,500
79	Claude Monet	Nymphéas	18,709,500
80	Edouard Manet	Portrait de Manet par lui-même, en buste (Manet à la palette)	18,702,500
81	Pablo Picasso	Mere et Enfant	18,700,000
82	Pablo Picasso	Les femmes d'Alger (J)	18,608,000
83	Pablo Picasso	Portrait de Germaine	18,608,000
84	Henri Matisse	Nu couché vu de dos	18,496,000
85	Paul Cézanne	Nature morte aux fruits et pot de gingembre	18,217,565

Present value**, USD	Year of make	Year of sale	Subject***	Size group****
20,765,484	1916	2003	Lscape	E
19,918,668	1941 - 1942	2004	A	D
22,478,717	1906	2000	Lscape	D
22,142,756	1880	2000	FemP	E
23,870,588	1888	1997	Nu	B
30,298,014	1955	1989	A	F
33,099,581	1888	1987	Lscape	C
29,814,535	1888	1989	Lscape	C
20,683,323	1906	2002	Lscape	D
19,121,466	1904	2004	Lscape	C
18,605,900		2005	Lscape	F
24,041,536	1932	1995	Nu	E
28,503,367		1990	FemP	D
21,974,729	1888	1999	Lscape	B
19,025,372	1906	2002	Lscape	D
21,544,660	1878	1997	SelfP	C
27,397,141	1921	1989	Fem&InfP	C
17,325,823	1955	2005	Nu	E
16,632,790	1902 -	2006	FemP	A
16,532,593	1927 -	2006	Nu	C
19,484,953	1895	2000	Slife	B

Rank	Artist	Title	Nominal value*, USD	
86	Constantin Brancusi	Danaïde	18,159,500	
87	Pierre-Auguste Renoir	La tasse de chocalat	18,150,000	
88	Pierre-Auguste Renoir	La promenade	17,427,945	
89	Mark Rothko	No. 6 (Yellow, white, blue over yellow on gray)	17,368,000	
90	Paul Cézanne	Portrait de Paul Cézanne	17,367,500	
91	Andy Warhol	Orange Marilyn	17,327,500	
92	Paul Cézanne	Pommes et serviette	17,176,765	
93	Henri Matisse	La robe persane	17,055,750	
94	Kasimir Malevich	Suprematist Composition	17,052,500	
95	Jasper Johns	False start	17,050,000	
96	Pablo Picasso	Famille de l'Arlequin	16,940,000	
97	Max Beckmann	Selbstbildnis mit Glaskugel (Self-portrait with crystal ball)	16,816,000	
98	Claude Monet	Le bassin aux nymphéas	16,808,000	
99	Paul Cézanne	Pichet et assiette de poires	16,784,500	
100	Amedeo Modigliani	Nu assis sur un divan (La belle Romaine)	16,777,500	
101	Fernand Léger	Le moteur	16,726,000	
102	Edgar Degas	Au musée du Louvre (Miss Cassatt)	16,509,500	
103	Paul Cézanne	Pichet de gres	16,502,500	
104	Paul Cézanne	Fillette à la poupee	16,502,500	
105	Edouard Manet	Le Banc (Le jardin de Versailles)	16,500,000	
106	Claude Monet	La plage à Trouville	16,469,840	
107	Mark Rothko	No.9 (White and black on wine)	16,359,500	

Present value**, USD	Year of make	Year of sale	Subject***	Size group****
18,619,855	1913	2002	S	-
25,021,300	1878	1990	FemP	D
26,114,247	1870	1989	OthP	C
16,466,181	1954	2004	A	F
17,138,692	1895	2003	SelfP	B
19,629,453	1964	1998	FemP	E
25,165,467	1879 - 1880	1989	Slife	B
18,063,779	1940	2000	FemP	C
18,337,901	1919 - 1920	2000	A	C
26,142,560		1988	A	F
24,818,586	1905	1989	Nu	B
15,655,864	1936	2005	SelfP	C
16,095,138	1917 - 1919	2004	Lscape	E
17,209,260	1890 - 1893	2002	Slife	A
18,385,175	1917	1999	Nu	C
17,384,893	1918	2001	A	E
16,927,141	1879	2002	OthP	B
18,083,779	1893 - 1894	1999	Slife	A
17,123,548	1902 - 1904	2001	Fem&InfP	B
23,556,502	1881	1990	Lscape	C
17,615,024	1870	2000	Lscape	B
16,143,542	1958	2003	A	G

Rank	Artist	Title	Nominal value*, USD
108	Marc Chagall	Anniversaire	16,335,000
109	Roy Lichtenstein	In the car	16,256,000
110	Canaletto	The Old Horse Guards, London, from St. James's Park	16,205,742
111	Francesco Guardi	Vue de la Giudecca et du Zattere à Venise	15,866,500
112	Roy Lichtenstein	Sinking sun	15,696,000
113	Willem de Kooning	Untitled XVI	15,696,000
114	Amedeo Modigliani	Fillette assise en robe	15,625,750
115	Willem de Kooning	Woman	15,622,500
116	Claude Monet	Dans la prairie	15,402,500
117	Pablo Picasso	La cage d'oiseaux	15,400,000
118	Amedeo Modigliani	Portrait de Jeanne Hébuterne	15,127,500
119	Andy Warhol	Mustard Race Riot (on 2 panels)	15,127,500
120	Henri Matisse	La pose hindoue	14,850,500
121	Edouard Manet	La Promenade	14,850,000
122	Pablo Picasso	Le sauvetage	14,792,000
123	Sir Joshua Reynolds	Portrait of Omai standing in a landscape, wearing robes and a headdress	14,749,038
124	Gustav Klimt	Litzlbergerkeller am Attersee	14,742,500
125	Fernand Léger	Contrastes de formes	14,600,250
126	Claude Monet	Le Parlement, soleil couchant	14,580,750
127	Henri de Toulouse-Lautrec	Danseuse assise aux bas roses	14,522,500
128	Pablo Picasso	Nu couché	14,522,500
129	Henri Matisse	Harmonie Jaune	14,520,000

Present value**, USD	Year of make	Year of sale	Subject***	Size group****
23,320,937	1923	1990	Othr	D
14,888,917	1963	2005	Othr	D
21,428,121		1992	Lscape	F
23,208,946		1989	-	F
14,027,654	1964	2006	Lscape	F
14,027,654	1975	2006	A	F
16,548,730	1918	2000	FemP	C
18,166,330	1949	1996	Nu	E
16,878,194	1876	1999	FemP	B
23,612,635	1923	1988	A	F
17,011,433	1919	1998	FemP	C
14,341,099	1963	2004	A	G
17,994,620	1923	1995	Nu	B
21,756,553	1880	1989	FemP	C
14,163,779	1932	2004	A	E
15,329,314		2001	MaleP	F
16,982,261	1915 - 1916	1997	Lscape	E
21,390,647	1913	1989	A	C
15,128,750	1902	2001	Lscape	D
16,728,795	1890	1997	FemP	B
16,583,777	1942	1997	Nu	F
18,861,127	1927 - 1928	1992	Othr	D

Rank	Artist	Title	Nominal value*, USD	
130	Gustave Caillebotte	L'homme au balcon, boulevard Haussmann	14,306,000	
131	Alberto Giacometti	Grande femme debout I	14,306,000	
132	Mark Rothko	Yellow over purple	14,305,750	
133	Claude Monet	Meules, derniers rayons de soleil	14,304,790	
134	Henri Matisse	La Mulatresse Fatma	14,302,500	
135	Claude Monet	Le Parlement, coucher de soleil	14,300,000	
136	Henri Matisse	La serpentine - Femme à la stele - L'araignee	14,030,750	
137	Edward Hopper	Chair car	14,016,000	
138	Claude Monet	Nymphéas	14,016,000	
139	Chaïm Soutine	Le boeuf écorché	13,829,075	
140	Alberto Giacometti	Grande tête de Diego	13,759,500	
141	Henri Matisse	LA VIS	13,752,500	
142	Pierre-Auguste Renoir	Jeune fille au Chapeau Garni de Fleurs des Champs	13,750,000	
143	Pablo Picasso	Nu jaune	13,736,000	
144	Pablo Picasso	Le peintre et son modèle	13,698,880	
145	Lodovico Carracci	Salmacis and Hermaphroditus	13,653,000	
146	Titian (Tiziano Vecelli)	Venus and Adonis (Titian and workshop)	13,553,180	
147	Edgar Degas	Les blanchisseuses	13,538,462	
148	Pablo Picasso	Tête et main de femme	13,456,000	
149	Alberto Giacometti	La forêt	13,209,500	
150	Willem de Kooning	Orestes	13,209,500	
151	Vincent van Gogh	Jeune homme à la casquette	13,202,500	

Present value**, USD	Year of make	Year of sale	Subject***	Size group****
15,380,175	1880	2000	MaleP	E
15,150,488	1960	2000	S	-
15,379,906	1956	2000	A	F
14,817,286	1890	2001	Lscape	C
18,291,956	1912	1993	FemP	D
21,306,139	1904	1989	Lscape	D
15,084,133	1909	2000	S	-
13,046,553	1965	2005	Othr	E
12,835,273	1907	2005	Lscape	E
12,593,792	1924	2006	A	D
14,105,951	1954	2002	S	-
17,395,405	1951	1993	A	E
20,486,672	1880	1989	FemP	B
12,578,568	1907	2005	Nu	A
12,216,857	1963	2006	Nu	F
12,175,893		2006	Relgs	E
18,128,685	1555	1991	Relgs	F
21,639,781	1874	1987	OthP	C
12,524,691	1921	2005	FemP	B
13,541,713	1950	2002	S	-
13,429,675	1947	2002	A	C
15,997,372	1888	1995	MaleP	A

Rank	Artist	Title	Nominal value*, USD
152	Claude Monet	Nymphéas	13,202,500
153	Claude Monet	Le jardin de l'artiste a Vetheuil	13,202,500
154	Pierre-Auguste Renoir	La liseuse	13,202,500
155	Willem de Kooning	Sail cloth	13,120,000
156	Henri de Toulouse-Lautrec	Fille a la Fourrure, Mademoiselle Jeanne Fontaine	12,980,000
157	Claude Monet	Le Grand Canal	12,896,000
158	Paul Gauguin	Incantation	12,679,421
159	René Magritte	L'Empire des lumières	12,659,500
160	Rembrandt Harmensz van Rijn	Portrait of a bearded man in a red doublet	12,656,000
161	Joan Miró	Portrait de Mme K.	12,656,000
162	Henri Matisse	Figure decorative	12,655,750
163	Paul Cézanne	Les toits de l'Estaque	12,652,500
164	Andy Warhol	Liz	12,616,000
165	Claude Monet	Le pont du chemin de fer à Argenteuil	12,573,746
166	Edgar Degas	La sortie du bain	12,454,874
167	Amedeo Modigliani	Nu assis au collier	12,432,500
168	Henri Matisse	Femme a l'ombrelle rouge, Assise de Profil	12,375,000
169	Michelangelo (Buonarroti)	The Risen Christ (+ study, verso)	12,320,348
170	Henri Matisse	Odalisque au fauteuil noir	12,109,962
171	Claude Monet	La Cathédrale de Rouen, effet d'après-midi (le portail, plein soleil)	12,107,656
172	Pablo Picasso	Garçon à la collerette	12,102,500

Present value**, USD	Year of make	Year of sale	Subject***	Size group****
15,351,828	1905	1996	Lscape	D
15,351,828	1881	1996	Lscape	D
13,698,111	1877	2001	FemP	B
12,211,574	1949	2005	A	B
18,531,115	1891	1990	FemP	B
11,808,451	1908	2005	Lscape	C
12,496,757	1902	2003	Nu	C
12,977,475	1952	2002	Lscape	D
13,325,814	1633	2001	MaleP	B
13,153,044	1924	2001	A	E
13,130,579	1908	2001	S	-
14,574,329	1883 - 1885	1997	Lscape	B
11,741,898	1963	2005	FemP	E
19,279,174	1873	1988	Lscape	C
11,106,137	1895	2006	Nu	B
15,064,192	1917	1995	Nu	C
18,173,766	1919 - 1921	1989	FemP	C
13,144,893		2000	Relgs	A
11,557,673	1942	2004	FemP	A
14,641,646	1894	1995	Lscape	D
14,530,599	1905	1995	OthP	C

Rank	Artist	Title	Nominal value*, USD
173	Claude Monet	Le Grand Canal	12,102,500
174	Pierre-Auguste Renoir	La loge	12,100,000
175	Claude Monet	Le Bassin aux Nymphéas	12,100,000
176	Pablo Picasso	Mère et enfant	11,992,500
177	Claude Monet	Meule	11,992,500
178	Edgar Degas	Petite danseuse de quatorze ans	11,882,500
179	Pablo Picasso	La statuaire	11,827,500
180	Paul Cézanne	Les grands arbres au Jas de Bouffan	11,776,000
181	Andy Warhol	Small torn Campbell's Soup Can (Pepper pot)	11,776,000
182	Pablo Picasso	Nu accroupi	11,768,000
183	Vincent van Gogh	L'allée des Alyscamps	11,767,500
184	Joan Miró	La caresse des étoiles	11,767,500
185	Gustav Klimt	Dame mit Facher	11,662,500
186	Jackson Pollock	Number 12, 1949	11,655,500
187	Paul Cézanne	Le château noir	11,552,500
188	Jackson Pollock	Number 8, 1950	11,550,000
189	Paul Cézanne	Pichet et Fruits sur une Table	11,550,000
190	Vincent van Gogh	Carriere pres de Saint-remy	11,550,000
191	Edgar Degas	Petite danseuse de quatorze ans	11,530,460
192	Leonardo da Vinci	Horse and rider	11,458,773
193	Andrea del Sarto	Head of Saint Joseph looking down, with a subsidiary study of his features (+ Two studies of legs, verso)	11,436,610
194	Rembrandt Harmensz van Rijn	Self-portrait with shaded eyes	11,381,592

Present value**, USD	Year of make	Year of sale	Subject***	Size group****
13,709,459	1908	1998	Lscape	D
18,028,271	1874	1989	FemP	A
15,717,606	1919	1992	Lscape	E
14,530,946	1922	1995	Fem&InfP	D
13,306,919	1891	1999	Lscape	C
13,816,646	1879 - 1881	1996	S	-
12,960,042	1925	1999	FemP	E
10,959,105	1885 - 1887	2005	Lscape	B
10,520,741	1962	2006	Othr	A
11,266,740	1959	2004	Nu	E
11,547,154	1888	2003	Lscape	C
11,154,188	1938	2004	A	B
14,581,288	1917 - 1918	1994	FemP	E
11,158,964	1949	2004	A	B
12,990,549	1904	1998	Lscape	C
17,208,805	1950	1989	A	E
17,208,805	1893 - 1894	1989	Slife	B
16,921,763	1889	1989	Lscape	B
12,330,272	1879 - 1881	2000	S	-
11,901,499		2001	Othr	A
10,588,361		2005	MaleP	A
11,204,669	1634	2003	SelfP	B

Rank	`Artist	Title	Nominal value*, USD	
195	Amedeo Modigliani	Garçon à la veste bleue	11,333,824	
196	Egon Schiele	Porträt des Malers Anton Peschka	11,312,041	
197	Claude Monet	Santa Maria della salute et le grand canal, Venise	11,309,624	
198	Canaletto	Le retour du Bucentaure le Jour de l'ascension	11,259,300	
199	Claude Monet	Nymphéas, temps gris	11,216,000	
200	Willem de Kooning	Spike's folly I	11,208,000	
201	Vincent van Gogh	Le pont de Trinquetaille	11,207,500	
202	Pablo Picasso	La maternité	11,164,897	
203	Canaletto	The Campo Santi Giovanni e Paolo, Venice, with the west end of the church and the Scuola di San Marco	11,155,155	
204	Claude Monet	Le pont japonais, bassin aux nymphTas	11,154,130	
205	Paul Gauguin	Te fare hymenee (La maison des chants)	11,124,220	
206	John Singer Sargent	Cashmere	11,112,500	
207	Joan Miró	Paysage sur les bords du fleuve amour	11,006,000	
208	Mark Rothko	No.2 (Blue, red and green)	11,005,750	
209	Edgar Degas	Danseuses	11,002,500	
210	Pablo Picasso	Les femmes d'Alger (Version "M")	11,002,500	
211	Paul Cézanne	L'Estaque vu à travers les pins	11,002,500	
212	Pablo Picasso	Femme nue	11,002,500	
213	Claude Monet	Les trois peupliers, temps gris	11,002,500	
214	Mark Rothko	No. 15	11,002,500	
215	Claude Monet	Garden House on the Banks of the Zaan	11,000,000	

Present value**, USD	Year of make	Year of sale	Subject***	Size group****
10,816,473	1918	2004	MaleP	C
11,862,632	1909	2001	MaleP	E
16,946,479	1908	1989	Lscape	C
14,241,207		1993	Lscape	E
10,019,753	1907 -	2006	Lscape	C
10,997,781	1959	2003	A	F
10,623,037	1888	2004	Lscape	C
16,357,554	1906	1989	Fem&InfP	C
11,819,036		2000	Lscape	B
17,102,493	1900	1988	Lscape	D
16,668,668	1892	1989	OthP	B
12,921,122	1908	1996	Othr	D
11,437,430	1927	2001	A	F
11,653,957	1953	2000	A	F
12,673,329	1899	1997	OthP	B
12,563,467	1955	1997	Nu	F
12,371,951	1882 - 1883	1998	Lscape	C
12,371,951	1909	1998	Nu	C
12,055,853	1891	1999	Lscape	C
12,055,853	1952	1999	A	G
16,389,338	1871	1989	Othr	B

Rank	Artist	Title	Nominal value*, USD	
216	Paul Gauguin	Entre les Lys	11,000,000	
217	Henri Matisse	L'asie	11,000,000	
218	Joseph Mallord William Turner	The Blue Rigi: Lake of Lucerne, sunrise	10,978,740	
219	Henri Matisse	Robe jaune et robe arlequin (Nezy et Lydia)	10,936,000	
220	Jasper Johns	0 Through 9	10,928,000	
221	Edvard Munch	Summer day	10,835,326	
222	Willem de Kooning	Untitled	10,656,000	
223	Edgar Degas	Danseuse	10,648,000	
224	André Derain	Bateaux dans le port, Collioure	10,614,035	
225	Henri Matisse	Nu couche I (Aurore)	10,452,500	
226	Claude Monet	Nymphéas	10,424,000	
227	Rembrandt Harmensz van Rijn	Portrait Of A Girl Wearing A Gold Trimmed Cloak	10,381,800	
228	Egon Schiele	Portrait of the art dealer Guido Arnot	10,377,920	
229	Vincent van Gogh	Intérieur d'un restaurant	10,342,500	
230	Paul Cézanne	Pommes et gâteaux	10,320,000	
231	Vincent van Gogh	La moisson en Provence	10,312,000	
232	Edgar Degas	Petite danseuse de quatorze ans	10,311,500	
233	Vincent van Gogh	Jardin a Auvers	10,245,900	
234	Maurice de Vlaminck	La Seine à Chatou	10,115,597	
235	Mark Rothko	Untitled	10,096,000	
236	Francis Bacon	Study for a Pope I	10,096,000	
237	Pablo Picasso	Arlequin au baton	10,096,000	

Present value**, USD	Year of make	Year of sale	Subject***	Size group****
16,115,965	1889	1989	Othr	C
14,288,732	1946	1992	Nu	D
9,788,161		2006	Lscape	A
10,011,513	1941	2005	OthP	B
10,357,935	1961	2004	A	E
9,864,302	1904 - 1908	2006	Lscape	E
9,754,808	1977	2005	A	G
10,504,853	1885 - 1890	2003	FemP	B
15,776,044	1905	1989	Lscape	C
10,843,581	1907	2001	S	-
10,227,971	1908	2003	Lscape	D
17,330,047	1632	1986	FemP	B
10,995,102	1918	2000	MaleP	E
12,202,559	1887 - 1888	1996	Othr	B
9,446,761	1873 - 1877	2005	Nu	B
10,117,998	1888	2003	Lscape	B
10,172,643	1879 - 1881	2003	S	-
13,318,554	1890	1992	Lscape	C
10,487,970	1906	2002	Lscape	C
9,393,519	1964	2005	A	F
9,241,397	1961	2005	MaleP	E
9,017,778	1969 -	2006	OthP	F

Rank	Artist	Title	Nominal value*, USD
238	Willem de Kooning	Untitled	10,096,000
239	Paul Cézanne	Portrait de femme	10,087,500
240	John William Waterhouse	St. Cecilia	9,960,407
241	Claude Monet	Nymphéas	9,906,000
242	Bruce Nauman	Henry Moore bound to fail (Back view)	9,906,000
243	Egon Schiele	Haut mit trockender Wäsche	9,906,000
244	Pablo Picasso	Compotier et guitare	9,905,750
245	Amedeo Modigliani	Portrait de Jeanne Hébuterne assise dans un fauteuil	9,902,500
246	Claude Monet	Le bassin aux nymphéas	9,902,500
247	Vincent van Gogh	Paysage au soleil levant	9,900,000
248	Marc Chagall	Au Dessus de la Ville	9,900,000
249	Fernand Léger	Les maisons sous les Arbres	9,900,000
250	Pablo Picasso	Nu couché	9,752,000
251	Claude Monet	La Jetee du Havre	9,682,500
252	Robert Ryman	Untitled	9,648,000
253	Alberto Giacometti	Grande femme debout IV	9,640,000
254	Piet Mondrian	Facade in tan and grey	9,625,000
255	Giovanni Segantini	Primavera sulle alpi	9,572,500
256	Pieter Brueghel II	The Procession to Calvary	9,520,200
257	Georges Braque	Femme lisant	9,484,121
258	Vincent van Gogh	Deux crabes	9,480,882
259	Chaïm Soutine	Le pâtissier de Cagnes	9,460,270
260	Claude Monet	Nymphéas	9,460,000
261	Pablo Picasso	Femme couchée à la mèche blonde	9,377,941

	Present value**, USD	Year of make	Year of sale	Subject***	Size group****
	9,017,778	1961	2006	A	F
	9,560,733	1900	2004	FemP	B
	10,650,439		2000	Othr	F
	10,276,308	1916 - 1919	2001	Lscape	F
	10,276,308	1967	2001	S	-
	10,293,687	1917	2001	Lscape	E
	10,647,545	1932	2000	Slife	E
	11,134,756	1918	1998	FemP	C
	11,134,756	1917 - 1919	1998	Lscape	E
	17,398,659	1889	1985	Lscape	C
	14,133,901	1915	1990	Othr	B
	13,647,982	1913	1990	A	C
	9,568,133	1932	2003	Nu	E
	12,382,247	1868	1993	Lscape	F
	8,616,988	1962	2006	A	-
	9,458,160	1960	2003	S	-
	14,101,469	1913	1989	A	C
	10,488,592	1897	1999	Lscape	F
	8,485,893	1607	2006	Relgs	F
	15,831,577	1911	1986	A	E
	9,046,941	1888 - 1889	2004	Othr	B
	8,920,389	1922 - 1923	2005	MaleP	B
	13,041,405	1907	1990	Lscape	D
	8,948,634	1932	2004	Nu	F

Rank	Artist	Title	Nominal value*, USD
262	Henri de Toulouse-Lautrec	L'abandon ou les deux amies	9,355,750
263	Amedeo Modigliani	Portrait du sculpteur Oscar Miestchaninoff	9,352,500
264	Claude Monet	Waterloo bridge, effet de Brouillard	9,352,500
265	Paul Cézanne	L'allee à Chantilly, I	9,352,500
266	Claude Monet	Asters	9,350,000
267	Paul Gauguin	Te Fare-la Maison	9,303,990
268	Kees van Dongen	Femme au grand chapeau	9,235,273
269	Andy Warhol	Jackie frieze (in 13 parts)	9,200,000
270	Norman Rockwell	Homecoming marine	9,200,000
271	Edgar Degas	Petite danseuse de quatorze ans	9,178,825
272	Meindert Hobbema	A wooded landscape with travellers on a path through a hamlet	9,162,904
273	Pierre-Auguste Renoir	Femmes dans un jardin	9,137,523
274	Constantin Brancusi	La muse endormie III	9,075,000
275	Joan Miró	L'Oiseau au plumage déployé vole vers l'arbre argenté	9,064,572
276	Claude Monet	Canotiers à Argenteuil	9,022,500
277	Francis Bacon	Study from Portrait of Pope Innocent X by Velazquez	9,016,584
278	Francis Bacon	Self-portrait	9,016,584
279	Francis Bacon	Portrait of George Dyer staring into a mirror	8,994,169
280	Constantin Brancusi	The kiss	8,968,000
281	Mark Rothko	No.15	8,967,500

	Present value**, USD	Year of make	Year of sale	Subject***	Size group****
	10,055,999	1895	2000	OthP	B
	11,228,190	1916	1995	MaleP	B
	10,376,955	1899 - 1903	1999	Lscape	C
	9,701,769	1888	2001	Lscape	C
	13,930,937	1880	1989	Slife	C
	12,454,015	1892	1991	-	C
	8,586,992	1906	2005	Nu	D
	8,419,939	1964	2005	FemP	F
	8,216,198	1945 -	2006	OthP	E
	8,923,114	1879 - 1881	2004	S	-
	9,515,676		2001	Lscape	E
	8,144,217	1873	2006	Lscape	B
	13,295,671	1917	1989	S	-
	8,249,853	1953	2006	A	E
	10,145,000	1874	1998	Lscape	B
	8,206,101	1959	2006	MaleP	E
	8,206,101	1969	2006	SelfP	A
	8,362,424	1967	2005	MaleP	F
	8,498,904	1908	2004	S	-
	8,583,818	1958	2004	A	G

Rank	Artist	Title	Nominal value*, USD
282	Camille Pissarro	Les quatre saisons: Le printemps, l'été, l'automne, l'hiver (4 works)	8,967,500
283	Claude Monet	Le bassin aux nymphéas	8,920,774
284	Joan Miró	Danseuse espagnole	8,916,000
285	Diego Rodriguez de Silva y Velasquez	Saint Rufina	8,912,500
286	Amedeo Modigliani	Portrait de Mario (Marios Varvoglis)	8,883,994
287	Mark Rothko	No.8 (White stripe)	8,856,000
288	Maurice de Vlaminck	Le jardinier	8,825,467
289	Pierre-Auguste Renoir	Berthe Morisot et sa fille, Julie Manet	8,806,000
290	Pablo Picasso	Le marin	8,802,500
291	Pierre-Auguste Renoir	La coiffure	8,802,500
292	Pierre-Auguste Renoir	Maternité ou Femme allaitant son enfant	8,800,000
293	Claude Monet	Alice Hoschede au Jardin	8,800,000
294	Piet Mondrian	Tableau Losangique Ii	8,800,000
295	Constantin Brancusi	La Negresse Blonde	8,800,000
296	Willem de Kooning	July	8,800,000
297	John Singer Sargent	Robert Louis Stevenson and his wife	8,800,000
298	Raphaël (Raphaël Urbinas Sanzio)	Study for the head and hand of an Apostle	8,752,900
299	Paul Cézanne	Nature morte: Pommes et poires	8,744,000
300	Ernst Ludwig Kirchner	Frauenbildnis in weissem Kleid (+ Adam und Eva, verso)	8,697,797
301	Cy Twombly	Untitled (New York City)	8,696,000
302	Edgar Degas	Danseuse jaune	8,692,500

Present value**, USD	Year of make	Year of sale	Subject***	Size group****
8,498,429	1872 - 1873	2004	Lscape	C
13,069,716	1917 - 1919	1989	Lscape	E
9,264,318	1924	2001	A	F
10,002,982		1999	FemP	B
14,066,035	1919 - 1920	1988	MaleP	D
8,688,350	1958	2003	A	G
8,205,292	1904	2005	Lscape	C
9,464,723	1894	2000	OthP	C
10,050,774	1943	1997	FemP	E
10,050,774	1888	1997	OthP	B
13,814,468	1886	1988	Fem&InfP	B
13,111,470	1881	1989	Lscape	C
12,563,467	1925	1990	A	E
12,563,467	1923	1990	S	-
12,131,540	1956	1990	A	F
8,423,351	1885	2004	OthP	B
10,176,867		1996	MaleP	A
8,578,377	1888 - 1890	2003	Slife	A
7,915,453	1908	2006	FemP	E
7,957,869	1968	2005	A	F
10,106,620	1885	1996	OthP	B

Rank	Artist	Title	Nominal value*, USD
303	Hendrick Avercamp	A winter scene with many figures skating on a frozen river	8,688,000
304	Lucas Cranach (the Elder)	Portrait of Kurfust Herzog Johann 'der Bestandige' von Sachsen (Folding diptych (currently detatched): Portait of Johann Fri)	8,615,166
305	Jan Van Huysum	A still life of fruit in a basket with flowers and other fruit, all upon a marble ledge before an urn and column	8,599,617
306	Francis Bacon	Studies of the human body	8,585,750
307	Vincent van Gogh	Oliviers avec les Alpilles au fond	8,573,864
308	Paul Cézanne	La Côte Du Galet, À Pontoise	8,527,500
309	Pierre-Auguste Renoir	Baigneuse (femme en jupe rouge s'essuyant les pieds)	8,525,000
310	Claude Monet	Meules, Effet de Neige, Le Matin	8,525,000
311	Fernand Léger	La Femme au Fauteuil	8,525,000
312	Canaletto	Venice, the Molo from the Bacino di San Marco with the Piazzetta and the Palazzo Ducale (+ another; pair)	8,513,877
313	Jean Honoré Fragonard	Le verrou	8,511,684
314	Pierre-Auguste Renoir	Jeune Fille Portant une Corbeille de Fleurs	8,496,436
315	Eugène Delacroix	Choc de cavaliers Arabes	8,481,571
316	Juan Gris	Le pot de géranium	8,479,500
317	Amedeo Modigliani	Giovanotto dai capelli rossi	8,479,500
318	Andy Warhol	Large flowers	8,476,000
319	Edouard Vuillard	La table de toilette (Dans les fleurs)	8,470,000
320	Alberto Giacometti	Femme Leoni	8,416,000

Present value**, USD	Year of make	Year of sale	Subject***	Size group****
8,491,175		2004	Lscape	C
12,186,399	1509	1990	MaleP	A
8,445,762	1730 - 1735	2003	Slife	B
8,905,874	1979	2001	Nu	F
9,394,100	1889	1999	Lscape	B
9,032,022	1879 - 1881	2000	Lscape	B
13,071,280	1888	1988	FemP	B
12,519,705	1891	1989	Lscape	C
12,170,859	1913	1990	A	E
9,733,182		1997	Lscape	B
9,325,952	1778	1999	Othr	A
10,850,035	1888	1993	FemP	C
9,595,111	1833 - 1834	1998	Othr	D
8,689,266	1915	2002	A	B
8,617,375	1919	2002	FemP	C
8,791,953	1964	2001	Othr	G
12,409,293	1895	1989	Othr	C
7,827,932	1947	2005	S	-

Rank	Artist	Title	Nominal value*, USD
321	Henry Moore	Three-piece reclining figure: Draped	8,408,000
322	Michelangelo (Buonar-roti)	A mourning woman (study)	8,386,482
323	Franz Marc	Der Wasserfall (Frauen unter einem Wasserfall)	8,377,193
324	Claude Monet	Nymphéas	8,365,750
325	Claude Monet	La Seine à Argenteuil	8,362,500
326	Jasper Johns	Corpse and mirror (two panels)	8,362,500
327	John Singer Sargent	In the garden, Corfu	8,362,500
328	Vincent van Gogh	Jardin de Fleurs	8,360,000
329	Alexej Jawlensky	Schokko (Schokko mit Tellerhut)	8,296,000
330	Vincent van Gogh	Le pont de Langlois à Arles	8,295,500
331	Henri Matisse	Figure decorative	8,259,500
332	Pablo Picasso	Chat à l'oiseau	8,252,500
333	Claude Monet	Waterloo Bridge, soleil voilé	8,252,500
334	Marc Chagall	Le village Russe, de la lune	8,252,500
335	Claude Monet	Les trois arbres, Automne	8,250,000
336	Frederic Edwin Church	Home by the lake (Scene in the Catskill Mountains)	8,250,000
337	Pablo Picasso	Au Moulin Rouge	8,250,000
338	Amedeo Modigliani	Jeanne Hebuterne con grande cappello	8,250,000
339	Paul Cézanne	Grand bouquet de fleurs	8,146,113
340	Gilbert Stuart	George Washington (The Constable-Hamilton portrait)	8,136,000
341	Paul Cézanne	Arlequin	8,080,808
342	Pablo Picasso	Sylvette au fauteuil vert	8,080,000

Present value**, USD	Year of make	Year of sale	Subject***	Size group****
7,967,752	1975	2004	S	-
8,708,834		2001	FemP	A
9,184,008	1912	1999	Nu	F
8,991,218	1908	2000	Lscape	D
9,631,730	1875	1997	Lscape	B
9,548,235	1974	1997	A	F
9,560,074	1909	1997	FemP	C
11,524,963	1888	1990	Lscape	B
8,138,486	1910	2003	FemP	B
8,137,995	1888	2003	Lscape	A
8,463,571	1908	2002	S	-
9,422,601	1939	1997	Othr	E
9,422,601	1903	1997	Lscape	C
9,041,889	1911	1999	Othr	E
12,292,003	1891	1989	Lscape	C
12,292,003	1852	1989	Lscape	D
12,115,844	1901	1989	FemP	B
11,778,251	1918	1990	FemP	A
7,918,351	1892 - 1895	2004	Slife	D
7,444,459	1794	2005	MaleP	-
12,390,206	1890	1988	MaleP	B
7,393,117	1954	2005	FemP	C

Rank	Artist	Title	Nominal value*, USD
343	Rembrandt Harmensz van Rijn	Portrait of Johannes Uyitenbogaert	8,077,295
344	Piet Mondrian	Composition in white, blue, and yellow: C	8,071,500
345	Jackson Pollock	Black and white no.6	7,980,750
346	Edgar Degas	Le baisser du rideau	7,975,000
347	Cy Twombly	Untitled (Rome)	7,968,000
348	Pierre-Auguste Renoir	Après le bain	7,960,526
349	Bartolomeo di Giovanni	The Argonauts in Colchis	7,944,732
350	Pablo Picasso	Le repos	7,925,750
351	Pablo Picasso	Demi-nu à la cruche	7,922,500
352	Jasper Johns	White numbers	7,922,500
353	Childe Hassam	Flags, afternoon on the avenue	7,922,500
354	Pablo Picasso	Nature morte à la bouteille de rhum	7,922,500
355	Paul Gauguin	Tahitiennes près d'un ruisseau	7,918,910
356	Amedeo Modigliani	Fillette au Tablier Noir	7,891,454
357	Pablo Picasso	Homme à la pipe assis et amour	7,865,801
358	Andy Warhol	Flowers	7,856,000
359	Juan Sánchez Cotán	Bodegón with a cardoon and francolin	7,854,572
360	Sir Alfred James Munnings	The Red Prince mare	7,848,000
361	Everett Shinn	Stage scene	7,848,000
362	Francisco José de Goya y Lucientes	Bullfight suerte de Varas	7,758,621
363	Claude Monet	Le bassin aux Nymphéas	7,758,443
364	Joan Miró	Le soleil rouge ronge l'araignée	7,744,000

Present value**, USD	Year of make	Year of sale	Subject***	Size group****
10,604,226	1633	1992	MaleP	E
7,961,199	1936	2003	A	B
8,277,878	1951	2001	A	E
12,227,972	1880	1988	Othr	B
7,290,435	1961	2005	A	E
11,832,033	1900	1989	Nu	B
11,621,269	1487	1989	Othr	E
8,390,775	1932	2000	FemP	A
9,124,797	1906	1997	Nu	D
9,045,697	1959	1997	A	E
8,973,464	1917	1998	Lscape	C
8,789,892	1914	1999	Slife	A
9,575,199	1893	1995	Lscape	C
11,561,672	1918	1989	FemP	C
7,008,751	1969	2006	Othr	E
7,306,070	1965	2005	Othr	G
7,470,211		2004	Slife	B
7,511,320	1921	2004	Othr	E
7,463,955	1906	2004	Othr	B
10,085,362	1824	1992	Othr	B
8,134,092	1917 - 1920	2001	Lscape	E
7,085,071	1948	2005	A	C

Rank	Artist	Title	Nominal value*, USD
365	Claude Monet	Nymphéas	7,730,882
366	Edvard Munch	Girls on a bridge	7,702,500
367	Lucian Freud	Red Haired Man on a Chair	7,700,297
368	Claude Monet	Nymphéas	7,700,000
369	Fernand Léger	Le Petit Dejeuner	7,700,000
370	Georges Braque	Atelier VIII	7,700,000
371	Pierre Bonnard	Place Clichy	7,686,182
372	Lyonel Feininger	Angler mit blauem Fisch II (Angler with blue fish II)	7,686,182
373	Paul Cézanne	Maisons dans la verdure	7,659,194
374	Fernand Léger	Les campeurs (1er état)	7,632,000
375	Maxfield Parrish	Daybreak	7,632,000
376	Pablo Picasso	Souvenir du Havre	7,629,129
377	Francesco Guardi	The Grand Canal, Venice, with the Palazzo Bembo	7,629,010
378	Edgar Degas	Les chevaux de courses	7,627,941
379	Claude Monet	Vétheuil	7,603,016
380	Henri Matisse	Deux Négresses	7,596,000
381	John Singer Sargent	Spanish Dancer	7,592,500
382	Wassily Kandinsky	Sketch for Composition Vii	7,582,651
383	Yves Tanguy	Les derniers jours	7,571,214
384	Claude Monet	Le Pont Japonais	7,562,500
385	Joan Miró	La table (nature morte au lapin)	7,546,252
386	Pierre-Auguste Renoir	Les rosiers à Wargemont	7,512,000
387	Pierre-Auguste Renoir	Gabrielle au chapeau de paille	7,502,000

Present value**, USD	Year of make	Year of sale	Subject***	Size group****
7,375,717	1914 - 1917	2004	Lscape	F
8,955,233	1902	1996	Lscape	E
7,258,043	1962 - 1963	2005	MaleP	D
11,281,176	1914 - 1917	1989	Lscape	F
10,306,967	1921	1991	Nu	E
10,166,786	1952 - 1955	1992	A	F
6,848,377	1906 - 1907	2006	Lscape	E
6,848,377	1912	2006	Othr	B
6,824,281	1881	2006	Lscape	C
7,097,325	1954	2005	Othr	F
6,813,432	1922	2006	OthP	D
12,194,347	1912	1987	A	B
7,058,231		2005	Lscape	B
7,277,409	1871 - 1872	2004	Othr	A
7,785,762	1880	2002	Lscape	C
7,891,826	1907 - 1908	2001	S	-
9,491,593		1994	FemP	F
9,856,620	1913	1992	A	D
7,136,121	1944	2005	A	E
10,796,730	1918 - 1924	1990	Lscape	E
9,124,455	1920	1995	Slife	E
7,117,909	1879	2004	Lscape	C
10,991,088	1900	1989	FemP	C

Rank	Artist	Title	Nominal value*, USD	
388	Pablo Picasso	Femme à la mandoline	7,500,000	
389	Claude Monet	Peupliers au Bord de l'epte, Effet du Soir	7,482,998	
390	Pablo Picasso	Femme assise pres d'une fenetre (insc. on stretcher)	7,482,500	
391	Michelangelo (Buonarroti)	Study of Christ and the Woman of Samaria, with a separate sketch of a man looking up (+ 2 other studies, verso)	7,482,500	
392	Alberto Giacometti	La forêt: sept figures et une tête	7,482,500	
393	Pierre Bonnard	Après le repas	7,480,000	
394	Edouard Vuillard	Le pot de grès	7,478,848	
395	Pablo Picasso	Tête de femme	7,474,747	
396	Pierre-Auguste Renoir	Jeune femme se baignant	7,422,059	
397	Henri Matisse	Danseuse dans le fauteuil, sol en damier	7,414,309	
398	Juan Gris	La console de marbre	7,400,000	
399	Pablo Picasso	La femme qui pleure	7,341,784	
400	Egon Schiele	Kniender weiblicher Halbakt	7,316,300	
401	Edvard Munch	Haus in Aasgaardstrand	7,315,823	
402	Philip Guston	The street	7,296,000	
403	Jan Van Huysum	Flowers in a terracotta vase on a marble ledge	7,296,000	
404	Lucian Freud	Naked Portrait	7,284,866	
405	Camille Pissarro	La rue Saint-Lazare	7,272,325	
406	Edgar Degas	Blanchissueses portant du linge	7,268,722	
407	Edgar Degas	Apres le bain	7,262,500	
408	Pablo Picasso	Les femmes d'Alger (Version "K")	7,262,500	

Present value**, USD	Year of make	Year of sale	Subject***	Size group****
11,499,660	1910	1988	A	C
9,323,054	1891	1994	Lscape	C
8,617,864	1932	1997	FemP	E
8,537,871		1998	FemP	A
8,412,927	1950	1998	S	-
11,468,994	1925	1988	Othr	E
6,663,257	1895	2006	Othr	C
11,460,941		1988	FemP	B
7,080,795	1888	2004	Nu	C
7,926,313	1942	2000	FemP	B
7,082,129	1914	2004	A	B
8,254,660	1937	1998	FemP	B
6,655,901	1917	2006	Nu	A
7,583,409	1905	2002	Lscape	E
6,784,208	1956	2005	A	F
6,650,782		2006	Slife	B
6,865,657	2002	2005	Nu	E
7,555,280	1893	2001	Lscape	B
11,508,574	1876	1988	OthP	B
8,443,506	1883	1996	Nu	A
8,291,889	1955	1997	Nu	F

Rank	Artist	Title	Nominal value*, USD
409	Pablo Picasso	Femme dans un fauteuil	7,260,916
410	Claude Monet	Saint-georges Majeur	7,260,000
411	Robert Rauschenberg	Rebus	7,260,000
412	Lucian Freud	Man in a string chair	7,255,205
413	Master of 1487	The Departure of the Argonauts	7,253,886
414	Pieter Brueghel II	The kermesse of St. George	7,201,556
415	Albert Bierstadt	Yosemite Valley	7,176,000
416	Mark Rothko	Untitled	7,175,500
417	Giorgio de Chirico	Il grande metafisico	7,175,500
418	Pablo Picasso	Mousquetaire à la pipe	7,175,500
419	Roy Lichtenstein	Happy tears	7,159,500
420	Amedeo Modigliani	Almaïsa	7,156,000
421	Pablo Picasso	Figure	7,156,000
422	Claude Monet	Nymphéas	7,155,750
423	Claude Monet	Les Meules, Giverny, effet du matin	7,152,500
424	Pablo Picasso	Les femmes d'Alger (Version "H")	7,152,500
425	René Magritte	Les valeurs personnelles	7,152,500
426	Jasper Johns	Two flags (in 6 parts)	7,152,500
427	Amedeo Modigliani	Portrait de Baranowski	7,150,117
428	Vincent van Gogh	L'homme est en mer	7,150,000
429	Willem de Kooning	Palisade	7,150,000
430	Paul Cézanne	Le Jas de Bouffan	7,150,000
431	Joan Miró	Les Echelles en Roue de Fue Traversant L'azur	7,150,000

Present value**, USD	Year of make	Year of sale	Subject***	Size group****
7,305,061	1932	2003	Nu	C
10,364,861	1908	1990	Lscape	C
9,904,882		1991	A	G
6,600,199	1988 - 1989	2006	MaleP	E
10,610,724	1487	1989	Othr	E
6,848,557	1628	2004	Othr	F
7,046,395	1866	2003	Lscape	E
7,038,266	1963	2003	A	F
6,867,054	1917	2004	A	C
6,798,743	1968	2004	OthP	E
7,274,407	1964	2002	FemP	D
7,434,329	1916	2001	FemP	B
7,421,778	1927	2001	A	E
7,421,519	1907	2001	Lscape	C
8,421,775	1889	1996	Lscape	C
8,166,254	1955	1997	Nu	F
8,041,768	1952	1998	Othr	D
7,935,319	1973	1999	Othr	F
8,088,407	1918	1998	FemP	C
10,500,398	1889	1989	Fem&InfP	B
10,207,817	1957	1990	A	F
9,856,876	1885 - 1887	1990	Lscape	B
9,856,876	1953	1990	A	E

Rank	Artist	Title	Nominal value*, USD	
432	Edgar Degas	Deux Danseuses en Jupes Vertes, Decor de Paysage	7,150,000	
433	Henri Matisse	Les huîtres	7,148,288	
434	Vincent van Gogh	Nature morte, vase avec oeillets	7,104,451	
435	Paul Gauguin	L'allée des Alyscamps, Arles	7,098,083	
436	Claude Monet	Les peupliers	7,046,000	
437	Constantin Brancusi	Mademoiselle Pogany II	7,042,500	
438	Edgar Degas	Danseuses se Baissant (Les Ballerines)	7,042,500	
439	Pablo Picasso	L'Indépendant (nature morte à l'éventail)	7,042,500	
440	Jasper Johns	White flag	7,040,000	
441	Pierre-Auguste Renoir	Enfant Assis en Robe Bleue (Portrait D'edmond Renoir,jr)	7,040,000	
442	Pierre-Auguste Renoir	L'Été; Jeune femme dans un champ fleuri	7,039,375	
443	Francis Bacon	Three studies for a self-portrait (triptych)	7,038,612	
444	Pierre Bonnard	La porte fenêtre or Matinée au Cannet	7,003,451	
445	Grant Wood	Spring plowing	6,960,000	
446	Andy Warhol	Self-Portrait	6,951,500	
447	Alberto Giacometti	L'homme qui marche I	6,895,280	
448	Claude Monet	Sur les planches de Trouville	6,885,394	
449	Piet Mondrian	Composition in black and whitewith blue square	6,875,000	
450	Paul Gauguin	Petit Breton a l'oie	6,862,133	
451	Pierre Bonnard	Compotiers et assiettes de fruits	6,848,000	
452	André Derain	Paysage à l'Estaque	6,848,000	

Present value**, USD	Year of make	Year of sale	Subject***	Size group****
9,287,676	1895	1992	FemP	E
6,368,114	1941	2006	Slife	B
6,998,850	1890	2003	Slife	A
10,883,405	1888	1988	Lscape	C
7,458,702	1891	2000	Lscape	D
8,110,931	1920 - 1925	1997	S	-
8,906,447	1885	1993	OthP	A
8,454,167	1911	1995	A	B
10,794,347	1955 - 1958	1988	A	F
9,705,232	1889	1990	OthP	B
6,270,871	1884	2006	FemP	C
6,270,189	1980	2006	SelfP	A
7,045,691	1932	2003	FemP	E
6,366,296	1932	2005	Lscape	B
6,652,459	1967	2004	SelfP	F
10,572,450	1960	1988	S	-
7,870,931	1870	1997	Lscape	B
9,815,209	1935	1990	A	C
10,053,628	1889	1989	Lscape	C
6,263,613	1930	2005	Slife	B
6,112,049	1906 -	2006	Lscape	B

Rank	Artist	Title	Nominal value*, USD
453	Pablo Picasso	Plant de tomate	6,840,000
454	Peter de Hooch	The courtyard of a house in delft with a young woman and two men drinking and smoking under an arbour...	6,830,177
455	Claude Monet	Le bassin aux nymphéas	6,826,000
456	Pablo Picasso	Buste de femme à la chemise	6,826,000
457	Sir Peter Paul Rubens	A portrait of a man as the god Mars	6,824,609
458	Maurice de Vlaminck	Paysage de Banlieue	6,822,500
459	Pablo Picasso	Le journal	6,822,500
460	Paul Cézanne	Saint-Henri et la baie de l'Estaque	6,820,000
461	Paul Gauguin	Ferme en Bretagne (II)	6,820,000
462	Edouard Manet	Un Bar aux Folies-bergere	6,802,937
463	Lucian Freud	Man with a feather (Self-portrait)	6,773,958
464	Pablo Picasso	Buste de femme	6,736,000
465	Andy Warhol	Flowers	6,736,000
466	Pablo Picasso	Femme assise dans un fauteuil	6,736,000
467	Amedeo Modigliani	Homme assis sur fond orange	6,729,466
468	Chaïm Soutine	Le chasseur de Chez Maxim's	6,728,000
469	Mark Rothko	Brown and blacks in reds	6,727,500
470	Gustave Caillebotte	Chemin montant	6,727,500
471	Andy Warhol	Large flowers	6,727,500
472	Pablo Picasso	La guenon et son petit	6,719,500
473	Yves Klein	"RE 1"	6,716,000
474	Claude Monet	Coin du bassin aux nymphéas	6,712,500
475	Nicolas Poussin	The Agony in the Garden	6,712,500

	Present value**, USD	Year of make	Year of sale	Subject***	Size group****
	6,545,640	1944	2004	Slife	C
	8,878,486	1658	1992	Othr	B
	7,335,160	1917 - 1919	2000	Lscape	F
	7,091,206	1922	2001	FemP	B
	6,979,888		2002	MaleP	C
	8,528,678	1905 - 1906	1994	Lscape	C
	7,569,073	1912	1999	A	A
	10,706,213		1988	Lscape	C
	10,161,389	1894	1989	Lscape	C
	8,475,483	1881	1994	FemP	B
	6,294,480	1943	2005	SelfP	B
	6,160,931	1939	2005	OthP	A
	6,160,931	1964	2005	Slife	G
	6,011,852	1960 -	2006	FemP	E
	5,994,166	1918	2006	MaleP	C
	6,374,296	1925	2004	MaleP	C
	6,634,332	1957	2003	A	F
	6,598,374	1881	2003	Othr	E
	6,437,864	1964	2004	Othr	G
	6,826,751	1951	2002	S	-
	7,109,075	1958	2000	A	F
	7,730,731	1918	1997	Lscape	E
	7,533,110	1650	1999	Relgs	B

Rank	Artist	Title	Nominal value*, USD
476	Francis Bacon	Study for portrait of Henrietta Moraes	6,712,500
477	Pierre-Auguste Renoir	Le premier pas	6,693,651
478	Pablo Picasso	Le garcon bleu	6,674,532
479	Paul Signac	Les Andelys. Les laveuses	6,673,985
480	Pierre-Auguste Renoir	Lajeune Mere	6,655,000
481	Claude Monet	Camille et Jean Monet au Jardin d'Argenteuil	6,633,772
482	Claude Monet	Paysage de printemps (Giverny)	6,628,161
483	Pablo Picasso	Au Moulin Rouge (Le Divan Japonais)	6,626,162
484	Claude Monet	Vétheuil, après-midi	6,624,000
485	Francis Bacon	Portrait of George Dyer talking	6,606,000
486	Paul Gauguin	Femmes au bord de la rivière	6,606,000
487	Amedeo Modigliani	La belle épicière	6,602,500
488	Fernand Léger	La pipe	6,602,500
489	Constantin Brancusi	La muse endormie II	6,602,500
490	Edgar Degas	Après le bain	6,602,500
491	Canaletto	The Grand Canal, Venice, looking east from the Campo di San Vio, with the Palazzo Corner, barges and gondolas	6,602,500
492	Claude Monet	La meule	6,602,500
493	Jan Davidsz de Heem	A lavish banquet still life, flanked by columns, before a landscape	6,600,000
494	Pierre-Auguste Renoir	Le jardin ou Dans le parc	6,600,000
495	Edgar Degas	Sur la scene	6,600,000
496	Claude Monet	La Berge a Argenteuil	6,600,000
497	Paul Cézanne	Carriere de Bibemus	6,600,000

Present value**, USD	Year of make	Year of sale	Subject***	Size group****
6,876,523	1964	2002	Nu	F
6,937,951	1876	2002	Fem&InfP	D
10,001,201	1905	1989	MaleP	C
6,201,364	1886	2005	Lscape	C
9,501,122	1898	1990	Fem&InfP	B
9,860,027	1873	1989	OthP	E
7,085,195	1894	2000	Lscape	C
5,901,931	1901	2006	OthP	B
6,157,973	1901	2005	Lscape	D
6,992,533	1966	2000	MaleP	F
6,850,872	1891 - 1893	2001	Lscape	A
7,925,781	1918	1995	FemP	C
7,925,781	1918	1995	A	C
7,538,080	1917	1997	S	-
7,477,887	1896	1998	Nu	C
7,212,085		2000	Lscape	B
6,847,239	1891	2001	Lscape	C
10,522,040	1642	1988	Lscape	F
10,360,851	1875	1988	Lscape	B
9,833,603	1879 - 1881	1989	FemP	B
9,692,675		1989	Lscape	B
9,669,579	1898	1989	Lscape	B

Rank	Artist	Title	Nominal value*, USD
498	Paul Gauguin	Nature morte aux mangos	6,571,533
499	Jan Van Huysum	Green grapes on the vine with morning glory, pink and white hollyhocks, a red opium poppy, a walnut, hazelnuts, a split melon...	6,555,091
500	Fernand Léger	Les acrobates (les perroquets)	6,527,171
501	Andy Warhol	5 Deaths twice I (Red car crash)	6,504,000
502	Canaletto	Venice, a view of the Piazza San Marco looking east towards the Basilica and the Campanile (+ Venice, The Grand Canal and the Rialto Bridge; pair)	6,478,553
503	Aelbert Cuyp	Orpheus charming the animals	6,456,918
504	Amedeo Modigliani	Le buste rouge (Cariatide)	6,419,556
505	Pablo Picasso	Tête d'homme	6,419,556
506	Franz Kline	Crow dancer	6,400,000
507	Gustave Caillebotte	Un soldat	6,389,500
508	Henri Matisse	Poissons chinois	6,382,500
509	Henri Matisse	Les deux femmes	6,382,500
510	Robert Rauschenberg	Red interior	6,382,500
511	Pablo Picasso	Les amants	6,331,000
512	Edvard Munch	Self-portrait (Against two-coloured background)	6,310,066
513	Michelangelo (Buonarroti)	The meeting of the infant Saint John the Baptist... [Verso: putti in amorous play...]	6,298,388
514	Francis Bacon	Study for a Pope	6,292,000
515	Pablo Picasso	Buveuse accoudée	6,288,000
516	Amedeo Modigliani	La rousse au pendentif	6,275,750

	Present value**, USD	Year of make	Year of sale	Subject***	Size group****
	6,105,939	1891 - 1896	2005	Slife	A
	6,062,571	1731	2005	Slife	B
	9,562,877	1933	1989	Nu	F
	6,161,835	1963	2004	Othr	E
	7,405,688		1997	Lscape	B
	8,022,552		1994	Relgs	E
	5,717,461	1913	2006	Nu	B
	5,717,461	1971	2006	FemP	D
	5,949,228	1958	2005	A	F
	6,545,161	1881	2002	MaleP	D
	7,661,589	1951	1995	A	E
	7,661,589	1938	1995	OthP	B
	7,286,811	1954 - 1955	1997	A	F
	6,701,177	1932	2000	Nu	E
	5,738,488	1904	2006	SelfP	B
	8,042,280	1530 - 1535	1993	Relgs	A
	9,218,332	1955	1989	MaleP	E
	5,750,202	1901	2005	FemP	B
	6,743,346	1918	2000	FemP	C

Rank	Artist	Title	Nominal value*, USD
517	Edgar Degas	Danseuses Russes	6,272,500
518	Pablo Picasso	Violon, Bouteille et Verre	6,272,500
519	Francis Bacon	Triptych May-June	6,270,000
520	Joaquín Sorolla y Bastida	La hora del baño (The bathing hour)	6,264,343
521	Jan van de Cappelle	A kaag and a smak in a calm, with fishermen pulling in their catch from a rowing-boat in the foreground, a Dutch frigate and other boats beyond	6,262,204
522	Henry Moore	Large four piece reclining figure	6,234,842
523	Juan Gris	Le guéridon	6,219,986
524	Hubert Robert	Colonnade et jardins du Palais Médici: Gentlemen sketching in an Italianate garden (+ Restes du palais du Pape Jules: An architectural capriccio with haymakers; pair)	6,213,960
525	Pablo Picasso	Guitare et compotier rose	6,183,635
526	George Wesley Bellows	Kids	6,168,000
527	Charles Willson Peale	George Washington	6,167,500
528	Georgia O'Keeffe	Calla lilies with red anemone	6,166,000
529	Pablo Picasso	Nu dans une forêt or La Dryade (study)	6,166,000
530	Lucian Freud	Bruce Bernard (Seated)	6,165,723
531	Pablo Picasso	Ma jolie: guitare, bouteille de Bass, grappe de raisin et verre	6,162,500
532	Pierre-Auguste Renoir	Les rosiers à Wargemont	6,162,500
533	Bernardo Bellotto	The fortress of Konigstein	6,144,144
534	Jacques-Louis David	Portrait of Suzanne Le Peletier de Saint-Fargeau	6,125,573

Present value**, USD	Year of make	Year of sale	Subject***	Size group****
8,020,319	1895	1993	OthP	B
7,840,881	1913	1994	A	B
9,341,922	1973	1989	Nu	G
6,143,599	1904	2003	Othr	D
5,791,027	1653	2005	Lscape	B
5,552,537	1972 - 1973	2006	S	-
6,439,314	1914	2001	A	B
5,533,893		2006	Lscape	B
9,059,568	1924	1989	A	D
5,864,638	1906	2004	Othr	D
5,901,375	1780 - 1782	2004	MaleP	E
6,394,147	1928	2001	Slife	D
6,404,961	1908	2001	Nu	A
5,606,886	1996	2006	MaleP	D
7,397,396	1914	1995	A	B
6,836,582	1879	1999	Lscape	C
8,218,385		1991	Lscape	F
7,045,718	1804	1997	FemP	B

Rank	Artist	Title	Nominal value*, USD
535	Sir Joshua Reynolds	Portrait of Mrs. Baldwin	6,122,612
536	Claude Monet	Paysage de printemps	6,118,321
537	Adriaen van Ostade	Peasants carousing and dancing outside an inn	6,112,062
538	Marc Chagall	La mariee sous le baldaquin	6,100,147
539	Pablo Picasso	Fillette au bateau (Maya)	6,073,864
540	Pablo Picasso	Nus	6,052,500
541	Edgar Degas	Danseuse à la barre	6,052,500
542	Fernand Léger	Composition (Le typographe)	6,052,500
543	Eugène Delacroix	Les Natchez	6,050,000
544	Pierre-Auguste Renoir	Jeune fille au chapeau de paille	6,050,000
545	Pablo Picasso	Femme nue assise	6,050,000
546	Roy Lichtenstein	Kiss II	6,050,000
547	Foujita Tsuguji (Tsuguharu Léonard)	Jeune fille dans le parc	6,050,000
548	Otto Dix	Bildnis Rechtsanwalt Dr. Fritz Glaser	6,010,427
549	Jan Van Huysum	Still life of fruit upon a marble ledge, a bird's nest to the right and a basket of flowers above, insects throughout	6,007,320
550	Canaletto	View of the Grand Walk, Vauxhall Gardens, with the orchestra pavillion, the Organ House, the Turkish dining tent and the statue of Aurora (+ The interior of the rotunda, Ranelaghr; 2 works)	5,978,733
551	Leonardo da Vinci	Personnage agenouille tourné vers la gauche (study)	5,973,260
552	Théodore Géricault	Portrait de Laure Bro Nee de Comeres	5,973,260

Present value**, USD	Year of make	Year of sale	Subject***	Size group****
5,849,092	1782	2004	FemP	E
9,167,767	1894	1989	Lscape	C
5,811,387	1660	2004	Othr	A
8,729,246	1949	1990	Othr	E
6,654,133	1938	1999	FemP	B
6,909,907	1934	1997	Nu	D
7,036,255	1885	1996	FemP	B
6,804,573	1917 - 1918	1998	A	G
8,863,781	1823 - 1834	1989	Othr	E
8,637,384		1990	FemP	B
9,276,392	1959	1988	Nu	E
8,637,384	1962	1990	Othr	F
8,637,384	1957	1990	OthP	B
6,588,522	1921	1999	MaleP	D
5,349,393		2006	Slife	B
6,612,738		1999	Lscape	B
8,737,470	1470 - 1475	1989	-	A
8,737,470	1817 - 1820	1989	-	A

Rank	Artist	Title	Nominal value*, USD	
553	Juan Gris	Paysage et maisons à Céret	5,956,824	
554	Kees van Dongen	Femme fatale	5,943,500	
555	Amedeo Modigliani	Portrait de Jeanne Hebuterne	5,942,500	
556	Paul Cézanne	Une moderne Olympia (or le pacha)	5,942,500	
557	Mark Rothko	No. 14, 1960	5,942,500	
558	Claude Monet	Paysage dans l'Ile Saint-Martin	5,942,500	
559	Claude Monet	Pont dans le jardin de Monet	5,942,500	
560	Egon Schiele	Sommerlandschaft	5,940,000	
561	Joan Miró	Danseuse espagnole	5,940,000	
562	Amedeo Modigliani	Portrait de Jeanne Hébuterne	5,935,108	
563	Rembrandt Harmensz van Rijn	Cupid blowing a soap bubble	5,933,600	
564	Pablo Picasso	Tête de femme	5,929,919	
565	Meindert Hobbema	Wooded landscape with cottages	5,857,993	
566	Gustav Klimt	Bauergarten (blumengarten)	5,842,442	
567	Lucian Freud	Large interior W11 (after Watteau)	5,832,500	
568	Alexander Calder	Untitled	5,831,500	
569	Claude Monet	Le jardin fleuri	5,830,000	
570	Francis Bacon	Study for portrait of van goghii	5,830,000	
571	El Greco (Domenikos Theotokopoulos)	Christ on the Cross	5,811,341	
572	Claude Monet	Nymphéas	5,777,500	
573	Pierre-Auguste Renoir	Jeune femme au corsage rouge	5,775,000	
574	Andrea Briosco Il Riccio	The Virgin and Child	5,752,931	
575	Maurice de Vlaminck	Péniche sur la Seine	5,730,952	

Present value**, USD	Year of make	Year of sale	Subject***	Size group****
5,533,388	1913	2005	A	C
5,630,209	1905	2004	Nu	C
7,319,038	1919	1994	FemP	B
6,784,272	1870	1997	Nu	B
6,784,272	1960	1997	A	G
6,680,854	1881	1998	Lscape	B
6,592,419	1895 - 1896	1999	Lscape	D
8,850,242	1917	1989	Lscape	E
8,188,789	1945	1990	A	E
5,513,161	1919	2005	FemP	A
7,127,156	1634	1995	Relgs	C
8,885,463	1921	1989	FemP	B
7,214,912		1994	Lscape	E
7,195,751	1905 - 1907	1994	Lscape	E
6,605,467	1981 - 1983	1998	Othr	F
5,718,591	1968	2003	S	-
9,318,631	1900	1987	Lscape	D
8,686,349	1957	1989	MaleP	F
6,196,884		2000	Relgs	B
6,595,820	1914 - 1917	1997	Lscape	E
8,481,091	1892	1989	FemP	B
5,856,285	1520 - 1525	2002	S	-
5,323,006	1905	2005	Lscape	B

Rank	Artist	Title	Nominal value*, USD
576	Joan Miró	Tête de paysan catalan	5,729,500
577	Henry Moore	Draped reclining mother and baby	5,728,000
578	Lucian Freud	Naked girl perched on a chair	5,728,000
579	Willem de Kooning	Two women (Study for Clamdigger)	5,728,000
580	Pierre-Auguste Renoir	Jeune fille assise en costume orientale	5,726,000
581	Fernand Léger	Les quatre constructeurs sur fond jaune	5,726,000
582	Claude Monet	Matinée sur la Seine	5,725,750
583	René Magritte	Le tombeau des lutteurs	5,722,500
584	Alberto Giacometti	Trois hommes qui marchent I	5,722,500
585	Henri Matisse	Nature morte aux citrons sur fond fleurdelisé	5,720,000
586	Jackson Pollock	Frieze	5,720,000
587	Claude Monet	Nymphéas	5,720,000
588	Pierre-Auguste Renoir	Leontine et coco (Claude Renoir)	5,720,000
589	Ferdinand Hodler	Eiger Mönch und Jungfrau über dem Nebelmeer	5,702,830
590	Franz Marc	Rote Rehe I	5,675,606
591	Bernardo Bellotto	The Gand Canal, Venice, looking east from the Palazzo Flangini to the Palazzo Vendramin Calergi, with the entrance to the Cannaregio	5,636,440
592	Jean François de Troy	La lecture de Molière	5,632,040
593	Cy Twombly	Untitled	5,619,500
594	Lucian Freud	Naked woman on a sofa	5,616,000
595	Amedeo Modigliani	Moïse Kisling seduto	5,616,000
596	Mark Rothko	Blue over red	5,616,000

Present value**, USD	Year of make	Year of sale	Subject***	Size group****
5,868,076	1924 - 1925	2002	A	A
5,322,994	1983	2005	S	-
5,236,791	1994	2005	Nu	D
5,110,074	1961 - 1962	2006	A	B
6,060,195	1905	2000	Nu	C
5,947,463	1950	2001	Othr	F
6,059,930	1896	2000	Lscape	D
6,433,415	1960	1998	Othr	E
6,269,043	1948	1999	S	-
8,979,404	1943	1988	Slife	B
8,770,407	1953 - 1955	1988	A	E
8,166,254	1914 - 1917	1990	Lscape	E
7,885,501	1909	1990	Fem&InfP	B
5,213,716	1908	2005	Lscape	C
6,380,672	1910	1998	Othr	D
6,340,487		1998	Lscape	C
6,936,501	1730	1994	Othr	C
5,707,612	1970	2002	A	F
5,218,621	1984 - 1985	2005	Nu	B
5,134,109	1916	2005	MaleP	D
5,134,109	1953	2005	A	D

Rank	Artist	Title	Nominal value*, USD	
597	Pablo Picasso	Tête de femme (Dora Maar)	5,616,000	
598	Alexander Calder	Flying dragon	5,616,000	
599	Frida Kahlo	Roots	5,616,000	
600	Joan Miró	Nocturne	5,615,750	
601	Jeff Koons	Michael Jackson and "Bubbles"	5,615,750	
602	Piet Mondrian	Composition No. 8	5,612,500	
603	Pierre-Auguste Renoir	Portrait de Mademoiselle Demarsy (femme accoudée)	5,612,500	
604	Francesco Guardi	The Punta della Dogana and Santa Maria della Salute (+ The island of San Giorgio Maggiore and the Giudecca from the Bacino di San Marco, Venice; pair)	5,612,500	
605	Camille Pissarro	La route de Rocquencourt	5,608,000	
606	John Singer Sargent	Venetian loggia	5,608,000	
607	Pablo Picasso	Femme dans un fauteuil, les bras croisés. Buste	5,593,130	
608	Wassily Kandinsky	Dünaberg	5,547,061	
609	Pablo Picasso	Homme à la pipe	5,547,018	
610	Alexej Jawlensky	Dunkle Augen	5,540,088	
611	Pablo Picasso	Homme à la pipe	5,523,065	
612	Jean-Michel Basquiat	Profit I	5,509,500	
613	Fernand Léger	Les deux acrobates	5,509,500	
614	Pablo Picasso	Buste d'homme	5,506,000	
615	Fitz Hugh Lane	Manchester Harbor	5,506,000	
616	Amedeo Modigliani	Buste de Manuel Humbert	5,504,000	
617	Philip Guston	Zone	5,504,000	

	Present value**, USD	Year of make	Year of sale	Subject***	Size group****
	5,009,877	1937 -	2006	FemP	B
	5,009,877	1975	2006	S	-
	5,009,877	1943 -	2006	SelfP	A
	5,822,982	1940	2001	A	A
	5,822,982	1988	2001	S	-
	7,015,525	1939 - 1942	1994	A	C
	6,798,883	1882	1995	FemP	B
	6,130,273	1770 - 1780	2000	Lscape	B
	5,529,104	1871	2003	Lscape	B
	5,365,365	1880 - 1882	2004	Othr	C
	4,979,581	1963	2006	FemP	E
	5,290,199	1909	2004	Lscape	A
	5,151,687	1968	2005	MaleP	E
	5,036,476	1912	2006	FemP	B
	5,020,955	1968	2006	MaleP	E
	5,642,380	1982	2002	Othr	G
	5,595,698	1918	2002	A	C
	5,709,060	1909	2001	OthP	B
	5,215,247	1853	2004	Lscape	C
	5,031,427	1916	2005	MaleP	B
	5,031,427	1953 - 1954	2005	A	E

Rank	Artist	Title	Nominal value*, USD	
618	Childe Hassam	The room of flowers	5,502,500	
619	Henri Matisse	Jeune femme au piano	5,502,500	
620	Piet Mondrian	Composition (no.5 on sub-frame)	5,502,500	
621	Amedeo Modigliani	Le fils du concierge	5,502,500	
622	Paul Cézanne	Cinq baigneuses sous des arbres	5,502,500	
623	Sir Peter Paul Rubens	The head of John the Baptist presented to Salome (4 parts)	5,502,500	
624	Claude Monet	Vue du bassin aux nymphéas avec saule	5,502,500	
625	Henri Matisse	Les roses Safrano (Nature morte devant la fenêtre ouverte, Nice, place Charles-Félix)	5,502,500	
626	Marc Chagall	La chambre jaune	5,502,500	
627	Pablo Picasso	Fillette au bateau (Maya)	5,502,500	
628	Roy Lichtenstein	Torpedo...los!	5,500,000	
629	Pierre Bonnard	La liseuse et la femme au chien	5,500,000	
630	Cy Twombly	Untitled	5,500,000	
631	Francis Bacon	Study for portrait	5,500,000	
632	Henri Matisse	Femme au bijou bleu (Helene Galitzine au cabochon)	5,500,000	
633	Pierre-Auguste Renoir	Jeune fille au chapeau de paille	5,500,000	
634	Joan Miró	Personnage: les freres fratellini	5,500,000	
635	Pablo Picasso	La dormeuse au miroir	5,500,000	
636	Marc Chagall	Le buveur (le saoul)	5,500,000	
637	Piet Mondrian	Composition C with red and grey	5,496,554	
638	Pierre-Auguste Renoir	Jeunes filles aux lilas	5,496,000	
639	Jeff Koons	Jim Beam J.B. Turner train	5,495,500	

Present value**, USD	Year of make	Year of sale	Subject***	Size group****
7,035,368	1894	1993	Othr	C
6,665,572	1925	1995	FemP	B
6,396,595	1939 - 1942	1996	A	B
6,336,665	1918	1997	OthP	C
6,281,734	1875	1997	Nu	B
6,277,847		1998	Relgs	D
6,185,976	1917 - 1919	1998	Lscape	F
6,104,091	1925	1999	Slife	C
6,027,926	1911	1999	Othr	D
6,027,926	1938	1999	FemP	C
8,057,983	1963	1989	Othr	F
8,057,983	1909	1989	Lscape	E
7,852,167	1971	1990	A	G
7,852,167	1957	1990	MaleP	E
7,852,167	1937	1990	FemP	A
7,852,167	1884	1990	FemP	B
7,852,167	1927	1990	A	E
7,582,212	1932	1990	Nu	E
7,582,212	1910 - 1912	1990	Othr	D
8,169,737	1932	1989	A	B
5,258,068	1890	2004	OthP	B
5,257,589	1986	2004	S	-

Rank	Artist	Title	Nominal value*, USD	
640	Sir Peter Paul Rubens	Meleager and Atalanta hunting the boar	5,469,729	
641	Gustav Klimt	Obstbäume am Attersee (Fruit trees by Lake Attersee)	5,457,025	
642	Franz Kline	Painting in black and white and color (Washington wall)	5,448,000	
643	Henri Edmond Cross	Vendanges (Var)	5,444,566	
644	Amedeo Modigliani	L'homme au verre de vin	5,436,293	
645	Pieter Brueghel II	A village kermesse	5,426,700	
646	Georges Braque	Bouteille et clarinette	5,424,368	
647	Fernand Léger	Nature morte à la lampe	5,422,470	
648	Kees van Dongen	Portrait de Fernande	5,405,504	
649	Gerhard Richter	Drei Kerzen	5,395,750	
650	John Singer Sargent	Rosina - Capri	5,395,750	
651	Amedeo Modigliani	Femme en robe écossaise	5,392,500	
652	Pierre-Auguste Renoir	Mademoiselle Grimprel au ruban bleu	5,392,500	
653	René Magritte	Le fils de l'homme	5,392,500	
654	Pierre Bonnard	Intérieur avec des fleurs	5,392,000	
655	Fernand Léger	Les constructeurs	5,392,000	
656	Pablo Picasso	L'aubade	5,384,000	
657	Thomas Eakins	Cowboys in the Badlands	5,383,500	
658	Joan Miró	Le rouge, le bleu, le bel espoir	5,383,500	
659	Cy Twombly	Untitled (Rome)	5,383,500	
660	David Hockney	The splash	5,378,348	
661	Pablo Picasso	Femme assise sur une chaise	5,359,578	
662	Vincent van Gogh	Femme dans un jardin	5,342,115	

Present value**, USD	Year of make	Year of sale	Subject***	Size group****
5,020,332		2005	Othr	A
6,237,519	1901	1997	Lscape	D
4,980,086	1959	2005	A	G
5,056,262	1892	2005	Lscape	E
8,080,169	1918 - 1919	1989	MaleP	C
5,633,086	1616	2001	Lscape	E
6,382,184	1910 - 1911	1996	A	B
5,106,569	1914	2005	Slife	B
4,812,057	1905	2006	FemP	B
5,594,620	1982	2001	Othr	E
5,594,620	1878	2001	Othr	B
6,106,941	1916	1998	FemP	C
6,062,256	1880	1998	OthP	A
6,062,256	1964	1998	MaleP	E
5,009,877	1919	2005	Slife	E
4,928,745	1950	2005	Othr	G
5,099,532	1967	2004	OthP	F
5,307,466	1888	2003	Lscape	D
5,150,291	1947	2004	A	B
5,099,058	1971	2004	A	F
4,787,811	1966	2006	Lscape	F
5,871,286	1938	1999	FemP	E
4,960,837	1887	2005	FemP	B

Rank	Artist	Title	Nominal value*, USD	
663	Frédéric Bazille	Pots de fleurs	5,328,000	
664	Marc Chagall	Two Bouquets	5,324,000	
665	Paul Cézanne	L'homme a la pipe	5,313,208	
666	Claude Monet	Au Parc Monceau	5,289,671	
667	Piet Mondrian	Composition (A) en rouge et blanc	5,289,500	
668	Paul Gauguin	Le toit bleu	5,286,000	
669	Amedeo Modigliani	Fillette assise	5,286,000	
670	Henri Matisse	La danseuse	5,286,000	
671	Henri Matisse	Femme couchée	5,286,000	
672	Edgar Degas	Preparation pour la classe	5,285,750	
673	James Tissot	Le banc de jardin	5,282,500	
674	Claude Monet	Waterloo Bridge, brouillard	5,282,500	
675	Claude Monet	Antibes vu de la Salis	5,282,500	
676	Jan Van Huysum	A still life of flowers in a terracotta vase upon a marble ledge before a niche	5,280,809	
677	Henri de Toulouse-Lautrec	La clownesse Cha-U-Kao	5,280,000	
678	Pierre-Auguste Renoir	Jeune fille portant une corbeille de fleurs	5,280,000	
679	Giorgio de Chirico	Evangelical still life	5,280,000	
680	Piet Mondrian	Blue facade, composition 9	5,280,000	
681	Canaletto	The Bacino di San Marco, looking east from the mouth of the Giudecca, the Dogana and the Riva degli Schiavone to the left and San Giorgio Maggiore to the right	5,280,000	
682	Roy Lichtenstein	Blue nude	5,280,000	

Present value**, USD	Year of make	Year of sale	Subject***	Size group****
5,097,121	1866	2004	Slife	D
7,600,898		1990	Slife	D
6,901,727	1890 - 1892	1992	MaleP	A
5,475,265	1878	2001	Lscape	B
5,416,685	1936	2002	A	A
5,678,834	1890	2000	Lscape	C
5,594,026	1918	2000	FemP	B
5,480,698	1925	2001	FemP	B
5,489,966	1917	2001	FemP	B
5,678,565	1882 - 1885	2000	FemP	B
6,514,515		1994	OthP	E
5,982,310	1903	1998	Lscape	C
5,859,928	1888	1999	Lscape	C
5,183,486	1734	2003	Slife	B
9,279,285	1895	1985	FemP	B
8,439,515	1888	1987	FemP	C
7,735,663	1916	1989	A	C
7,735,663	1913 - 1914	1989	A	C
5,000,682		2005	Lscape	C
4,905,504	1995	2005	Nu	F

Rank	Artist	Title	Nominal value*, USD	
683	Jeff Koons	New Hoover convertibles, green, red, brown, new Hoover deluxe shampoo polishers yellow, brown doubledecker	5,280,000	
684	Ernst Ludwig Kirchner	Akte in der Sonne, Moritzburg	5,279,416	
685	Jackson Pollock	Number 17, 1949	5,272,000	
686	Pablo Picasso	Femme endormie	5,272,000	
687	Yves Klein	"RE 2"	5,271,500	
688	Jasper Johns	Gray numbers	5,271,500	
689	Wassily Kandinsky	Das Jüngste Gericht	5,227,500	
690	Lodovico Carracci	The Pietà	5,227,500	
691	Leonardo da Vinci	Personnage debout tourné vers la droite (study)	5,226,600	
692	Max Beckmann	Dame mit Spiegel (Lady with a mirror)	5,214,485	
693	Sir Peter Paul Rubens	A forest at dawn with a deer hunt	5,196,032	
694	Paul Delvaux	Le miroir	5,189,431	
695	Paul Klee	Auftrieb und Weg (Segelflug)	5,188,679	
696	Frederic Remington	A reconnaissance	5,172,500	
697	Pablo Picasso	Le petit Pierrot aux fleurs (Portrait du fils de l'artiste)	5,170,000	
698	Jean Dubuffet	Pese Cheveu	5,170,000	
699	Robert Delaunay	Premier Disque	5,170,000	
700	Camille Pissarro	Paysage, la moisson, Pontoise	5,168,000	
701	Claude Monet	Le pont japonais	5,168,000	
702	Berthe Morisot	Cache-Cache	5,168,000	
703	Alexej Jawlensky	Sizilianerin mit grünem Shawl (Sicilian woman with green shawl)	5,168,000	

Present value**, USD	Year of make	Year of sale	Subject***	Size group****
4,709,284	1981 - 1987	2006	Inst	-
5,403,335	1910	2002	Nu	E
5,197,387	1949	2003	A	B
5,169,217	1932	2003	FemP	A
5,196,894	1958	2003	A	E
5,168,726	1957	2003	A	B
6,274,577	1910	1995	A	D
5,709,568		2000	Othr	E
7,645,283	1470 - 1475	1989	-	A
4,910,121	1943	2005	FemP	C
7,600,569		1989	Lscape	C
5,684,807	1936	1999	Nu	E
7,774,780	1932	1989	A	D
5,737,846	1902	1999	Lscape	C
7,927,099	1929	1988	OthP	C
7,381,037	1962	1990	A	F
6,920,392	1912	1991	A	-
4,723,381	1873	2005	Lscape	C
4,723,381	1918 - 1924	2005	Lscape	E
4,723,381	1873	2005	Fem&InfP	B
4,723,381	1912	2005	FemP	B

Rank	Artist	Title	Nominal value*, USD	
704	Jean-Michel Basquiat	El gran espectaculo - The history of black people (in 3 parts))	5,168,000	
705	Francis Bacon	Three studies for Self-portrait (in 3 parts)	5,168,000	
706	Andy Warhol	S&H Green Stamps (64 S&H Green Stamps)	5,168,000	
707	Jean Dubuffet	Trinité-Champs-Elysées	5,168,000	
708	Francis Bacon	Study for a Pope VI	5,141,286	
709	Paul Cézanne	Ferme en Normandie,été (Hattenville)	5,140,117	
710	Claude Monet	La Promenade d'Argenteuil	5,135,833	
711	Pieter Brueghel the Elder	The drunkard pushed into the pigsty	5,121,031	
712	Roy Lichtenstein	Step-on can with leg (in 2 attached parts)	5,104,000	
713	Jean Honoré Fragonard	Girl holding a dove (Marie-Catherine Colombe?)	5,102,447	
714	Pablo Picasso	Buste de femme (Dora Maar)	5,094,896	
715	George Stubbs	Portrait of The Royal tiger	5,073,927	
716	Francisco José de Goya y Lucientes	A still life of dead hares	5,069,500	
717	Frida Kahlo	Self-portrait	5,065,750	
718	Claude Monet	Antibes vue de la salis	5,065,750	
719	Claude Monet	Nymphéas	5,062,500	
720	Pierre-Auguste Renoir	La jeune fille au cygne	5,062,500	
721	Vincent van Gogh	Bâteaux de pêches sur la plage à Saintes-Maries-de-la-Mer, Mediterranée	5,062,500	
722	Paul Cézanne	Environs de Gardanne	5,062,500	
723	Piet Mondrian	Composition in a square with red corner. Picture No. 3	5,060,000	

Present value**, USD	Year of make	Year of sale	Subject***	Size group****
4,723,381	1983	2005	A	G
4,723,381	1976	2005	SelfP	A
4,609,086	1962	2006	A	A
4,609,086	1961	2006	A	E
4,994,846	1961	2004	MaleP	E
5,911,770	1882	1997	Lscape	C
5,808,998		1998	Lscape	B
5,235,121		2002	-	A
4,882,526	1961	2004	Othr	E
5,402,660		2000	FemP	B
4,949,712	1942	2004	FemP	B
6,134,084		1995	OthP	F
5,136,709		2003	Slife	B
5,441,947	1929	2000	SelfP	B
5,360,677	1888	2000	Lscape	C
5,884,868	1908	1996	Lscape	D
5,779,195	1886	1997	FemP	B
5,733,047	1888	1998	Othr	A
5,438,451	1886 - 1890	2000	Lscape	B
8,454,167	1937 - 1938	1986	A	F

Rank	Artist	Title	Nominal value*, USD
724	Paul Cézanne	Dans la vallée de l'Oise	5,060,000
725	Paul Cézanne	Les reflets dans l'eau	5,060,000
726	Frank Stella	Tomlinson Court Park	5,060,000
727	Henry Moore	Large four piece reclining figure	5,056,000
728	Claude Monet	Près Monte-Carlo	5,056,000
729	Pablo Picasso	Homme à l'épée	5,052,474
730	Pierre-Auguste Renoir	La baigneuse	5,050,641
731	Pablo Picasso	Femme nue assise dans un fauteuil	5,048,000
732	George Wesley Bellows	The knock out	5,048,000
733	Andy Warhol	Marlon	5,047,500
734	Amedeo Modigliani	Cariatide (+ Cariatide; pair)	5,006,500
735	Claude Monet	Vétheuil, après-midi d'automne	5,002,001
736	Claude Monet	Matinée sur la Seine, près de Giverny	4,977,048
737	Claude Monet	La berge du petit-gennevilliers	4,975,047
738	Jean Honoré Fragonard	Two girls on a bed playing with their dogs	4,974,120
739	Paul Gauguin	Femmes au bord de la rivière	4,968,862
740	Norman Rockwell	Rosie the riveter	4,959,500
741	Andy Warhol	Big electric chair	4,959,500
742	Gerhard Richter	Der Kongress (Professor Zander)	4,956,000
743	Wassily Kandinsky	Berglandschaft mit Dorf I	4,956,000
744	Pablo Picasso	Tête de femme (Fernande)	4,956,000
745	Pablo Picasso	Femme à la collerette	4,955,750
746	Pablo Picasso	La toilette de Vénus	4,952,500
747	Henri Matisse	Les glaieuls	4,952,500

Present value**, USD	Year of make	Year of sale	Subject***	Size group****
7,758,437	1873 - 1874	1988	Lscape	C
7,431,051	1888 - 1890	1989	Lscape	C
7,413,344	1959	1989	A	G
4,508,889	1972 - 1973	2006	S	-
4,508,889	1883 -	2006	Lscape	C
4,757,097	1969	2005	MaleP	F
5,602,603	1909	1999	Nu	C
4,780,841	1965	2004	Nu	E
4,798,427	1907	2004	Othr	B
4,975,749	1966	2003	MaleP	E
4,713,673	1911 - 1912	2005	Nu	C
4,859,331	1901	2004	Lscape	D
5,151,306	1896	2001	Lscape	D
7,288,880	1875	1989	Lscape	B
4,426,893		2006	Nu	B
5,963,985	1892	1995	Othr	A
5,078,142	1943	2002	FemP	E
5,036,128	1967	2002	Othr	F
5,244,400	1965	2000	MaleP	F
5,146,843	1908	2001	Lscape	C
5,146,843	1909	2001	S	-
5,244,135	1938	2000	FemP	B
5,653,560	1923	1997	Nu	D
5,240,692	1928	2000	Slife	E

Rank	Artist	Title	Nominal value*, USD	
748	Jasper Johns	Jubilee	4,950,000	
749	Pierre Bonnard	Paysage du Cannet	4,944,000	
750	David Smith	Jurassic bird	4,944,000	
751	Lucas Cranach (the Elder)	St. Barbara in a wooded landscape	4,944,000	
752	Paul Delvaux	La ville inquiète	4,941,793	
753	Fernand Léger	Le disque rouge	4,936,000	
754	Claude Monet	Le Pont Routier, Argenteuil	4,926,641	
755	Johann Joseph Zoffany	The Dutton Family in the drawing room of Sherborne Park, Gloucester-shire	4,900,556	
756	Jusepe de Ribera	The martyrdom of St Bartholomew	4,892,368	
757	Claude Monet	Nymphéas	4,876,563	
758	Edgar Degas	Femme assise devant un piano	4,876,563	
759	Giovanni Paolo Panini	Interior of Saint Peter's, Rome, looking west towards the tomb of Saint Peter, with numerous worshippers and other figures in the nave (+ Interior of San Paolo fuori le Mura, Rome, looking down the nave towards the altar, with numerous worshippers, workmen and other figures in the nave; pair)	4,872,287	
760	Pierre-Auguste Renoir	La jeune fille au banc	4,871,937	
761	Johann Joseph Zoffany	A group portrait of John, 14th Lord Willoughby de Broke, and his family	4,855,746	
762	Juan Gris	Tasse, verres et bouteille (Le journal)	4,853,520	
763	Francesco Guardi	The Villa Loredan, near Paese, with elegant couples out walking	4,849,630	
764	Henri Matisse	Nature morte, serviette à carreaux	4,849,500	

Present value**, USD	Year of make	Year of sale	Subject***	Size group****
6,625,907	1959	1991	A	E
4,518,016	1928	2005	Lscape	F
4,518,016	1945	2005	S	-
4,430,571		2006	Relgs	B
5,558,725	1940 - 1941	1998	Nu	G
4,674,610	1919	2004	A	B
7,322,654	1874	1989	Lscape	B
5,072,040		2001	Othr	E
6,920,395	1634	1990	Relgs	E
5,409,405	1908	1999	Lscape	D
5,409,405	1882 - 1885	1999	FemP	B
4,653,159	1741	2004	Relgs	D
5,404,270	1875	1999	FemP	B
7,114,095	1765	1989	OthP	E
5,383,831	1914	1999	A	B
7,093,864		1989	Lscape	B
4,924,214	1903	2002	Slife	B

Rank	Artist	Title	Nominal value*, USD	
765	John Singer Sargent	Capri girl (Dans les oliviers, à Capri)	4,842,500	
766	Amedeo Modigliani	Jeune fille asisse en chemise	4,842,500	
767	Auguste Rodin	Eve	4,842,500	
768	Pierre-Auguste Renoir	Géraniums dans une bassine de cuivre	4,842,500	
769	Winslow Homer	The red canoe	4,842,500	
770	Jackson Pollock	Search	4,840,000	
771	Pierre-Auguste Renoir	Jeune femme à l'ombrelle japonaise	4,840,000	
772	Pierre-Auguste Renoir	Le printemps ou la conversation	4,840,000	
773	Pablo Picasso	Cruche, bol et citron	4,840,000	
774	Georges Braque	Nature morte	4,840,000	
775	Georges Braque	La calanque de Figuerolles, La Ciotat	4,840,000	
776	Cy Twombly	Untitled	4,840,000	
777	Jasper Johns	Device Circle	4,840,000	
778	Franz Xaver Messer-schmidt	Ill humored man	4,832,000	
779	Claude Monet	Les bords de la Seine à Argenteuil	4,832,000	
780	Chuck Close	John	4,832,000	
781	Fernand Léger	Esquisse pour Le grand déjeuner	4,832,000	
782	Vincent van Gogh	A pair of shoes	4,831,707	
783	Claude Monet	Plage de Juan-les-Pins	4,829,244	
784	George de Forest Brush	The Indian and the lily	4,824,000	
785	Paul Gauguin	Les trois huttes, Tahiti	4,818,100	
786	Jacob Isaacksz van Ruysdael	Two undershot water-mills with men opening a sluice	4,804,669	
787	Gerhard Richter	Untitled	4,798,662	

Present value**, USD	Year of make	Year of sale	Subject***	Size group****
5,700,894	1878	1996	FemP	B
5,483,784	1918	1998	Nu	B
5,304,575	1880 - 1881	1999	S	-
5,304,575	1880	1999	Slife	C
5,304,575	1889	1999	Lscape	A
7,597,957	1955	1988	A	F
7,597,957	1876	1988	FemP	B
7,421,114	1876	1988	Othr	B
7,107,962	1907	1989	Slife	B
7,091,025	1918	1989	Slife	C
7,091,025	1907	1989	Lscape	B
6,672,347	1962	1990	A	G
6,478,665	1959	1991	Lscape	E
4,575,092	1770	2005	S	-
4,488,014	1872	2005	Lscape	B
4,488,014	1971 - 1972	2005	MaleP	G
4,415,334	1920 - 1921	2005	Othr	C
5,292,747	1886	1999	Othr	A
4,604,694	1888	2004	Lscape	C
4,585,184	1887	2004	MaleP	B
7,701,216	1891 - 1892	1987	Lscape	B
4,566,782	1653	2004	Lscape	B
4,360,496	1967	2006	A	F

Rank	Artist	Title	Nominal value*, USD
788	Max Beckmann	Anni (Mädchen mit Fächer)	4,787,637
789	Henri de Toulouse-Lautrec	Danseuse ajustant son maillt (Le premier maillot)	4,787,500
790	Pablo Picasso	Les courses à auteuil	4,783,501
791	Jan van de Cappelle	Shipping in a calm at flushing with a states yacht firing a salute	4,783,475
792	Pablo Picasso	Le baiser	4,760,606
793	Claude Monet	La Seine à Vétheuil	4,750,661
794	Telemaco Signorini	L'alzaia (The tow-path)	4,748,012
795	Jean Dubuffet	Paris Montparnasse	4,739,500
796	Pablo Picasso	Buste de femme assise sur une chaise	4,736,000
797	Joan Miró	La po,tesse	4,732,500
798	Frederic Edwin Church	Untitled	4,732,500
799	Claude Monet	Fleurs à Vétheuil	4,730,000
800	Frederic Remington	Attack on the supply wagons	4,730,000
801	Gerrit Dou	A sleeping dog beside a terracotta jug, a basket, a pair of clogs and a pile of kindling wood	4,720,000
802	Bernardo Bellotto	The Piazza San Marco, Venice	4,720,000
803	Vincent van Gogh	Les Toits	4,720,000
804	Yves Klein	RE 46 (SIII)	4,720,000
805	Auguste Rodin	Les bourgeois de calais, grandmodele	4,719,000
806	Ferdinand Hodler	Linienherrlichkeit	4,714,828
807	Claude Monet	La maison de l'artiste à Giverny	4,711,500
808	Alexander Calder	Baby flat top	4,711,500
809	Andy Warhol	Last Supper	4,710,990

	Present value**, USD	Year of make	Year of sale	Subject***	Size group****
	4,444,386	1942	2005	FemP	B
	5,895,892	1890	1994	FemP	B
	4,256,697	1901	2006	Othr	B
	6,398,359	1645	1991	Lscape	C
	4,687,403	1969	2003	Nu	E
	4,316,731	1881	2006	Lscape	C
	4,654,712	1865	2003	Othr	E
	4,852,447	1961	2002	A	F
	5,087,289	1939	2000	FemP	B
	5,732,392	1940	1995	A	A
	5,249,519	1848	1999	-	E
	7,252,452	1880	1988	Lscape	B
	6,929,865	1905 - 1909	1989	Othr	D
	4,383,642	1650	2005	Othr	A
	4,297,428		2006	Lscape	C
	4,208,296	1882	2006	Lscape	A
	4,208,296	1960	2006	A	E
	6,737,159		1990	S	-
	4,195,382	1908	2006	Nu	E
	4,461,675	1913	2004	Lscape	C
	4,461,675	1946	2004	S	-
	4,280,563	1986	2006	Othr	E

Rank	Artist	Title	Nominal value*, USD
810	Bartolomé Esteban Murillo	Saint joseph and the christ child	4,696,293
811	Egon Schiele	Liebespaar (Mann und Frau I)	4,677,500
812	Henri Matisse	Nu au turban (Henriette)	4,677,500
813	Georges Braque	Paysage à l'Estaque	4,675,000
814	Joan Miró	Personnages et l'étoile	4,667,443
815	Lucian Freud	Naked portrait with reflection	4,651,144
816	Amedeo Modigliani	Jeune fille à la chemise rayé	4,632,749
817	Pablo Picasso	Les courses	4,629,500
818	Donald Judd	Untitled (in 6 parts)	4,629,500
819	Paul Gauguin	Cabane sous les arbres	4,629,500
820	Andy Warhol	Lavender Marilyn (1)	4,629,500
821	Andy Warhol	Group of five Campbell's Soup cans	4,626,000
822	Robert Delaunay	Les fenêtres simultanees	4,625,750
823	Vincent van Gogh	Flowers in a vase	4,625,750
824	Amedeo Modigliani	Paul Guillaume	4,625,750
825	Pablo Picasso	Femme couchee a la meche blonde	4,622,500
826	Pablo Picasso	Femme au costume turc dans un fauteuil	4,622,500
827	Maurice de Vlaminck	La danseuse du 'rat mort	4,622,500
828	Claude Monet	Matin sur la Seine a Giverny	4,620,000
829	Wassily Kandinsky	Engel des jüngsten gerichts	4,620,000
830	Pierre-Auguste Renoir	Portrait de gabrielle (jeune fille aux fleurs)	4,620,000
831	Henri Matisse	Anémones au miroir noir	4,610,325

	Present value**, USD	Year of make	Year of sale	Subject***	Size group****
	6,474,235		1990	Relgs	F
	5,914,438	1914	1993	Nu	E
	5,123,737		1999	Nu	C
	6,965,468	1906	1989	Lscape	B
	4,595,529	1949	2003	A	B
	5,231,626	1980	1998	Nu	D
	6,941,768	1917	1989	FemP	C
	4,739,600	1901	2002	Othr	B
	4,739,600	1966 - 1967	2002	S	-
	4,700,386	1892	2002	Lscape	B
	4,700,386	1962	2002	FemP	A
	4,894,773	1962	2000	Othr	A
	4,968,711	1912	2000	A	D
	4,968,711	1890	2000	Slife	A
	4,894,508	1916	2000	MaleP	A
	5,777,492	1932	1994	Nu	F
	5,548,047	1955	1995	FemP	D
	5,276,656	1906	1997	FemP	B
	6,883,522	1893	1989	Lscape	C
	6,883,522	1911	1989	A	B
	6,768,705	1900	1989	FemP	B
	4,787,422	1918 - 1919	2001	Slife	B

Rank	Artist	Title	Nominal value*, USD	
832	Gerard (I) Ter Borch	The music lesson	4,609,650	
833	Amedeo Modigliani	Donna con collana rossa	4,608,000	
834	Pablo Picasso	Sylvette	4,608,000	
835	Jeff Koons	Aqualung	4,608,000	
836	Jean-Michel Basquiat	Untitled (Two heads on gold)	4,600,000	
837	Tamara de Lempicka	Portrait de Mrs. Bush	4,599,500	
838	Marc Chagall	Au cirque	4,598,000	
839	Henri Matisse	Figure decorative	4,598,000	
840	Edgar Degas	Les trois danseuses jaunes	4,590,529	
841	Alexej Jawlensky	Lola	4,576,166	
842	Paul Cézanne	Les cinq baigneurs	4,566,038	
843	Pablo Picasso	Dora Maar aux ongles verts	4,564,757	
844	Sir Peter Paul Rubens	A night scene with an old lady holding a basket and a candle, a young boy at her side about to light his candle from hers	4,550,580	
845	Henri Matisse	Nature morte, nappe rose, vase d'anemones, citrons et ananas	4,547,934	
846	Henri Matisse	Torse nu or Femme en buste, bras levés	4,539,706	
847	Jacob Isaacksz van Ruysdael	A view of Bentheim Castle from the north-west	4,535,721	
848	Franz Kline	Ninth Street	4,519,500	
849	Pablo Picasso	Buste de femme à la frange	4,516,000	
850	Willem de Kooning	Woman (Blue eyes)	4,516,000	
851	Alberto Giacometti	La place	4,515,750	
852	Andy Warhol	Dollar Sign	4,515,282	

	Present value**, USD	Year of make	Year of sale	Subject***	Size group****
	5,294,765		1997	Othr	B
	4,279,270	1918	2005	FemP	C
	4,108,099	1954 -	2006	FemP	C
	4,108,099	1985	2006	S	-
	4,509,380	1982	2003	Othr	G
	4,399,207	1929	2004	FemP	D
	6,736,473	1976	1989	Othr	E
	6,564,412		1990	S	-
	4,320,777	1897	2005	OthP	B
	4,071,577	1912	2006	FemP	B
	5,931,172	1880 - 1882	1992	Nu	B
	5,131,274	1936	1998	FemP	B
	4,345,447	1616 - 1617	2004	OthP	C
	5,197,929	1925	1997	Slife	D
	4,328,190	1923	2004	Nu	A
	4,190,357		2005	Lscape	B
	4,588,472	1951	2002	A	F
	4,850,671	1938	2000	FemP	A
	4,778,231	1953	2000	FemP	B
	4,850,402	1948	2000	S	-
	4,102,129	1981 - 1982	2006	Othr	G

Rank	Artist	Title	Nominal value*, USD	
853	Claude Monet	Vue de Rouen	4,512,500	
854	Canaletto	The Molo looking west with the column of Saint Theodore (+ The Riva degli Schiavoni looking east, Venice; pair)	4,512,500	
855	Frans Jansz Post	View of the town and homestead of Frederik in Paraiba, Brazil	4,512,500	
856	Childe Hassam	Central Park	4,512,500	
857	Joan Miró	L'espoir	4,512,500	
858	Claude Monet	Un verger au printemps	4,510,000	
859	Francesco Guardi	View of Punta Della Dogana and Santa Maria della Salute; view of the Island of San Giorgio Maggiore	4,510,000	
860	Pablo Picasso	Guitare sur une table and le portail, fontainbleau: a double-sided painting	4,510,000	
861	Henri Matisse	La robe persane	4,510,000	
862	Karl Schmidt-Rottluff	In der Dämmerung	4,506,015	
863	Henri Matisse	Nature morte, fleurs et tasse	4,506,015	
864	Francis Bacon	Two figures at a window	4,505,721	
865	Wassily Kandinsky	Milieu accompagne (centre with accompaniment)	4,497,697	
866	Edvard Munch	Sommernatt, Åsgårdstrand (Summer night, Åsgårdstrand)	4,496,000	
867	Edgar Degas	La loge	4,496,000	
868	Stuart Davis	Rue de l'échaudé	4,496,000	
869	Paul Gauguin	Vase de fleurs et gourde	4,496,000	
870	Pablo Picasso	Mousquetaire et nu couché	4,492,632	
871	Pablo Picasso	Femme assise au chapeau de paille	4,492,632	

	Present value**, USD	Year of make	Year of sale	Subject***	Size group****
	5,415,951	1872	1995	Lscape	B
	5,228,724		1997	Lscape	B
	5,228,724	1638	1997	Lscape	C
	5,075,595		1998	Lscape	B
	5,005,355	1946	1999	A	B
	6,719,628	1886	1989	Lscape	C
	6,623,328	1770 - 1780	1989	Lscape	B
	6,438,777	1921	1990	A	D
	6,134,882	1940	1991	FemP	C
	4,182,079	1912	2005	Nu	E
	4,182,079	1924	2005	Slife	B
	4,093,412	1953	2006	Othr	E
	5,742,101	1937	1993	A	E
	4,174,897	1902	2005	Lscape	E
	4,174,897	1880	2005	Othr	B
	4,107,287	1928	2005	Lscape	C
	4,007,901	1890 -	2006	Slife	B
	4,363,747	1967	2004	Nu	F
	4,363,747	1938	2004	FemP	B

Rank	Artist	Title	Nominal value*, USD
872	Joseph Mallord William Turner	Fort Vimieux	4,492,632
873	Jean-Michel Basquiat	Untitled	4,491,815
874	Sir Joshua Reynolds	Portrait of Mary Wordsworth, Lady Kent	4,488,585
875	Claude Monet	Bateaux sur le galet	4,488,000
876	Henri Matisse	Nu au fauteuil	4,488,000
877	Jasper Johns	Flag	4,488,000
878	Lyonel Feininger	Zeitungsleser (Newspaper readers II)	4,484,653
879	Francis Bacon	Three studies for a portrait of John Edwards	4,484,150
880	Jasper Johns	Small false start	4,477,000
881	Joan Miró	Personnages Oiseaux	4,477,000
882	Francis Bacon	Portrait - Man screaming (study)	4,475,843
883	Camille Pissarro	Les peupliers, Matin, Éragny	4,472,499
884	Georges Braque	L'Arlequin	4,465,959
885	John Frederick Lewis	The midday meal, Cairo	4,463,705
886	Donatello (Donato di Niccolo di Betto Bardi)	The Madonna and Child	4,440,000
887	Pierre-Auguste Renoir	Gabrielle a la rose	4,410,740
888	Gustave Caillebotte	Le pont de l'Europe	4,409,500
889	Paul Cézanne	L'Estaque vu à travers les arbres	4,409,500
890	Andy Warhol	Silver Liz (in 2 parts)	4,409,500
891	Andy Warhol	Liz	4,406,000
892	Pablo Picasso	Femmes et enfants au bord de la mer	4,402,500
893	Jasper Johns	Decoy	4,402,500

	Present value**, USD	Year of make	Year of sale	Subject***	Size group****
	4,290,020		2004	Lscape	D
	4,282,455	1982	2004	A	G
	4,419,143	1777	2003	FemP	E
	4,292,388	1884	2004	Othr	C
	4,249,689	1921	2004	Nu	A
	4,249,689	1971	2004	A	B
	4,355,984	1916	2004	Othr	D
	4,698,607	1984	2001	MaleP	F
	6,559,198	1960	1989	A	B
	6,391,664	1972	1990	A	G
	4,782,383	1952	2000	MaleP	B
	3,979,017	1893	2006	Lscape	B
	6,543,021	1912	1989	A	B
	4,142,671	1875	2005	Othr	E
	4,041,629	1450	2006	Relgs	B
	6,321,531	1910	1990	Nu	A
	4,476,558	1876	2002	Othr	C
	4,476,558	1878 - 1879	2002	Lscape	A
	4,476,558	1963	2002	FemP	E
	4,661,689	1963	2000	FemP	E
	5,566,529	1932	1993	Othr	D
	5,025,387	1971	1997	A	F

Rank	Artist	Title	Nominal value*, USD
894	Georges Braque	L'Olivier près de l'Estaque	4,402,500
895	Vincent van Gogh	Les chaumières à Auvers	4,402,500
896	Paul Signac	Concarneau, calme du matin - Op. 219 (Larghetto)	4,402,500
897	Fernand Léger	Les trois femmes au bouquet	4,402,500
898	Pablo Picasso	Nu couché et femme se lavant les pieds	4,402,500
899	Amedeo Modigliani	Portrait de Louise	4,402,500
900	Vincent van Gogh	Arles, vue des Champs de Ble	4,402,500
901	Paul Klee	Geschwister	4,401,631
902	Pablo Picasso	Buste de femme souriante	4,400,000
903	Pablo Picasso	Femme assise (Woman in a red hat)	4,400,000
904	Francesco Guardi	View of the island of San Cristoforo with the islands of San Michele and Murano in the distance	4,400,000
905	Giacomo Balla	La scala degli addii (salutando)	4,400,000
906	Edouard Manet	Bouquet de pivoines	4,400,000
907	Claude Monet	Nymphéas, reflets de Saule	4,400,000
908	Henri Rousseau	Portrait de Joseph Brummer	4,397,662
909	Andrew Wyeth	South Cushing	4,384,000
910	Edgar Degas	Avant la course	4,376,000
911	Edgar Degas	La promenade des chevaux	4,376,000
912	Frank Stella	Bethlehem's hospital	4,375,500
913	Vincent van Gogh	Nature morte, branche d'amandier	4,375,500
914	Maurice de Vlaminck	Le verger	4,368,832
915	Pierre-Auguste Renoir	Canotiers à Argenteuil	4,360,933

	Present value**, USD	Year of make	Year of sale	Subject***	Size group****
	4,985,258	1906	1998	Lscape	B
	4,948,780	1890	1998	Lscape	A
	4,948,780	1891	1998	Lscape	C
	4,883,273	1922	1999	Othr	C
	4,728,597	1944	2000	Nu	E
	4,563,615	1917	2001	FemP	A
	4,563,615	1888	2001	Lscape	A
	5,178,300	1929	1996	A	B
	6,907,234		1988	FemP	B
	6,746,467	1934	1988	Nu	F
	6,461,783		1989	Lscape	C
	6,281,734	1908	1990	Othr	E
	6,065,770	1882	1990	Slife	B
	6,065,770	1920	1990	Lscape	F
	5,560,408	1909	1993	MaleP	E
	3,907,704	1955 -	2006	Othr	C
	4,185,090	1882 - 1888	2004	Othr	A
	4,185,090	1892	2004	Othr	B
	4,312,316	1959	2003	A	G
	4,288,943	1888	2003	Slife	A
	3,886,457	1905	2006	Lscape	B
	4,383,624	1873	2003	Lscape	B

Rank	Artist	Title	Nominal value*, USD
916	Jean Dubuffet	Georges limbour roi mexicain	4,356,000
917	Maurice de Vlaminck	Les regates a bougival	4,356,000
918	August Macke	Zwei Frauen vor dem Hutladen	4,341,527
919	Claude Monet	Le pont japonais	4,310,280
920	Joachim Beuckelaer	The four Elements: A greengrocer's stall with the Flight in Egypt beyond (+ 3 similar; set of 4)	4,306,038
921	Vincent van Gogh	Une liseuse de romans	4,301,859
922	Bartolomé Esteban Murillo	Christ the Man of Sorrows	4,300,626
923	Gustave Caillebotte	Le bassin d'Argenteuil	4,299,500
924	Pierre Bonnard	Nu sur fond jaune	4,295,750
925	Pierre-Auguste Renoir	Baigneuse debout	4,292,500
926	Frederic Remington	The last lull in the fight (The last stand)	4,292,500
927	Sir Alfred James Munnings	Lord and Lady Mildmay of Flete, with their children, Helen and Anthony, with a view towards Ermington in Devon-shire	4,292,500
928	Jasper Johns	Gray rectangles	4,290,000
929	Francis Bacon	Three studies of Isabel Rawsthorne (triptych)	4,282,794
930	Mary Cassatt	Mother and two children	4,272,000
931	Rembrandt Harmensz van Rijn	Study of an elderly woman in a white cap	4,272,000
932	Maxfield Parrish	The lantern bearers	4,272,000
933	Paul Cézanne	Nature morte au melon vert	4,264,285
934	Pablo Picasso	Femme assise	4,264,000

	Present value**, USD	Year of make	Year of sale	Subject***	Size group****
	6,218,916		1990	MaleP	E
	6,218,916	1905	1990	Lscape	B
	4,407,402	1913	2002	FemP	A
	4,605,244	1918 - 1924	2000	Lscape	C
	4,558,400	1569 - 1570	2000	Othr	F
	3,991,925	1888	2005	FemP	C
	3,944,136		2005	Relgs	B
	4,401,057	1882	2002	Lscape	C
	4,613,784	1915	2000	Nu	D
	4,942,598	1887	1997	Nu	B
	4,701,783	1903	1999	Othr	E
	4,701,783		1999	Othr	E
	6,577,805	1957	1988	A	G
	4,082,843	1966	2004	FemP	A
	3,917,785	1906	2005	Fem&InfP	C
	3,888,149	1640	2006	FemP	A
	3,807,506	1908	2006	Othr	D
	6,389,656	1902 - 1906	1989	Slife	A
	4,077,793	1949	2004	FemP	E

Rank	Artist	Title	Nominal value*, USD	
935	Pablo Picasso	Dés, verre, bouteille de Bass, carte à jouer et carte de visite	4,264,000	
936	Pablo Picasso	Femme au petit chapeau rond, assise	4,259,015	
937	Amedeo Modigliani	Tête de jeune fille	4,249,332	
938	Claude Monet	Le Palais Contarini	4,237,500	
939	Claude Monet	Le bassin aux nymphéas	4,235,000	
940	Marc Chagall	Les amoureux	4,232,426	
941	Pablo Picasso	Chat et homard	4,212,894	
942	Claude Monet	Prairie de Limetz	4,204,963	
943	Amedeo Modigliani	Beatrice Hastings devant une porte	4,189,500	
944	Edgar Degas	Le petit déjeuner après le bain	4,186,000	
945	Frederic Edwin Church	Mount Newport on Mount Desert Island	4,186,000	
946	Alexander Calder	Stegosaurus	4,185,750	
947	Paul Gauguin	L'aven - travers pont-aven	4,182,500	
948	Claude Monet	Le palais da mula	4,182,500	
949	Frank Weston Benson	The sisters	4,182,500	
950	Piet Mondrian	Composition No. III (insc. on stretcher)	4,182,500	
951	Willem de Kooning	Two standing women	4,182,500	
952	Georges Braque	Violon et verre	4,182,500	
953	Jasper Johns	Diver	4,180,000	
954	Amedeo Modigliani	Lunia Czechowska (la main gauche sur la joue)	4,180,000	
955	Claude Monet	Aux Petites Dalles	4,180,000	
956	Claude Monet	L'Arbre en boule, Argenteuil	4,161,498	

Present value**, USD	Year of make	Year of sale	Subject***	Size group****
4,037,228	1914	2004	A	A
4,867,536	1942	1997	FemP	C
5,424,844	1916	1993	FemP	B
4,997,857	1908	1996	Lscape	C
6,204,647	1917	1989	Lscape	E
4,979,126	1916	1996	Othr	B
3,964,089	1965	2005	Othr	C
4,356,118	1888	2002	Lscape	C
4,252,730	1915	2002	FemP	B
4,495,743	1894	2000	Nu	C
4,495,743	1850 - 1859	2000	Lscape	B
4,428,339	1972 - 1973	2000	S	-
5,227,254	1888	1994	Lscape	C
5,227,254	1908	1994	Lscape	C
5,065,834	1899	1995	OthP	E
4,815,865	1929	1997	A	B
4,774,118	1949	1997	Nu	C
4,735,995	1913	1998	A	B
6,561,872	1962	1988	A	G
6,409,144	1918	1988	FemP	B
6,227,948	1884	1989	Lscape	C
3,701,337	1876	2006	Lscape	B

Rank	Artist	Title	Nominal value*, USD
957	Mark Rothko	White, orange and yellow	4,160,000
958	Jean Dubuffet	La calipette	4,151,625
959	Claude Monet	Nymphéas	4,151,500
960	Vincent van Gogh	Still Life: Vase with gladioli and lilacs	4,146,886
961	August Macke	Markt in Tunis	4,144,956
962	Lucas Cranach (the Elder)	Venus and Cupid	4,142,531
963	Pablo Picasso	Carafe et plant de tomate	4,127,941
964	Salvador Dalí	Ma femme nue regardant son propre corps devenir marches, trois vertèbres d'une colonne, ciel et architecture	4,122,517
965	Henri de Toulouse-Lautrec	"Hélène V..."	4,121,389
966	Paul Klee	Die Sangerin I. als Fiordiligi	4,117,280
967	Foujita Tsuguji (Tsuguharu Léonard)	Enfants à la poupée	4,114,000
968	Sir Alfred James Munnings	Gypsies on epsom downs, derby week	4,104,000
969	Claude Monet	Charing cross bridge, la tamise	4,086,493
970	Claude Monet	Vétheuil, vu de l'à®le Saint-Martin	4,076,000
971	Georgia O'Keeffe	Black cross with stars and blue	4,076,000
972	Fernand Léger	Variation de formes	4,076,000
973	Roy Lichtenstein	Ball of twine	4,075,750
974	David Smith	CUBI V	4,072,500
975	Mary Cassatt	In the box	4,072,500
976	Pablo Picasso	Femme écrivant	4,072,500
977	Henry Moore	Reclining figure	4,072,500

	Present value**, USD	Year of make	Year of sale	Subject***	Size group****
	3,707,309	1953	2006	A	C
	5,940,931	1961	1990	Othr	E
	4,068,997	1914 - 1917	2003	Lscape	F
	3,688,291	1886	2006	Slife	A
	4,387,639	1914	2000	Othr	B
	3,825,821	1525	2005	Relgs	A
	3,934,961	1944	2004	Slife	C
	4,363,852	1945	2000	Nu	B
	4,403,145	1888	2000	FemP	B
	6,032,177	1923 - 1939	1989	FemP	A
	6,027,371	1955	1989	-	B
	3,675,360		2006	Othr	E
	5,376,406	1900 - 1903	1992	Lscape	C
	4,224,705	1880	2001	Lscape	B
	4,224,705		2001	Othr	D
	4,231,849	1913	2001	A	B
	4,231,589	1963	2001	A	D
	5,089,695	1963	1994	S	-
	4,793,934		1996	OthP	B
	4,648,483	1932	1997	FemP	D
	4,517,028	1969 - 1970	1999	S	-

Rank	Artist	Title	Nominal value*, USD
978	Henry Moore	Two piece reclining figure: Points	4,072,500
979	Cy Twombly	Untitled	4,072,500
980	Henri Matisse	Les tulipes	4,072,500
981	Henry Moore	Working model for unesco reclining figure	4,070,000
982	Salvador Dalí	Assumpta corpuscularia lapislazulina	4,070,000
983	Ferdinand Hodler	Am Genfersee	4,055,737
984	Marc Chagall	Le jongleur	4,048,000
985	Paulus Potter	Cattle in a field, with travellers in a wagon on a track beyond and a church tower in the distance, a rain storm approaching	4,048,000
986	Georg Flegel	Irises, tulips, anemone, snake's head fritillaria, lilies, columbine, narcissus, carnations, turk's cap lilies, violets, rosemary, bellflowers, jonquils, a pink rose, a red peony, a chrysanthemum, foxglove, clematis, snapdragons and other flowers in a decorated pewter jug with a black and red striped beetle, on a ledge in a stone niche with a cylindrical glass goblet of white wine, a sliced roll, cherries, a stag beetle and a knife.	4,048,000
987	Yves Klein	Ant 127	4,048,000
988	Pablo Picasso	Femme au chapeau de paille	4,046,206
989	Vincent van Gogh	Eglogue en Provence - Un couple d'amoureux	4,046,206
990	Pablo Picasso	Partition, guitare, compotier	4,040,404
991	Pablo Picasso	Personnage à la pipe	4,040,000
992	Alberto Giacometti	Homme qui marche III	4,039,500

Present value**, USD	Year of make	Year of sale	Subject***	Size group****
4,460,665	1969	1999	S	-
4,460,665	1959	1999	A	F
4,221,072	1914	2001	Slife	C
5,810,604	1957	1990	S	-
5,810,604	1952	1990	Othr	F
3,614,033	1908	2006	Slife	C
3,696,559	1943	2005	Othr	D
3,683,510	1652	2006	Lscape	A
3,625,012		2006	Slife	B
3,607,111	1960	2006	A	F
4,186,710	1937	2001	FemP	B
4,186,710	1888	2001	Othr	A
6,195,103	1924	1988	Slife	A
3,959,515	1971	2003	OthP	E
3,980,599	1950	2003	S	-

Rank	Artist	Title	Nominal value*, USD	
993	Luis Meléndez	Arbutus berries on a plate, apples, a wood barrel and bread rolls on a wooden table	4,039,500	
994	Claude Monet	Paysage de printemps à Giverny	4,039,500	
995	Francisco José de Goya y Lucientes	The death of a picador	4,030,072	
996	Pablo Picasso	Femme avec oiseaux	4,015,000	
997	Gustav Klimt	Dame im Fauteuil	4,012,679	
998	Claude Monet	A travers les arbres, ile de la grande jatte	4,002,079	
999	Dante Gabriel Rossetti	Pandora (on 2 sheets)	3,987,557	
1000	Pablo Picasso	Paysage de Cannes au crespuscule	3,986,820	

Notes:
* Nominal value - auction price, converted to USD and including buyer's premium with no time value adjustment made
** Present value - auction price, converted to USD and excluding buyer's premium, indexed according to the time value calculating process (described in section 2.4.1)
**** All paintings are segregated into 7 groups by their size evaluated in square meters (see Exhibit 3.5 at page 76 for definitions of size groups)

Present value**, USD	Year of make	Year of sale	Subject***	Size group****
3,944,060		2004	-	A
3,862,718	1894	2004	Lscape	C
4,731,872		1996	Othr	A
5,535,015	1939	1990	FemP	C
4,158,976	1897 - 1898	2001	FemP	B
5,682,846	1878	1990	Lscape	B
4,259,955	1869	2000	Relgs	C
5,705,098	1960	1990	Lscape	F

*** Definitions of the labels used in the "Subject" column:

FemP: Female portrait
MaleP: Male portrait
Fem&InfP: Female with a child portrait
SelfP: Self-Portrait
OthP: Other portraits
Lscape: Landscape
Nu: Nude
Slife: Still life
Relgs: Religious
A: Abstraction
S: Sculpture
Inst: Intallation
Othr: Others

Schedule B

Skate's Top 50 Artists by Market Value

Rank	Artist	Number of works*	Total value**, USD	
1	Pablo Picasso	123	1,576,826,984	
2	Claude Monet	102	872,355,182	
3	Vincent van Gogh	35	589,524,173	
4	Paul Cézanne	37	483,069,812	
5	Pierre-Auguste Renoir	44	438,024,266	
6	Amedeo Modigliani	37	338,283,273	
7	Henri Matisse	36	302,869,289	
8	Edgar Degas	28	245,645,007	
9	Paul Gauguin	19	199,429,850	
10	Andy Warhol	20	151,770,272	
11	Mark Rothko	14	149,998,500	
12	Fernand Léger	18	146,969,390	
13	Willem de Kooning	13	140,664,500	
14	Edouard Manet	8	134,889,187	
15	Canaletto	11	128,719,453	
16	Joan Miró	17	122,408,517	
17	Francis Bacon	18	118,015,994	
18	Sir Peter Paul Rubens	6	104,214,734	
19	Jasper Johns	14	95,354,500	
20	Gustav Klimt	7	94,407,534	
21	Egon Schiele	8	92,302,239	
22	Piet Mondrian	12	90,803,054	
23	Alberto Giacometti	10	87,986,530	
24	Constantin Brancusi	7	86,103,500	
25	Rembrandt Harmensz van Rijn	7	81,378,438	
26	John Singer Sargent	8	75,241,750	

Average price***, USD	Weighted ERR****	Nationality	Year of birth	Year of death
12,819,732	(2.26%)	Spanish	1881	1973
8,552,502	(2.25%)	French	1840	1926
16,843,548	(5.48%)	Dutch	1853	1890
13,055,941	(0.26%)	French	1839	1906
9,955,097	(5.78%)	French	1841	1919
9,142,791	6.35%	Italian	1884	1920
8,413,036	(0.37%)	French	1869	1954
8,773,036	(2.38%)	French	1834	1917
10,496,308		French	1848	1903
7,588,514	(4.00%)	American	1928	1987
10,714,179		American	1903	1970
8,164,966	3.09%	French	1881	1955
10,820,346		American	1904	1997
16,861,148		French	1832	1883
11,701,768	(5.97%)	Italian	1697	1768
7,200,501	(0.99%)	Spanish	1893	1983
6,556,444	5.88%	Irish	1909	1992
17,369,122	(11.59%)	Flemish	1577	1640
6,811,036	(3.73%)	American	1930	living
13,486,791	7.99%	Austrian	1862	1918
11,537,780	9.64%	Austrian	1890	1918
7,566,921	(2.01%)	Dutch	1872	1944
8,798,653	(4.40%)	Swiss	1901	1966
12,300,500		Rumanian	1876	1957
11,625,491	7.68%	Dutch	1606	1669
9,405,219		American	1856	1925

Rank	Artist	Number of works*	Total value**, USD
27	Henri de Toulouse-Lautrec	7	73,463,139
28	Marc Chagall	10	69,792,573
29	Roy Lichtenstein	8	65,121,250
30	Lucian Freud	9	57,007,692
31	Wassily Kandinsky	7	55,420,908
32	Joseph Mallord William Turner	3	51,327,372
33	Georges Braque	9	50,014,449
34	Max Beckmann	4	49,373,872
35	Pierre Bonnard	8	49,149,384
36	Jackson Pollock	6	47,018,250
37	Maurice de Vlaminck	7	44,841,847
38	Francesco Guardi	6	42,867,640
39	Cy Twombly	7	42,079,500
40	George Wesley Bellows	3	38,918,500
41	Henry Moore	7	37,641,842
42	Edvard Munch	5	36,659,715
43	Gustave Caillebotte	5	36,132,000
44	Georges Seurat	1	35,202,500
45	Michelangelo (Buonarroti)	4	34,487,719
46	Jan Van Huysum	5	33,738,836
47	Juan Gris	5	32,909,830
48	David Smith	3	32,832,500
49	Camille Pissarro	5	31,488,324
50	René Magritte	4	30,927,000

Notes:
* Number of artist's works included in Skate's Top 1000
** Total value of artist's works included in Skate's Top 1000

Average price***, USD	Weighted ERR****	Nationality	Year of birth	Year of death
10,494,734		French	1864	1901
6,979,257	(3.24%)	Russian / French	1887	1985
8,140,156	(5.12%)	American	1923	1997
6,334,188		British	1922	0
7,917,273		Russian	1866	1944
17,109,124		British	1775	1851
5,557,161		French	1882	1963
12,343,468		German	1884	1950
6,143,673	4.06%	French	1867	1947
7,836,375	6.53%	American	1912	1956
6,405,978	(2.55%)	French	1876	1958
7,144,607		Italian	1712	1793
6,011,357	(7.29%)	American	1928	0
12,972,833		American	1882	1925
5,377,406	19.73%	British	1898	1986
7,331,943		Norwegian	1863	1944
7,226,400		French	1848	1894
35,202,500		French	1859	1891
8,621,930		Italian	1475	1564
6,747,767		Dutch	1682	1749
6,581,966		Spanish	1887	1927
10,944,167		American	1906	1965
6,297,665	1.12%	French	1830	1903
7,731,750		Belgian	1898	1967

*** Average price of artist's work included in Skate's Top 1000
**** Annualized ERR weighted by initial purchase price

Schedule C

Skate's Index of Repeat Sales

Artist	Title	Year of make	
Pablo Picasso	Le miroir	1932	
Claude Monet	Dans la Prairie	1876	
Claude Monet	Nymphéas	1906	
Pierre-Auguste Renoir	La liseuse	1877	
Vincent van Gogh	Le pont de Trinquetaille	1888	
Vincent van Gogh	La moisson en Provence	1888	
Amedeo Modigliani	Garçon à la veste bleue	1918	
Claude Monet	Nymphéas	1907	
Pierre-Auguste Renoir	Jeune femme se baignant	1888	
Edgar Degas	Petite danseuse de quatorze ans	1879	
Canaletto	Venice, the Molo from the Bacino di San Marco with the Piazzetta and the Palazzo Ducale (+ another; pair)		
Jasper Johns	Two flags (in 6 parts)	1973	
Claude Monet	Le Grand Canal	1908	
Henri Matisse	Robe jaune et robe arlequin (Nezy et Lydia)	1941	
Paul Cézanne	La Côte Du Galet, À Pontoise	1879	
Claude Monet	Le Parlement, soleil couchant	1902	
Claude Monet	Le Grand Canal	1908	
Claude Monet	La plage à Trouville	1870	
Claude Monet	Nymphéas	1908	
Edgar Degas	Petite danseuse de quatorze ans	1879	
Edgar Degas	Petite danseuse de quatorze ans	1879	
Jasper Johns	0 Through 9	1961	
Edgar Degas	Les chevaux de courses	1871	
Claude Monet	Nymphéas	1907	

Inital purchase price, USD	Holding period, years	Year of sale	Hammer price, USD	Seller's commission	Annualized ERR
26,400,000	6	1995	18,200,000	(396,000)	(6.27%)
24,344,569	11	1999	14,000,000	(365,169)	(4.87%)
22,552,500	3	2002	17,000,000	(338,288)	(9.46%)
15,730,000	11	2001	11,996,818	(235,950)	(2.46%)
15,402,500	5	2004	10,000,000	(231,038)	(8.57%)
14,681,401	6	2003	9,200,446	(220,221)	(7.29%)
12,705,000	14	2004	10,112,789	(190,575)	(1.71%)
12,705,000	16	2005	12,500,000	(190,575)	(0.20%)
12,432,500	7	2004	6,620,142	(186,488)	(8.68%)
12,377,500	3	2003	9,200,000	(185,663)	(8.55%)
12,100,000	8	1997	7,737,616	(181,500)	(5.97%)
12,100,000	10	1999	6,500,000	(181,500)	(6.47%)
11,550,000	16	2005	11,500,000	(173,250)	(0.12%)
11,317,455	6	2005	9,750,000	(169,762)	(2.55%)
11,002,500	4	2000	7,750,000	(165,038)	(8.76%)
10,890,000	11	2001	13,249,773	(163,350)	1.59%
10,890,000	8	1998	11,000,000	(163,350)	(0.06%)
10,780,000	12	2000	14,967,127	(161,700)	2.73%
10,505,051	15	2003	9,300,446	(157,576)	(0.91%)
10,175,000	11	1999	11,250,000	(152,625)	0.78%
10,120,000	9	1996	10,800,000	(151,800)	0.59%
9,909,500	2	2004	9,750,446	(148,643)	(1.56%)
9,842,199	13	2004	6,803,965	(147,633)	(2.91%)
9,680,000	11	2001	6,499,773	(145,200)	(3.69%)

Artist	Title	Year of make
Pierre-Auguste Renoir	Gabrielle à sa coiffure	1910
Amedeo Modigliani	Jeanne hébuterne (Au chapeau)	1919
Joan Miró	L'Oiseau au plumage déployé vole vers l'arbre argenté	1953
Henri Matisse	Nu couche I (Aurore)	1907
Paul Cézanne	La Cote du Gallet, a Pontoise	1879
Rembrandt Harmensz van Rijn	Portrait of a bearded man in a red doublet	1633
Sir Peter Paul Rubens	A portrait of a man as the god Mars	
Paul Cézanne	Les grands arbres au Jas de Bouffan	1885
Maurice de Vlaminck	La Seine à Chatou	1906
Claude Monet	Nymphéas	1908
Pierre-Auguste Renoir	Baigneuses	1892
Camille Pissarro	Les quatre saisons: Le printemps, l'été, l'automne, l'hiver (4 works)	1872
Pierre-Auguste Renoir	Femmes Dans Un Jardin	1873
Claude Monet	Les Meules, Giverny, effet du matin	1889
Maurice de Vlaminck	Péniche sur la Seine	1905
Robert Rauschenberg	Rebus	
Henry Moore	Three-piece reclining figure: Draped	1975
Vincent van Gogh	Une liseuse de romans	1888
Paul Cézanne	L'Estaque vu à travers les arbres	1878
Alberto Giacometti	Grande femme debout I	1960
Edgar Degas	Préparation pour la classe	1882
Gustav Klimt	Schloss Kammer am Attersee II	1909
Claude Monet	Nymphéas	1908

Inital purchase price, USD	Holding period, years	Year of sale	Hammer price, USD	Seller's commission	Annualized ERR
9,680,000	8	1998	3,100,000	(145,200)	(12.69%)
9,572,500	9	2006	27,026,457	(143,588)	11.89%
9,350,000	16	2006	8,079,082	(140,250)	(0.99%)
9,242,500	1	2001	9,496,818	(138,638)	0.81%
9,240,000	9	1996	10,000,000	(138,600)	0.75%
9,077,500	3	2001	11,500,000	(136,163)	7.68%
8,252,500	2	2002	6,195,554	(123,788)	(11.59%)
7,954,930	9	2005	10,500,000	(119,324)	3.00%
7,865,000	12	2002	9,190,542	(117,975)	1.16%
7,416,147	10	1999	4,430,966	(111,242)	(5.05%)
6,860,707	8	1998	3,100,000	(102,911)	(9.75%)
6,820,000	13	2004	8,000,000	(102,300)	1.12%
6,712,500	7	2000	6,100,000	(100,688)	(1.47%)
6,710,000	6	1996	6,500,000	(100,650)	(0.72%)
6,686,088	4	2005	5,102,635	(100,291)	(6.90%)
6,325,000	2	1991	6,600,000	(94,875)	1.12%
6,167,500	1	2004	7,500,446	(92,513)	19.73%
5,610,620	2	2005	3,826,660	(84,159)	(18.08%)
5,502,500	5	2002	4,000,000	(82,538)	(5.91%)
5,445,000	1	1990	3,600,000	(81,675)	(34.88%)
5,445,000	8	1998	3,998,666	(81,675)	(3.91%)
5,280,845	10	1997	21,418,080	(79,213)	14.42%
5,062,500	5	2000	7,599,773	(75,938)	9.06%

Artist	Title	Year of make
Marc Chagall	Le grand bouquet (Bouquet des ferme)	1966
Pierre-Auguste Renoir	Les laveuses	1912
Roy Lichtenstein	Step-on can with leg (in 2 attached parts)	1961
Pablo Picasso	Tête de femme	1921
Vincent van Gogh	Nature morte, vase avec oeillets	1890
Edouard Vuillard	Le pot de grès	1895
Vincent van Gogh	Les toits	1882
Claude Monet	La Promenade d'Argenteuil	
Amedeo Modigliani	Fillette au tablier noir	1918
Gustav Klimt	Obstbäume am Attersee (Fruit trees by Lake Attersee)	1901
Pablo Picasso	Buste de femme (Dora Maar)	1942
Berthe Morisot	Cache-Cache	1873
Edgar Degas	Preparation pour la classe	1882
Maxfield Parrish	Daybreak	1922
Vincent van Gogh	Flowers in a vase	1890
Andy Warhol	Shot Red Marilyn	1964
Alberto Giacometti	Grande femme debout I	1960
Jackson Pollock	Number 12, 1949	1949
Barnett Newman	White fire I	1954
Berthe Morisot	Cache-cache	1873
Pablo Picasso	Compotier et guitare	1932
Francis Bacon	Portrait of George Dyer staring into a mirror	1967
Henri Matisse	Anémones au miroir noir	1918
Kees van Dongen	Femme au grand chapeau	1906

Inital purchase price, USD	Holding period, years	Year of sale	Hammer price, USD	Seller's commission	Annualized ERR
5,023,650	16	2006	3,000,000	(75,355)	(3.24%)
4,952,500	12	2005	2,651,545	(74,288)	(5.35%)
4,849,500	1	2004	4,550,446	(72,743)	(5.12%)
4,840,000	5	1994	2,966,752	(72,600)	(9.52%)
4,746,611	7	2003	6,336,564	(71,199)	3.99%
4,732,500	8	2006	6,663,257	(70,988)	4.40%
4,707,110	16	2006	4,200,000	(70,607)	(0.80%)
4,664,818	8	1998	4,666,667	(69,972)	(0.18%)
4,653,846	3	1989	7,174,049	(69,808)	16.94%
4,631,940	8	1997	4,958,659	(69,479)	0.66%
4,549,646	3	2004	4,542,318	(68,245)	(0.56%)
4,405,750	5	2005	4,600,000	(66,086)	0.56%
4,401,033	2	2000	4,799,773	(66,015)	3.92%
4,292,500	10	2006	6,800,000	(64,388)	4.54%
4,072,500	2	2000	4,199,773	(61,088)	0.79%
4,070,000	6	1994	3,300,000	(61,050)	(4.00%)
3,960,000	10	2000	13,000,000	(59,400)	12.46%
3,960,000	15	2004	10,400,000	(59,400)	6.53%
3,859,500	1	2003	3,300,446	(57,893)	(15.81%)
3,852,500	2	2000	3,999,773	(57,788)	1.50%
3,850,000	8	2000	8,999,773	(57,750)	10.98%
3,850,000	15	2005	8,016,222	(57,750)	5.03%
3,742,500	3	2001	4,185,750	(56,138)	3.30%
3,672,227	8	2005	8,231,493	(55,083)	10.41%

Artist	Title	Year of make	
Pablo Picasso	Au Moulin Rouge (Le Divan Japonais)	1901	
Alfred Sisley	Bords du Loing à Saint-Mammès	1885	
Pierre-Auguste Renoir	La coiffure	1888	
Jasper Johns	Colored alphabet	1959	
Piet Mondrian	Composition II, with red (Composition in a square)	1926	
Vincent van Gogh	Femme dans un jardin	1887	
Vincent van Gogh	Le moissonneur (d'après Millet)	1889	
Pierre Bonnard	Intérieur avec des fleurs	1919	
Paul Cézanne	Carriere de Bibemus	1898	
Balthus	Nu aux bras levés	1951	
Alberto Giacometti	Grande femme debout I	1960	
Fernand Léger	Nature morte à la lampe	1914	
Jean Dubuffet	Paris Montparnasse	1961	
Alberto Giacometti	Homme qui marche III	1950	
Francis Bacon	Three studies for Self-portrait (in 3 parts)	1976	
Cy Twombly	Untitled (Bolsena)	1969	
Pablo Picasso	L'atelier	1956	
Pablo Picasso	Femme dans un fauteuil	1932	
Egon Schiele	Porträt des Malers Anton Peschka	1909	
Kees van Dongen	Femme fatale	1905	
Pablo Picasso	Les courses à auteuil	1901	
Georg Flegel	Irises, tulips, anemone, snake's head fritillaria, lilies, columbine, narcissus, carnations, turk's cap lilies, violets, rosemary, bellflowers, jonquils, a pink rose, a red peony, a chrysanthemum, foxglove, clematis, snapdragons and other flowers in a decorated pewter jug with a black and red striped beetle, on a ledge in a stone niche with a cylindrical glass goblet of white wine, a sliced roll, cherries, a stag beetle and a knife.	n/a	

Inital purchase price, USD	Holding period, years	Year of sale	Hammer price, USD	Seller's commission	Annualized ERR
3,632,500	11	2006	5,901,931	(54,488)	4.53%
3,630,000	18	2006	2,590,617	(54,450)	(1.98%)
3,520,000	11	1997	8,000,000	(52,800)	7.61%
3,520,000	12	2001	3,399,773	(52,800)	(0.41%)
3,520,000	15	2004	2,657,079	(52,800)	(2.01%)
3,412,500	9	2005	4,755,460	(51,188)	3.75%
3,410,000	7	1995	3,597,232	(51,150)	0.58%
3,302,500	9	2005	4,800,000	(49,538)	4.06%
3,190,000	3	1989	6,000,000	(47,850)	27.75%
3,085,750	4	2004	3,276,913	(46,286)	1.21%
3,080,000	3	1989	4,950,000	(46,200)	20.06%
3,080,000	14	2005	4,827,205	(46,200)	3.09%
3,042,284	5	2002	4,300,000	(45,634)	7.00%
2,972,500	5	2003	3,600,000	(44,588)	3.60%
2,947,708	6	2005	4,600,000	(44,216)	6.99%
2,869,500	2	2004	2,600,446	(43,043)	(7.29%)
2,860,000	12	2000	3,199,773	(42,900)	0.81%
2,860,000	10	2003	6,592,196	(42,900)	8.34%
2,828,218	14	2001	10,278,219	(42,423)	9.64%
2,760,085	14	2004	5,300,000	(41,401)	4.68%
2,312,500	11	2006	4,256,697	(34,688)	5.76%
1,980,000	16	2006	3,600,000	(29,700)	3.65%